ALSO BY JEANNE LESEM

The Pleasures of Preserving and Pickling

PRESERVING IN TODAY'S KITCHEN

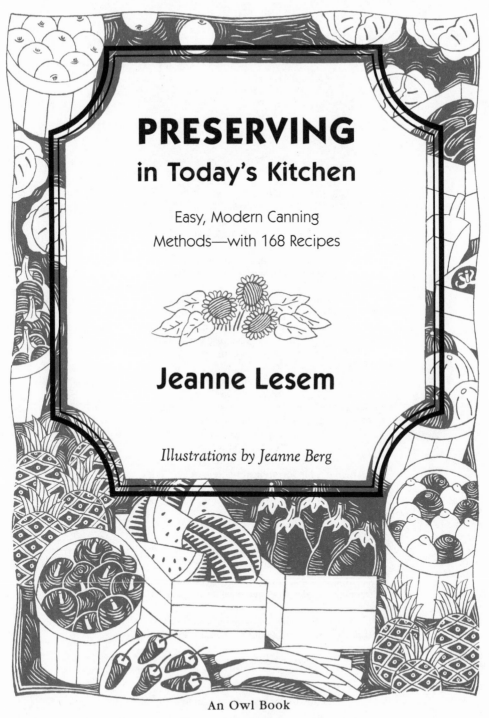

PRESERVING
in Today's Kitchen

Easy, Modern Canning
Methods—with 168 Recipes

Jeanne Lesem

Illustrations by Jeanne Berg

An Owl Book

Henry Holt and Company ı New York

Henry Holt and Company, Inc.
Publishers since 1866
115 West 18th Street
New York, New York 10011

Henry Holt® is a registered
trademark of Henry Holt and Company, Inc.

Library of Congress Cataloging-in-Publication Data
Lesem, Jeanne.
Preserving in today's kitchen: easy, modern canning methods with
168 recipes / Jeanne Lesem; illustrated by Jeanne Berg.—1st Owl book ed.
p.   cm.
"An Owl Book."
Rev. ed. of: Preserving today. 1992.
Includes bibliographical references and index.
1. Canning and preserving. I. Lesem, Jeanne.   Preserving today.
II. Title.
TX601.L387 1997   96-29834
641.4'2—dc21   CIP

ISBN 0-8050-4881-2

First published in hardcover in 1992 by
Alfred A. Knopf, Inc., under the title *Preserving Today*.

First Owl Book Edition—1997

Printed in the United States of America
All first editions are printed on acid-free paper.∞

3 5 7 9 10 8 6 4 2

To Isabel Sobol,

for help far above and beyond

the call of friendship

A blessing be upon the cook, who,
Seeing, buys this little book,
And buying, tries and tests its wares;
And testing, throws away her cares;
And care-free, tells her neighbor cook
To get another such a book!

Good Things to Eat,
published by the Members
of the Chancel Chapter of
Grace Cathedral, Topeka,
Kansas, 1921, revised,
enlarged second edition

ACKNOWLEDGMENTS

I am deeply indebted to the friends and acquaintances who helped locate historical and literary references for this book, and who patiently answered questions about everything from the etymology of bread-and-butter pickles to the origins of apple butter, beet preserves, and jelly roll, and who sometimes even made room in their freezers for jars of this and that when my own freezer developed gridlock: Carolyne Bowers, Cara De Silva, Bess Dewing, Marilyn Einhorn, Rick Ellis, Ella Elvin, Karen Hess, Sheila Johnson of the Brooklyn Public Library, Barbara Kirshenblatt-Gimblett, Joyce Lambert, Mary Lyons, Anne Mendelson, Lawrence Maxwell, Joan Nathan, Ruth and Jim Nesi, Jacqueline Newman, Anne Pascarelli, the staffs of the New York Academy of Medicine Library and Rare Book Room, Peter G. Rose, Alice Ross, Alison Ryley of the New York Public Library, Isabel Sobol, Joyce Toomre, Jeanne Voltz, William Woys Weaver, and Jacqueline Wilke.

Thanks also to my copy editor, Evie Righter, whose sharp-eyed reading of the manuscript reminded me that I had lost track of several recipes in my computer; to my editor, Judith Jones, for patiently helping me meet an early deadline without compromising our high standards; and to computer expert and friend Steve Miller, whose skill at the keyboard and unfailing good humor helped me survive computer glitches and learn a new word-processing program.

My gratitude also goes to many food world professionals who answered questions and located and sometimes supplied such unusual ingredients as citron, pummelos, and feijoas: the United States Department of Agriculture research staff; Robert A. Baker, research chemist at the USDA Citrus and Subtropical Products Laboratory, South Atlantic Area; Lisa Barmann, Beth Chase, and Stephanie Connors of the United Fresh Fruit and Vegetable Association; Sally Brunot of Dole Packaged Foods Co.; Barbara Dunbar Bristow of the U.S. Sugar Co., Inc.; Philip G. Crandall, Ph.D., University of Arkansas; Carol Hacker of Kerr; Stephanie Johnson of J. R. Brooks and Son; Bess Petlak of

Frieda's-by-Mail; John O. Kirkpatrick of Lindcove Ranch; Jim Magee of Dacus, Inc.; Steve Nelson of Kaprelian Brothers Packing Co.; Mark J. O'Brien of General Foods; Roberta Phillips of Rival Manufacturing Co.; Joan Randle of Ball Corp.; Barbara C. Robison of Sunkist Growers; Caryl Saunders for The Fresh Garlic Association; Professor D. P. H. Tucker, extension horticulturist, University of Florida Citrus Research and Education Center in Lake Alfred, Florida; and Jane Uetz and Jean Brady of Best Foods.

CONTENTS

INTRODUCTION

Nineteenth Century cooking was no lark. It was done in wretched conditions, without running water, decent lighting or proper refrigeration. The wood stove and open fireplace, however romantic to us, involved endless hours of heavy labor.

Lucille Fillin, in her introduction to *Cookbooks,*
A Special Collection, the catalog for a 1976 exhibit
at Hofstra University Library, Hempstead, New York

Why put up pickles and preserves at home when you can easily buy them at every food store, some gift shops, and even drugstores?

Superior flavor is one reason. And no worry about additives and preservatives, excess sugar or salt is another.

It's too much trouble, you say? Not anymore. Food processors and microwave ovens have helped turn a time-consuming and labor-intensive chore into a leisure activity that provides luxuries for our tables that earlier generations of women could only dream of.

Back to point one: If you have never tasted homemade strawberry jam, for example, you may not know that its flavor is enhanced by the fragrance of fresh, ripe berries. Homemade pickles, chutneys, and other relishes are also far superior to anything money can buy. But the big plus is that you—and not some faceless manufacturer—make the decision about ingredients.

If you prefer low-sugar or no-sugar jams, yet want to avoid sugar substitutes, go directly to the chapter on Fruit Butters and Reduced-calorie Spreads (pages 101 to 123). There you will find recipes that use unsweetened fruit juice concentrates or boiled apple cider to replace some or all of the sugar.

If salt is a concern, see pages 144 and 145 for recipes for salt-free sour pickles and dill pickles. Or you can choose recipes in which a little salt is used only for seasoning, not for its preservative properties; that small amount can be eliminated without compromising the safety of the pickles, although you may then want to increase the herb and spice content in the recipe to compensate for the flavor loss.

Until the end of World War II many of us still thought it was a housewife's or cook's duty to put up enough jars of food during the summer and fall to last through the winter and spring. Now we know better. We no longer need—or want—to fill hundreds, or even dozens, of jars of anything any time of year. If local crops are ready for preserving but we are not, we can easily precook small batches of fruit and vegetables quickly in a microwave oven, and freeze them in premeasured amounts to be finished at our convenience—one jar at a time, or as needed. We can make Peach Melba Jam (page 54) in January as easily as in June; Seville Orange Marmalade (page 99) in midsummer as well as midwinter, and Chili Corn Relish (page 167) whenever we want it, using frozen kernels when fresh corn is scarce or pricey. Frozen unsweetened fruit and berries from a supermarket can easily be substituted for the fresh any time of year. I have given directions for doing this in a variety of recipes.

Tedious handwork—chopping, grating, and slicing of ingredients—has been taken over by food processors, blenders, and electric food grinders that complete chores in minutes that used to take hours. Microwave ovens can reduce cooking time for many recipes to a few minutes; they also allow us to cook many fruits and berries in their own juices, without added water, to produce intensely colorful, flavorful, aromatic spreads. Some recipes are even microwavable from start to finish, including a few that are so much better made by microwave that I don't recommend preparing them any other way.

As you read my book, you will also learn how to put up preserves and pickles easily and quickly, using family-size pots, pans, and microwave cooking containers; and slow cookers or the slow-cook setting on countertop ovens.

Ingredients today range far beyond the familiar apples and oranges, peaches, plums, pears, cherries, and grapes of my childhood. Subtropical and tropical fruit and heirloom varieties of produce that used to be found rarely, if at all, in specialty shops now appear regularly in upscale supermarkets and at growing numbers of farmers' markets and farmstands. And the new vegetables! My favorite, snap peas, makes wonderful refrigerator pickles, to cite just one example.

As our immigration patterns continue to change, our culinary horizons are expanding. Thanks to thousands of recent arrivals from Asia, the Pacific, and Hispanic nations, we can now find Chinese cabbage, bok choy, daikon, fresh ginger, leaf coriander (aka Chinese parsley and cilantro or culantro), tomatillos, fresh chiles, carambolas, guavas, feijoas, blood oranges, mangoes, cactus pears, kiwifruit, and papayas side by side in supermarket produce departments with more familiar fruits, vegetables, and fresh herbs.

The earliest method of fruit preservation probably was drying. Evidence exists that sliced apples were dried in Neolithic Britain, C. Anne Wilson writes in *The Book of Marmalade* (1985). Salting, brining, and smoking were other early methods of food preservation. From colonial times onward women were preserving food in all four ways, as well as packing it into stone and pottery jars and crocks and wooden barrels.

Home preserving as we now know it began to increase significantly in the first half of the nineteenth century, thanks to two Frenchmen and an American tinsmith. The Frenchmen were Emperor Napoleon Bonaparte, who offered a prize of 12,000 francs to anyone who could find a way to provide nourishing food for his armies, and Nicolas Appert, an obscure Paris confectioner who won the prize for developing a method of food preserving by sterilization. About forty years later, John Landis Mason of Brooklyn, New York, designed and patented a glass jar with a shoulder and screw-top lid—a combination that made it easy to achieve and keep an airtight seal. Mason's jars at first supplemented, and eventually replaced, stone and pottery vessels, and his name became generic for canning jars. The tapered jars we now use were introduced after World War II, when freezer lockers and home freezers became commonplace. Unlike jars with shoulders, the tapered containers can be emptied without defrosting the contents.

English and Dutch settlers who introduced home preserving to the colonies were soon joined in the eighteenth and nineteenth centuries by religious refugees from Germany, Poland, Russia, and Switzerland. Members of these Protestant sects—the Shakers, the Quakers, the Mennonites, and the Amish—supplemented their plain meat-and-potatoes meals with generous numbers of "sweets and sours"—homemade jams, jellies, preserves, syrups, pickles, relishes, sauces, and condiments. Many of these families became known as the Pennsylvania Dutch because they settled in eastern Pennsylvania, an area that has become a major tourist attraction because of its food and craft traditions.

Some Amish and Mennonite families moved on to the Midwest—to Kansas, Oklahoma, and as far north as the Dakota Territory—introducing their simple food and frugal preserving habits wherever they settled. Some went north to Canada, others traveled south to Virginia.

In my research I consulted many community cookbooks that provide windows on the Old World. For example, in a Mennonite cookbook* published in Kansas in 1974 one woman recalled that a group of Polish settlers was so poor that women saved the brine and seasonings from their homemade dill pickles to

---

Melting Pot of Mennonite Cookery, by Edna Ramseyer Kaufman (North Newton, Kansas: Bethel College Women's Association, 1974)

recycle over wedges of cooked cabbage. In another community cookbook,* an unidentified North Dakota woman recalled that her grandmother put sour apples in the sauerkraut. "I don't know whether they were used to flavor the kraut or whether that was supposed to preserve the apples but they tasted very good, they were sour (the apples)."

When I began collecting historical material for this book, I was in a sense tracing my own roots. My mother's family had emigrated from Cracow in the nineteenth century when Poland was part of Austria. My father's parents came from the German Rhineland and the French province of Alsace, which have a common border. As I learned more about Pennsylvania Dutch preserving, I realized that many of my mother's recipes must have come from my paternal grandmother, Amelia Gottlieb Lesem, who was a Rhinelander.

Later generations from many other nations have continued to adapt Old World cooking to the ingredients and customs of the New World. Today as we look for ways to eliminate rich and salty things from our diets, we are finding delicious substitutions in ethnic condiments and sauces such as salsas and pestos.

Nowadays we also hear of a return to the popularity of "grandmother" food—meat loaf, mashed potatoes, and simply cooked vegetables. This kind of menu would have been accompanied by an assortment of preserved and pickled fruits and vegetables in the early decades of the century. In fact, the custom continued well into the fifties, even in the New York metropolitan area, where family-style restaurants like Patricia Murphy's would bring a relish tray to the table, along with the bread. The temptation to taste the relishes before ordering no doubt reduced appetites for the richer, fattier fare that followed. Not a bad strategy for today.

Another old custom worth reviving: hot chile- and herb-spiked sauces and condiments with meats and poultry to replace the flavor lost when you reduce the amount of fat in a recipe or skip it altogether. Chiles have been so widely used for so many years by the poor in India, China, Southeast Asia, and Africa that we tend to forget their American origins.

I won't suggest that you give up chocolate in all its luscious forms, but the next time you have a yen for something sweet, skip the fudge sauce and pour homemade preserves or jams or a homemade fruit sauce over your ice cream or frozen yogurt instead. For an even more refreshing and lighter trade-off, use these spreads and sauces as toppings for fresh or partly defrosted fruit or berries.

And instead of giving up jam on your breakfast toast, skip the butter or margarine. Both fats have twice as many calories as the same amount of jam, preserves, jelly or marmalade, and none of the fruity flavor. And, of course, the

*Food 'N Folklore, by Beata Mertz, published by the North Dakota Historical Society of Germans from Russia to commemorate the 1973 centennial of Germans from Russia in the Dakota Territory

calorie count is even lower if you eat homemade fruit butters and low-sugar or no-sugar spreads. Don't just take my word for it. Health experts at the U.S. Department of Agriculture and the American Dietetic Association take the same position.

Jeanne Lesem
New York, New York
March, 1991

GETTING STARTED

Can comes from the Middle English word canne, *which comes from the Old High German word* channa. *It means a tinplate container or a jar used to preserve food or other products for later use.*

Canning became the verb-form of the noun just as today's language gives us the word programming for the action of writing a program for a computer.

"Putting up" food has also aroused its share of curiosity as a term. It is believed to have originated as the housewife finished her canning and then put up her jars on a shelf in a darkened area for later use . . .

William F. Brantley, *A Collector's Guide to Ball Jars,* 1975

 t is no exaggeration to say that home preserving today requires only one special tool—a jar lifter that will probably cost less than $5. A wide-necked canning funnel is more a convenience than a necessity, as is a bubble releaser—a long flat plastic stick for releasing air bubbles from filled jars before you seal them. Any nonmetal gadget such as the plastic handle of a rubber scraper can be substituted for the latter.

The jar lifter lets you remove canning jars from a pot full of boiling water without scalding yourself or destroying the sterility of the jars as you would if you used regular kitchen tongs.

Preserving kettles

Chances are your kitchen already contains a variety of pots, pans, baking dishes, and casseroles that are suitable for every recipe in this book. For range top preserves and other sweet spreads, a 4- or 5-quart saucepan at least 8 inches in diameter is preferable. A 2- or 3-liter glass-ceramic casserole with ovenproof glass lid works equally well on range tops or in microwave ovens (for a detailed discussion of microwave utensils, see pages 34–35). Most range top recipes in this book were cooked in a 4- or 4½-quart saucepan 8 inches in diameter or a 1½-quart saucepan 6 inches in diameter across the top. All three are made of heavy-gauge aluminum with nonstick interiors, but other sizes and other materials are also acceptable. Anodized pans work fine (Calphalon and Magnalite Professional are two brands that come to mind). So do enameled steel or stainless steel, especially if the latter has a bottom core of copper or aluminum for better heat conduction.

Do not use unlined aluminum pans. They can be pitted by salty brine left standing in them, and aluminum may also affect the color of some fruits cooked in it. Unlined copper, iron, and tin can create toxic substances and darken mixtures cooked in them.

Enameled iron poses no toxicity problems (assuming that the enamel is not chipped in the interior), but its weight is a disadvantage. Lifting a large pot can be dangerous when it is very heavy.

A wok or a straight-sided 12-inch skillet or sauté pan makes a great preserving kettle for finishing sweet spreads, once the sugar has been added. The extra-wide surface cuts cooking time dramatically because it speeds up evaporation. For the same reason, it is less desirable for precooking, because extra liquid is needed for this step.

A pressure cooker has limited use. Because the high temperature (240 degrees Fahrenheit) resulting from 15 pounds' pressure destroys the pectin naturally present in fruit, it should not be used to precook any spread you want to jell. But it makes quick work of any fruit you want to purée for a butter.

Variables on cooking time

Don't expect a recipe to require exactly the same cooking time whenever you make it. The size and width (diameter) of the pan you use, seasonal variations in rainfall, or the amount of watering you do if the fruit is from your own garden or orchard are among the factors that affect cooking time.

RULE OF THUMB

Whatever pot or pan you choose for preserving sweet spreads should have a capacity at least four times that of the food to be cooked in it. Heavily sweetened spreads foam up alarmingly and may boil over, messing up your range top or microwave oven so badly you may be tempted to swear off preserving forevermore.

Jar sterilizers

You need a pot either deep enough to hold jars upright or wide enough to hold jars on their sides on a low rack or folded dishtowel. The rack or towel protects jars from direct contact with the bottom of the pot, which could cause breakage. Possibilities include deep spaghetti or chowder pots for upright jars or large Dutch ovens or deep, covered roasters for jars on their sides. All should allow at least three inches of headspace above the jars—one inch for water and two more for air space to prevent boilovers.

Other utensils

You will need spoons—wooden, nylon, or stainless steel—for stirring and testing for gel, and graduated measuring spoons, preferably a set that includes measures for ⅛ teaspoon and ½ tablespoon.

A colander is handy for draining raw fruit, but a large strainer works just as well, and can be used both for draining liquids and straining cooked fruit to remove seeds and skin.

A soup ladle is best for filling jars, although in a pinch you can substitute a stainless steel 1- or 2-cup dry measure.

Graduated measuring cups, metal or plastic, should be used for measuring sugar, which should be leveled with the straight cutting edge of a knife. Pitcher-style glass or plastic liquid measures are customary for measuring wet ingredients; you can make do with just the graduated set, but it's much more convenient to measure water and other liquids in a container that won't splash over the edge.

You can, of course, use an old-fashioned hand-cranked food grinder for preparing ingredients for relishes and some jams. But you will save time and effort by using either the grinder attachment that comes with an electric

How to sterilize jars

First, a safety check. Run a finger around rims and threads of jars, and discard any with cracks or scratches; they would prevent a perfect seal. Always use new lids; the sealant might fail on used ones. Bands (rings) may be reused if they are undented and free from rust. Now, wash the glasses, lids, and rings in hot, soapy water, and rinse. Fill the sterilizer of your choice with hot water, and use a jar lifter to lower jars into it, leaving enough room between each jar for water to circulate freely. Add more hot water if needed to cover the jars by one inch, and leave headspace of at least two inches. Cover, bring to a full, rolling boil, and adjust heat so water boils steadily for at least 10 minutes. The jars should be kept hot until filled. Always use a jar lifter to remove them, and set them on a folded towel (cloth or paper), never directly on a solid metal surface, where thermal shock might crack them. Lid manufacturers' directions, which vary from brand to brand, are on the boxes in which the closures are packed. Old glass-lined zinc lids should not be used. The rubber rings on metric jars (liters and fractions thereof) should be replaced with each new use. They are easier to put on the lids if first softened by a quick dip in very hot water.

kitchen center appliance or a blender or a food processor, which is the ideal tool for chopping or puréeing raw or cooked fruit that has already been peeled and pitted or seeded. My processor has a workbowl five inches deep and seven inches in diameter. If yours is smaller, you will sometimes have to process ingredients in batches. A processor can also be used to slice and shred ingredients for most recipes. I have warned against using it in recipes where it does a poor job.

For small slicing and shredding jobs, an inexpensive plastic mandoline with stainless steel blades and a hand guard works beautifully and produces more even slices than most of us can achieve with even the best knife.

A food mill with medium holes is useful for simultaneously puréeing and straining seeds and peel from cooked mixtures. A strainer or a China cap (a cone-shaped metal colander) will also do this job.

A plastic chopping board is easier to keep clean and safer than wooden ones. Cross-contamination can be a problem with wooden boards that are also used for cutting raw meat, poultry, and fish. Plastic, on the other hand, comes clean easily with detergent and water.

A grater with small, medium, and large holes is useful for grating citrus peel, and preparing small amounts of other ingredients when you don't want to use a food processor. I assume you also have on hand small, sharp paring knives, a citrus reamer (juicer) or an electric juicer, and a swivel-blade vegetable peeler.

If you do not have a kitchen scale, preferably the kind with its own bowl and a stand that can be reset to zero when adding ingredients, now is the time to treat yourself to one. If you garden or shop often at farmstands and farmers' markets, you will find the scale indispensable for getting the correct weight from pint and quart baskets whose contents can sometimes vary as much as a quarter pound.

Other optional tools that pay for themselves in time and labor savings are a grapefruit knife for preparing pineapple wedges, a grapefruit spoon for scraping pith from citrus peels, a melon ball cutter for cleanly coring apple, pear, and quince halves, and a jelly bag with metal stand that clips onto the rim of a bowl.

The jelly bags of my youth were muslin sacks in which sugar and flour were packed for retail sale. You can make a perfectly acceptable substitute by sewing two large white cotton handkerchiefs together on three sides, and making a casing for a drawstring around the top. Use it with the seam allowances on the outside, so pulp won't get trapped in the seams. Alternatively, you can line a strainer with one large white cotton handkerchief or even four thicknesses of woven cheesecloth.

If you make cherry jam or preserves regularly, you will want a plunger-type cherry pitter. Equally useful, if optional, are a tweezer-type strawberry huller, a potato masher or piecrust blender (for mashing raw fruit and berries to start the juice flowing), a wire mesh tea ball with chain and hook for segregating whole spices that should be removed before packing the food (or tie the spices in cheesecloth instead); and an aluminum ruler, which is more convenient than a spoon handle for measuring the depth of a mixture to be boiled down by half. The rulers are sold at sewing notions shops and hardware stores.

I couldn't manage without heat-resistant rubber spatulas, for cleaning sides of pans and bowls of sugar crystals, and for salvaging the maximum amount of product when cooking is done.

Gel (or jell) testing

When you make jellies without commercial pectin, you will need to test the cooked product to determine when it reaches the right stage for setting. Overcooking makes jellies rubbery, undercooking leaves them runny.

Testing by temperature is complicated, and works no better in my experience than the old-fashioned sheet test: Using a clean, dry metal spoon, scoop up a small amount of jelly and hold it above the steam rising from the kettle. Tilt the spoon so the jelly runs off the side of its bowl. If it falls in two separate drops, keep cooking. If two drops merge and fall as one sheet, the jelly is done.

I usually back up the sheet test by placing about 1/2 teaspoonful (a drop or two more or less makes no difference) on a chilled saucer in either the coolest part of the refrigerator or in the freezer for a minute or more. If, when it has cooled, the jelly wrinkles when you push it gently with a finger, it is done.

Don't panic if jelly made without commercial pectin takes as much as 24 hours to set. And if after 24 hours it has not set properly, simply empty it back into a saucepan, melt it down, and cook it a few minutes more before making another gel test. Or, you can always serve runny jelly as a dessert sauce, thinned still more with a little liqueur or cordial.

When making the sheet test, never use a spoon that has set jelly clinging to it or you may get a false positive. I keep a tall glass of cool water nearby to put the spoon in between tests so it cleans itself and cools off.

Step-by-step guide to packing and sealing jars

- Sterilize jars (page 5) and follow lid manufacturer's package instructions for preparing lids. If using European glass-lidded jars, dip new rubber rings in hot water to soften, and ease them into place.
- Grip a jar with a jar lifter just below its neck, or around its circumference if you have had to sterilize it on its side. Tilt the jar to empty water back into the sterilizer, and set the jar, right side up, on a wooden surface or a folded towel.
- Scald jar funnel and ladle in boiling water before using.
- Use ladle to fill jars within ¼ inch of the rim for jams and other sweet spreads. For pickles and syrupy recipes with chunks of solid ingredients, allow ¾- to 1-inch headspace—the air space between the jar rim and the surface of solid contents—and fill the jars almost to overflowing with liquid, so that solids are covered. Whole fruit and large pieces of fruit tend to float at first, then sink as they absorb syrup. A piece of wadded parchment paper or waxed paper may be placed on the surface to keep solids immersed. Do not use aluminum foil or plastic wrap. Too little is known about their possible chemical reactions with the hot syrups.
- Clean rims and threads with a dampened paper towel. Seal with lids as manufacturer directs. Follow recipe directions for inverting jars when indicated. Otherwise, set jars an inch or more apart on a counter to cool. Test for seal as lid package directs. Label, and store in a cool, dry, dark spot or the refrigerator or freezer, as recipe indicates.
- Labels packed with canning jars often come with directions for removing them before reusing the jars. If they do not, or if you use self-stick labels designed for packages or file folders, always remove them before you put the jars in a dishwasher. Very hot water sets their adhesive so firmly that the residue must be removed with cotton pads soaked with liquid spot remover or adhesive solvent from a hardware store. Both products are flammable, and never should be used near a range or hotplate or by anyone who is smoking. Some products leave an oily, smelly film that must be washed off with very hot, soapy water.

Jars and lids

Canning jars have come a long, long way in the 133 years since John L. Mason improved on other inventors' work by developing a jar and a closure that together produced an airtight seal. His achievement also made his name synonymous with all canning jars with threaded necks and lids.

The newest designs are 4-ounce quilted crystal jelly jars, perfect for one- and two-person households, and for gift-giving. Four to six of these little jars filled with homemade spreads make a welcome present, especially to those of us who like variety and are bored with bland, oversweetened supermarket preserves.

Two manufacturers now make wide-mouthed tapered canning jars in the 8-ounce size, which are easier to fill than standard tapered jars.

And 12-ounce jars now come in quilted crystal and floral designs, pretty enough to bring to the table.

Variables in contents

Batches of preserves, pickles, and relishes rarely come out even with the number of jars you have prepared to hold them. I keep small storage jars with plastic lids on hand for the extras, and refrigerate them for immediate use.

Storage temperature

The ideal temperature range for room temperature storage is 40 to 50 degrees Fahrenheit for homemade preserves and pickles made with traditional amounts of sugar and other natural sweeteners and/or vinegar of 5 percent acidity or fermented salt brine. Up to 70 degrees Fahrenheit is safe for unopened jars, but quality and color in the case of red jams, jellies, and preserves deteriorate rapidly in the 50- to 70-degree range, and harmful bacteria thrive between 70 and 140 degrees. You can retard the oxidation or darkening of red spreads by using ascorbic acid mixture (commercial powders combining powdered vitamin C with sugar and an anti-caking agent) to some extent, but not totally. Refrigeration or freezing is the best preventive measure for this problem.

For refrigerator or freezer preserves and pickles, the choice of containers is even better. French *confiture* glasses—called "working glasses" in some shops and stores—make beautiful presentation containers. They come with plastic lids, hold 12 to 13 ounces (plus headroom), and can be stored in a refrigerator or freezer. European-style glass-lidded jars with rubber rings and wire closures are available in sizes ranging upwards from 200 milliliters (about 1 cup) to 2 liters (2 generous quarts) or more. Like the *confiture* glasses, they look good enough to bring to the table and can also be refrigerated or frozen. The glass-topped jars are particularly good for pickles and relishes with high vinegar or alcohol content, both of which can corrode metal lids.

If you want to pack gift spreads in glass stemware—a nice touch if the spread is a wine jelly—make the jelly shortly before you plan to give it away, cover it with plastic wrap, and refrigerate it.

If you reuse commercial jars, sterilize them as you would new canning jars.

Other types of jars

Most commercial pint- and quart-size mayonnaise or salad dressing jars may be used with two-piece lids for canning acid foods. However, you should expect more seal failures and jar breakage. These jars have a narrower sealing surface and are tempered less than Mason jars. They may also be weakened by repeated contact with metal spoons or knives used in dispensing mayonnaise or salad dressing. Mayonnaise-type jars are not recommended for use with foods to be processed in a pressure canner because of excess jar breakage.

USDA Complete Guide to Home Canning, 1988

As for paraffin, forget it. It has outlived its usefulness in home preserving, and it was never very satisfactory anyway: difficult to use, given to weeping (breaking its seal) in warmish storage, and letting mold form. The jellies you would have sealed with paraffin can more easily and safely be refrigerated or frozen instead. Just be sure to leave about ¾-inch headroom in the jars to allow the jellies to expand as they freeze.

Beeswax

Before the invention of paraffin, beeswax was used to seal preserving jars made of glazed pottery. Melted beeswax in the grooved necks of the jars hardened to form an airtight seal.

Use two-part lids to seal commercial jars as well as regular canning jars. Follow the manufacturer's directions for preparing them for sealing. The threaded rings (bands) may be reused indefinitely, as long as they are not bent or rusty; the lids should be discarded after a single use because the sealant around the edges may not work a second time.

Lids from peanut butter, pickle, and olive jars may be used and will sometimes even create a vacuum seal, but there is no way of testing for this. They should, therefore, be reserved only for refrigerator or freezer storage. These lids tend to retain odors from the original contents of their jars. Leaving them upside down on a sunny windowsill for several days usually deodorizes them.

To process or not to process

Until sometime in the 1970s, open-kettle preserving was the officially recommended method for putting up preserves, pickles, and relishes such as chutneys. The open-kettle system works this way: You prepare the preserves or pickles as usual, and fill hot, sterilized jars within ¼ inch of the rim for preserves and other sweet spreads, or as directed in individual recipes. Seal, following the lid manufacturer's directions; cool and label. After 24 hours, check the lids for a seal. If the center of the lid remains flat when pressed with a finger, it is okay. Remove the ring, and clean it and the jar threads. The jars may be stored without the rings, but I find it more convenient to refasten the rings, making sure not to overtighten them, which would break the seal.

Sometime in the 1970s the U.S. Department of Agriculture and State Cooperative Extension Agents began recommending water bath processing as a safety precaution for preserving and pickling all acid fruits and vegetables.

If you put up larger amounts of food than your refrigerator or freezer can accommodate at one time, processing according to USDA recommendations is an important safety factor.

Extensive testing at the University of Minnesota Extension indicates that all fruit spreads and pickled products should be water bathed for 10 minutes for room temperature storage of 8-ounce jars. Consult an extension agent for timing for larger jars.

The recommendation is based on extensive tests to determine the effect on such homemade products' rate of spoilage and texture. The researchers found texture in fruit spreads was not adversely affected (although they become firmer during prolonged storage than the same spreads packed the open-kettle way), but that pickles tend to be less crisp and crunchy. They concluded that a reduced rate of spoilage outweighed the crispness factor. They also found fruit solids tended to separate from the jelly in water bath preserves, float to the top of the jar and remain there.

To water bath jars of homemade preserves and pickles, pack the hot, cooked food in clean, hot jars and seal with lids as manufacturer directs. Set the jars on an open rack at least ½ inch high in a saucepan or stockpot or water bath canner deep enough to allow for one to two inches of boiling water above the lids and an inch or two of air space above that. Allow a little air space between jars to permit even penetration of heat. Fill pan with very hot water to one or two inches above lids, cover pan tightly, bring to a boil,

Freezer storage

Freezers that maintain a temperature of zero degrees Fahrenheit or lower are easy to identify by their appearance. All chest and upright freezers fall into this class, along with refrigerator-freezers that have separate outer doors. The freezer compartments of single-door refrigerators range in temperature from 10 to 15 degrees Fahrenheit, which is safe for short-term storage of a few weeks to a month or so. Beyond that time, quality tends to deteriorate.

and adjust heat to maintain a steady boil for 10 minutes. Immediately remove jars with a jar lifter to an open rack, wood surface, or wood- or towel-covered surface to cool. Label and store.

Special handling is necessary for preserving with reduced amounts of sugar, vinegar, or salt. Most may be safely refrigerated for a few weeks to a month or so. For long-term storage the modern alternative to water bath processing of low-sugar, low-salt, and low-acid foods is freezing at zero degrees Fahrenheit or lower. Freezing retards the development of bacteria, enzymes, yeasts, and molds that can spoil even acid foods like pickles and preserves. It also retains color more effectively and for longer periods than the old-fashioned water bath method of processing.

However, it is always necessary to use the (boiling) water bath process for long-term storage when freezer space is not available, or when the freezer temperature is above zero degrees Fahrenheit.

Pressure canning creates an even higher temperature (240 degrees Fahrenheit) than a water bath, and that temperature is necessary for safe packing of all lowacid foods—canned vegetables, meat, fish, poultry, and seafood, for instance. But I am not concerned with such foods in this book.

Replacements for the old stone crock

Large glass, plastic, and stainless steel bowls make fine substitutes for old-fashioned stone crocks for fermenting pickles. Metal or plastic buckets, waste-baskets, or garbage pails are safe to use ONLY if you line them with new, undamaged food storage bags because pickling brines can react with metal and some plastics to create toxic substances. Food storage bags are always labeled as such. Be sure to read the labels before buying; the typical supermarket shelves have food bags beside garbage, trash, wastebasket, and lawn and leaf bags, any of which may react with brine to create toxic substances. Don't be tempted to reuse plastic bread bags or shopping bags of any type. Even lightweight ones that are safe for carrying raw food home should not be used for brining pickles because they may have invisible punctures through which brine can leak. And, anyway, they were not designed for liquid storage.

Spoilage

One thing that can spoil any home-packed product is a bad spot left on food when you prepare it. Bruises on cucumbers can lead to soft, rotten pickles. Pick your fruit and vegetables carefully, and trim away bruised or moldy areas if they are small. If they are large, discard the piece of fruit or vegetable entirely rather than risk spoiling a whole batch of preserves or pickles. When I have to use packaged instead of loose produce, I always buy a little extra to make up for possible loss. Some varieties of fruit are especially susceptible to hidden spoilage. In individual recipes calling for them, I have mentioned this hazard and recommended buying a larger quantity than is actually needed for the recipe.

Mold sometimes attacks both preserves sealed with paraffin and sour or brined pickles that are not completely covered with liquid. These pickles should always be discarded without tasting. So should moldy preserves, according to the latest advice from the U.S. Department of Agriculture. For years the Department considered preserves (and jams, jellies, and marmalades) safe to eat if the mold content was scanty and removable and the spread smelled and looked normal, but they are obviously being more cautious now.

Most preserves and related spreads in opened but covered containers keep well at room temperature if they are served every day or so and used completely within a few weeks. If resealed jars are left that way for long periods at warm room temperatures, the contents tend to mold. Refrigeration helps prevent this, but if you eat preserves only occasionally, the quality as well as the shelf life will be better if you pack them in containers just large enough for a few servings.

If pickles become slippery to touch or develop an off-odor, discard them without tasting and in such a way that neither humans nor pets can get at them. Most pickles in opened jars keep satisfactorily at cool room temperature under the same conditions as preserves, but they generally taste better when chilled. Crispness is more pronounced, especially with dills, bread-and-butter pickles, and almost any pickles that are packed in sweet-and-sour syrup.

Altering recipes

All the recipes in this book can be doubled, but you will get better results if you follow my directions for small batches.

The quality of preserves and pickles remains higher if they are packed in containers that hold only enough food for two or three meals. Once a jar is opened, the flavor and the color of food left in it gradually deteriorate.

Many recipes can be halved without difficulty. It is especially simple to divide the ingredients for recipes meant to be cooked in two batches, although you may have to use a little more than half the seasonings in a divided recipe. Do rely on your personal taste in this area, but remember that most pickles and relishes mellow and lose their sharpness when they are permitted to stand for a few weeks in a cool, dark spot.

IMPORTANT

Most preserved and pickled foods with reduced acidity or sweetness require special processing, storage, and handling to avoid spoilage that can lead to food poisoning in general and deadly botulism poisoning in particular. Botulin toxin thrives in low-acid food in an airless environment such as that of a vacuum-sealed canning jar.

To avoid this risk, never reduce the amount of vinegar in a recipe that is too tart for your taste. Add sugar or corn syrup or honey instead.

Never reduce the amount of salt in a brine.

If you want to reduce sweetness or replace sugar with a noncaloric or low-calorie substitute, either use recipes developed especially for these purposes or consult your County Cooperative Extension Agent for directions for converting specific recipes to a high-temperature method of processing. Special storage and handling may also be necessary. Agents usually are listed by title in the white pages of the telephone directory. If your community does not have a Cooperative Extension Agent, ask the consumer service department of your local public utility (gas and electric company) for the address of the nearest one.

Sources for low-sugar or sugar-free recipes include manufacturers of sugar substitutes, whose addresses can be found on their product packages.

Timing

Timing is flexible in recipes that call for a mixture to stand anywhere from a few hours to 24 or more. A difference of an hour or two will not ruin your pickles or preserves. Of course, in very hot weather or in an unusually warm kitchen, you should refrigerate unfinished mixtures to keep them from fermenting if you must hold them much longer than a recipe suggests.

Overcooking or undercooking can be more troublesome. Overcooked fruit spreads may become cloudy, sticky, rubbery, dark, tough, or even caramelized. Some preserving mixtures made without added pectin can be recooked briefly if they aren't quite thick enough or have not set, but some will darken unappetizingly

What to do when the jelly won't gel

Sometimes jellies, marmalades, and preserves will fail to gel, or set, as firmly as you wish. You can either return them to the pot, and reboil until gel tests done; or you can add one tablespoon of commercial liquid pectin or a homemade pectin extract (pages 19 to 21) for each cup of jelly or marmalade, and reboil until gel tests done. If a test of unsweetened juice or marmalade mixture indicates too little pectin is present, simply add liquid pectin or homemade pectin a tablespoon at a time for each cup of juice or marmalade mixture, and retest to determine the amount of sugar needed before you cook the spread. *Always discard test mixture without tasting.*

Savor the flavor

I seldom use commercial pectin by the full box or pouch because the rich, full flavor of the fruit and berries is overwhelmed by the amount of sugar required. Boiling down the fruit and its juices instead really concentrates the flavor and enhances the aroma and that, for me, is preferable to the higher yields obtained with commercial pectins.

during the second cooking. Rather than risk this, I usually serve too-thin preserves at refrigerator temperature, which thickens them a little, or use them as sauces for desserts, pancakes, waffles, or French toast.

Overcooked pickles and relishes become mushy, and some darken badly. Undercooked ones can be reheated without risk, but remember that crispness is one of the most desirable qualities in a good pickle product.

Follow the manufacturer's directions when you use liquid and powdered pectins by the box or pouch for regular high-yield recipes, but please note that I use a different technique than theirs in my reduced-calorie spreads, where the pectin is used as a bulking agent and the spreads are not meant to gel.

Happily for people who must avoid added sugar for health reasons or who prefer sharply reduced sugar content, there are now at least four brands of low-methoxyl pectin that may be used with or without sugar or sugar substitutes. Low-methoxyl pectins have been chemically treated to remove a natural component that requires a lot of sugar to gel. Earlier versions of this type of pectin required a tiresome two-step method. The new ones do not. You may notice a slight difference in texture with these products; some produce a more brittle, Jell-O-like texture, and others result in a slightly softer gel than usual.

All four brands are white powders which are difficult to divide if you want to put up a smaller amount of jelly than the manufacturer recommends. In all of my tests using less than a full package or pouch, I have had less than desirable results. But nothing beats these products for making unusual jellies out of bottled juices, from grape to the more exotic tropical blends that are all fruit or fruit juice reconstituted from concentrates. Juice drinks may lack enough acidity to work well with the reduced-calorie pectins.

If you use the low-methoxyl pectins, and lack enough refrigerator space to store full batches (the yields tend to range from 4 to 10 cups, depending on brand of pectin and type of fruit or juice being used), either process the extras as the pectin manufacturer directs, or give them away for immediate use.

Blended sugar

Blended sugar is available in many supermarkets and may be used in most of the recipes in my book, just as you would use pure cane sugar. In recipes where it is unsuitable, Candied Citrus Peel, for example, I have so noted and explained why.

Blended sugar is made from pure cane sugar mixed with sugar from other sources (such as beets). It is hygroscopic—it attracts moisture from the air, which makes the sugar crystals sticky and subject to melting even at low temperatures.

For that reason blended sugar is also unsuitable for meringues, meringue-type cookies, cooked crystalline candies, and brownies, which get their chewiness from the cane sugar they contain. Some baked goods also brown more quickly when they are made with blended sugar.

Saving calories

One tablespoon of butter contains 102 calories; the same amount of jelly made with the regular amount of sugar, only 49; jams or preserves, 54. If you make your own, the calorie savings will usually be greater than these figures indicate, as they are based on store-bought jams, jellies, and preserves, many of which are made with added pectin that requires extra sugar.

Stocking the freezer

With the number of one- and two-person households at an all-time high in the United States—and growing every year—most of us do not need or want dozens of jars of anything.

If you live in a hot, humid climate or have neither air conditioning nor a cool, dry cellar for storage, a capacious freezer makes an ideal food bank for storing fruits and berries precooked at the height of their individual harvest seasons. Pack them in premeasured amounts to make into sweet or savory spreads, sauces, conserves, and relishes at your convenience. The same principle applies

Handy freezer containers

Empty half-gallon paper milk cartons make handy freezer containers for storing small bags of cooked fruits and berries to be made into preserves, jams, jellies, or marmalades at a later date. Rinse the cartons well, open the tops completely, and stack with sealed freezer bags containing ½, 1, 1½, or 2 cups of the cooked fruit. When the milk carton is full, reseal it with freezer tape, label, and date. The cartons stack efficiently, and help protect the contents from freezer burn.

to exotica such as Seville (sour) oranges, blood oranges, Chinese pummelos, mangoes, guavas, and feijoas in their seasons.

Few pickles and relishes freeze successfully because freezing destroys their crispness. Most of the pickling recipes retained from the first edition of this book can be halved successfully, as I have indicated in many cases. You can also make cucumber pickles with Kirby cucumbers, a small unwaxed variety that is in markets all year. And all the new pickling recipes yield small amounts.

To save freezer space for more unusual produce, I seldom freeze peaches, raspberries, strawberries, blueberries, dark sweet cherries, rhubarb, corn, and small boiling onions because all of them are generally available in supermarket freezer cases. They may be substituted, ounce for ounce, for the fresh fruit, berries, and vegetables in my recipes. The pectin content of frozen fruit and berries tends to be lower than that of fresh fruit because they are picked when fully ripe. To compensate when you substitute frozen fruit for the fresh, test the cooked mixtures for pectin and acid content before adding sugar, and adjust as necessary.

Charts rating fruit for pectin and acid content are at best approximate because there are variables such as weather changes, particularly rainfall, that affect the fruit. Keep this in mind as you choose ingredients from the following lists:

Fruit high in pectin and acid

Apples

Blackberries, mature but
  unripe

Citron (*C. medica*)

Cranberries

Currants, red and white

Gooseberries

Grapefruit

Grapes, Concord and wild

Guavas, partially ripe

Lemons

Limes, Persian and Key

Oranges, sour or Seville

Plums, damson

Quinces, unripe

Fruit high in pectin, low in acid

Apples, sweet

Blackberries, ripe

Blueberries

Cherries, sweet

Guavas, ripe

Oranges, sweet

Papayas, semi-ripe

Pummelos

Quinces, ripe

Tangerines

Fruit high in acid, low in pectin

Apricots

Cherries, sour

Pineapple

Rhubarb

Strawberries

Fruit low in both acid and pectin

Bananas

Carambolas

Mangoes, ripe

Mulberries

Nectarines

Papayas, ripe

Peaches

Pears

Raspberries

All overripe fruit

French chemist Henri Braconnot, who discovered pectin in 1825, was the first person to make artificial jellies with pectin derived from carrots. Liquid pectin was developed 88 years later by Robert Douglas, son of a Scottish marmalade and jelly manufacturer. Douglas had spent years trying to develop a process for recycling apple pomace, a by-product of his own upstate New York cider vinegar manufacturing business. The liquid pectin he developed was first marketed commercially in 1921, and sold to General Foods eight years later.

Pectin: what it is, how it works

Pectin is the substance in fruit and berries that combines with sugar and acid to make jellies, jams, preserves, and marmalades gel. The amount of pectin varies according to the species of the fruit or berry, its degree of ripeness, and even growing conditions. A wet season produces juicier fruit with lower pectin content than does a dry season, when the fruit will have less juice but more pectin.

In most of my preserving recipes, you will find a specific amount of sugar or a combination of sugar and corn syrup recommended. These recommendations are based on tests for acid and pectin that are quick and easy to perform.

For acid level, taste a spoonful of your preserving mixture; it should taste as tart as a mixture of 1 part fresh lemon juice diluted with 3 parts water. If it does not, add ½ to 1 tablespoon of fresh lemon juice for each cup of your preserving mixture. Bottled lemon juice may be substituted, but the flavor suffers. Before testing for pectin, cook the mixture at least 5 minutes, and cool. The pectin content of uncooked juice will not register, nor will that of hot or warm juice.

To determine pectin level, measure into a small cup a teaspoonful of rubbing alcohol and 1 teaspoonful of cooked juice cooled to room temperature. Shake the cup gently to coat the juice with the alcohol, and let stand at least 60 seconds. Then, pour the mixture into a saucer. If a solid mass of gelatin forms (this rarely occurs) the pectin level is high, and you should use 1 cup of sugar for each cup of cooked juice or fruit with its juice; if large, broken flakes of gelatin form, you will need ½ to ¾ cup of sugar for each cup of unsweetened fruit or juice. If the mixture remains thin or if gelatin flakes are small and sparse, your options are: Reduce the juice or fruit by boiling, to concentrate what pectin there may be; or boost the pectin content by adding 1 tablespoon of liquid pectin for each cup of fruit mixture; or 4 to 6 tablespoons of homemade Lemon Pectin Extract (page 20) or Apple Pectin Extract (page 20). Repeat the rubbing alcohol pectin test until you are satisfied with the pectin level.

> Always discard the contents of the pectin test without tasting.
> Wash the cup and the measuring spoon in warm soapy water,
> and rinse and dry them before repeating the test.

Pectin extracts

The recipes that follow for homemade pectin extracts are simply apple juice and lemon peel concentrates. The former is made from tart, preferably underripe fruit. If you use sweet apples instead, you may need to add lemon or lime juice for acidity in the ratio indicated on page 19. Citrus pectin extracts can be made from other citrus fruit, but I find lemon the most useful. Both recipes are based on information in a Louisiana Extension Service booklet whose authors suggest a 15-minute water bath for extracts that will not be used immediately. Freezing works equally well for their preservation.

MAKES ABOUT 3 CUPS

4 pounds sliced, unpeeled apples, tart, firm ones such as greenings in winter or Granny Smiths in summer
2 quarts water

Wash and dry apples. Remove stems and slice apples, including peels and cores, into a 4-quart saucepan. Add water, cover tightly, bring to a boil, and boil 20 minutes. Strain into a 2-quart measure, reserving pulp, if desired, to make apple butter.* You should have about 6 cups of juice.

Wash and dry the saucepan, return the juice to it, and measure depth. Boil the juice, uncovered, until reduced by half. Drip the juice through a dampened jelly bag or two thicknesses of dampened cheesecloth. Do not squeeze the bag.

Refrigerate the extract in a tightly covered container if you plan to use it within a few days; or freeze in small containers.

*To prepare apple butter, purée the pulp in a food mill to remove seeds and skin, and add 2/3 cup of sugar or sugar to taste for each cup of purée, remembering that the sweetness will be concentrated as the butter boils down. See Fruit Butters chapter (pages 101 to 123) for cooking methods. Because much of the apple flavor has gone into the juice, you may want to add a little ground cinnamon, allspice, cloves, and nutmeg toward the end of the cooking time.

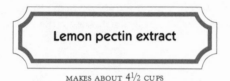

MAKES ABOUT 4 1/2 CUPS

Seeds and coarsely ground white pith of 5 to 6 large, thick-skinned lemons, about 1 1/2 pounds, or the equivalent weight in smaller lemons

3 tablespoons citric or tartaric acid
(citric acid, made from citrus fruit
and labeled sour salt, can be found
in the spice rack at most supermarkets; tartaric acid, made from
grapes, is sold by wine supply
shops)
6 quarts water

With a swivel-blade peeler, remove and discard the zest (shiny yellow outer peel) from the lemons, but do not cut deeply—the pectin is in the white pith beneath the zest. It won't matter if the peeled fruit is tinged a pale yellow.

Squeeze the lemons, reserving seeds, pulp, and pith. (I usually sweeten the juice and freeze it to make lemonade later.) Grind the pulp and pith coarsely, and measure. You should have about 2 cups, packed. Place this, the seeds, 1 tablespoon of the citric or tartaric acid, and 2 quarts of water in a straight-sided 4-quart saucepan. Let stand, uncovered, at least 2 hours, then measure the depth of the pan's contents and make a note of it. (An aluminum marking guide for home sewing is good for measuring because it can be scalded or sterilized.)

Bring the mixture to boil over medium heat, stirring often to prevent sticking. Boil rapidly until it is reduced by half. Stir often toward the end of the cooking period, which will take at least an hour or more. When the depth measures half the original figure, pour the extract through a strainer or colander lined with 4 thicknesses of damp cheesecloth into a bowl of at least 2-quart capacity.

Return the pomace (pulp) to the saucepan, add another tablespoon of citric or tartaric acid and 2 more quarts of water, and measure and cook as you did the first batch. No presoaking is necessary for this or the third and final batch. The second and third batches tend to reduce more rapidly than the first. Strain each batch when done into the first one.

When you strain the third batch, squeeze the pomace to extract as much liquid as possible. Put the extract through a clean, dampened jelly bag or 2 thicknesses of dampened cheesecloth, without squeezing. Let it drip several hours, until you have about 6 cups of cloudy liquid. If you plan to use it within a few days, refrigerate the extract in clean, tightly covered containers. Freeze for longer storage.

High-altitude preserving

The jelling or setting point is reached faster at altitudes of 2,500 feet or higher because the humidity level is lower there and liquids evaporate faster. Water also boils at a lower temperature than it does at sea level, making it necessary for safety's sake to follow your local Cooperative Extension Service or utility company home economist's recommendations for water bathing any preserves, pickles, or relishes that are to be stored at room temperature instead of in the refrigerator or freezer.

Consult your local Cooperative Extension Agent or utility company home economist for advice.

Measurements and equivalents

Pinch = as much as can be picked up between thumb and index finger

⅓ tablespoon	= 1 teaspoon
½ tablespoon	= 1½ teaspoons
1 tablespoon	= 3 teaspoons
⅛ cup	= 2 tablespoons
¼ cup	= 4 tablespoons
½ cup	= 8 tablespoons
¾ cup	= 12 tablespoons
⅓ cup	= 5 tablespoons plus 1 teaspoon
⅔ cup	= 10 tablespoons plus 2 teaspoons
1 cup	= 16 tablespoons
1 pint	= 2 cups
1 quart	= 4 cups
1 gallon	= 4 quarts
32 ounces (liquid)	= 1 quart
16 ounces (avoirdupois)	= 1 pound

MARKET GUIDE

The following alphabetized list indicates when fruits, berries, vegetables, and herbs are available nationally, and offers tips on how to recognize ripeness and quality. Because peak seasons vary regionally, local grocers and County Cooperative Extension Agents are your best sources of information about shopping for local and regional produce. The list was compiled from information supplied by the United Fresh Fruit and Vegetable Association, J.R. Brooks & Son, Sunkist Growers, John Kirkpatrick, and Frieda's Finest.

Apples — Skin color differs according to variety. Avoid bruised and blemished fruit. Summer varieties tend to be more tart and tender than those harvested in the fall. Season: All year.

Beets — Firm, round, with slender main root, deep red or gold flesh and smooth surface. Avoid oval-shaped beets with scaly top surface, indicating toughness. Season: All year.

Blackberries — Ideally, blackberries for preserving should be a mixture of three-quarters fully ripe and one-quarter mature but unripe, reddish turning to

A pint's a pound — almost always

A pint of most fruits and vegetables weighs a pound — usually. Cherries and most berries are exceptions. They are usually packed in cardboard or plastic pint and quart baskets or trays, and the weight of a pint, for example, may range from 10 to 12 ounces or more. Citrus fruit usually is sold by the piece or bag, but I have specified weights for it in most ingredient lists because a fruit that looks small to me might seem medium size to someone else. While measurements need not be accurate to the ounce in preserving and pickling, an inexpensive kitchen scale eliminates guesswork.

purplish-black. Avoid berries that show signs of mold. Season: May through January.

Blueberries — Deep blue with whitish bloom, nature's waxy protective coating. Unripe berries are reddish-blue. Season: June through September.

Broccoli — Dark green florets and crisp leaves and stems. Avoid broccoli whose heads show signs of opening into yellow flowers. Season: All year.

Cabbage, Chinese — See Chinese cabbage.

Cabbage, green — Firm, hard heads, heavy for their size, good pale to deep green color, depending on variety, and free from blemishes. Season: All year.

Cactus pears — See prickly pears.

Cantaloupes — Netted skin with no signs of mold or bruising. A stem end that gives slightly to finger pressure, and a fruity aroma are signs of ripeness. Season: February through November.

Carambolas — Choose firm, shiny-skinned fruit and ripen at room temperature until a bright golden yellow. Browning on the sharp edges of star doesn't matter. The edges may be trimmed with scissors, if desired. Whole fruit keeps at room temperature 1 or 2 days, and up to 2 weeks refrigerated in covered containers or plastic wrap. Season: Late August through March.

Carrots — Well formed, smooth, firm, brightly colored, free from splits or wilting. Season: All year.

Cauliflower — Compact, solid white to creamy white curds, bright green jacket leaves. Avoid speckled or discolored heads. Season: All year.

Celery — Light green color with crisp leaves and no signs of wilting. Season: All year.

Cherries — Dark sweet ones are a deep red, almost black, when ripe. Unripe ones are bright red. Sour cherries are bright red, soft and juicy when ripe. Because they bruise easily they should be put up as soon as possible after picking or purchase. Chokecherries (*Prunus virginiana*) grow wild all over North America. The red to black fruit are pea-size, and grow in clusters. Avoid the leaves and pits, which are toxic. Season: May through August for domestic sweet cherries, January for imports; late June/early July for sour cherries; late summer/early fall for chokecherries.

Chestnuts — Glossy brown unsplit shells. Breaks in the shell or sprouting may indicate mold or other spoilage. Refrigerate for a few days or freeze for several months. Chestnuts bought early in the season tend to have less spoilage than later. Season: Mid-September through January.

Chinese cabbage (napa) — Firm heads with crisp, curly leaves on the ribbed stems. Season: All year.

Citron (*C. medica*) — Etrog is a variety of the true citron, which should not be confused with *citron,* the French word for lemon, or with the citron melon that grows wild in the United States and whose rind is pickled like watermelon rind. Citron recipes in old American cookbooks almost invariably are for the melons. Most of us know citron as a candied fruit peel used largely in baking, but etrog has had an important role in the Jewish Feast of the Tabernacles, or Sukkot, since ancient times. Fruit that fails to meet the strict standards for religious use also may end up in the preserving kettle. Etrog resembles a lemon, but unlike a lemon, it is mostly peel, half an inch to an inch or more thick. The size ranges from less than 8 ounces to a pound or more, depending on variety. Flavor and aroma are strongest at the green or green-to-yellow or orange stage. Most fresh fruit obtainable today in the United States is imported from Israel and elsewhere in the Mediterranean area for religious use. John Kirkpatrick, a citrus grower in California's San Joaquin Valley, has planted citron trees and sells through retail sources any fruit whose appearance is not acceptable for the Jewish ritual. For information about availability, write to Mr. Kirkpatrick at P.O. Box 845, Exeter, CA 93221. Fax: (209) 732-1927

> *After the holiday of Sukkot was over, the etrog's thick skin was eaten pickled in vinegar or boiled to a pulp. A perfume was extracted from its peel, which was also highly valued as an antidote for snakebite. If you have a leftover etrog, add it to grapefruit and orange peel for citrus preserves (in ancient times, this confection was made from etrog and citron, but it is rather bitter). A folk custom relates that a woman who bites into an etrog will become pregnant within a year.*   •
>
> Joan Nathan, *The Jewish Holiday Kitchen*
> (New York: Schocken Books, 1979)

Corn — Fresh-looking husks with bright color, silk ends free from injury or decay, and kernels that are plump but not too mature. Season: All year.

Crabapples — Pink blush on a yellow ground indicates ripeness. Use the largest fruit you can find — the size of a Ping-Pong ball or larger — to save time and effort in preparing the fruit for cooking. Season: Fall.

Cranberries — Deep burgundy red color and unblemished. Unripe berries are bright red. Season: October through December.

Cucumbers — Firm, good green to whitish green color, smallish diameter, and unwaxed skin. Avoid cucumbers that are yellowish or have shriveled ends, indicating bitterness and toughness. Season: All year.

Currants, red and white — Bright red or white berries, unbruised. Season: Midsummer.

Eggplant — Firm, with very dark purple or white skin. Season: All year.

Feijoas—Sometimes called pineapple guavas; the two fruits are not related botanically, although both are members of the Myrtle family, and both are fragrant when ripe. Feijoas are more egg-shaped than guavas, and can be used the same way in cooking. Feijoa seeds are smaller than guava seeds, and need not be removed. The texture of the  pulp is gritty like a pear. The musky aroma and flavor can be pleasantly toned down by combining feijoas with lemon peel and juice. Season: March through June for imports; September through January for California fruit.

Garlic—White- or pink-skinned, depending on variety. Avoid heads that are sprouting or show darkish spots that may indicate softness or spoilage. Season: All year.

Gingerroot—Choose firm, fresh-looking roots with no wrinkling of the skin. Young ginger will have pink tips and a more delicate flavor than the older roots. For short-term storage (a week or so), wrap the roots loosely in paper towels, and then in a plastic bag in the refrigerator vegetable crisper. For longer storage, and for recipes using  ginger juice, scrape away the skin, wrap closely in plastic freezer wrap, and freeze. Ginger is easily grated while frozen, and gives far more juice than roots that have not been frozen. A slice of fresh, unfrozen ginger about 2 inches in diameter and 1 inch long will yield about 3 tablespoons of finely chopped ginger, or slightly more than 1 tablespoon of grated ginger. Season: All year.

Ginger as houseplant

Sprouting ginger can be turned into a pretty houseplant. Set the roots, sprout ends down, just below the surface of potting soil in a shallow pot, and keep soil damp and out of direct sunlight until green shoots emerge.

Gooseberries—A midsummer fruit highly prized by English settlers, the berries range in size from that of a blueberry to a dark sweet cherry. They may be white, green, or pinkish purple; the latter two colors are more common in American markets. Gooseberries' high acid and pectin content makes them ideal for preserves, jams, and jellies, but historically they have also been used in sauces and soups. They should be firm and dry when purchased; they keep well for two weeks in a refrigerator and will soften slightly during that time.

Grapefruit—Look for fruit heavy for its size; this indicates juiciness. A large fruit that seems light for its size is likely to be dry and have little flavor. Blemishes on the peel—russet spots and green streaks—are freaks of nature, and do not affect the flavor, quality, or juice content. Season: All year.

Grapes, Concord — Deep purple when ripe; mature but unripe grapes are dark red. Season: Late August to October.

Guavas — May have white, yellow, or green skin, and white, yellow, pink, or red flesh. Ripe fruit will give slightly when squeezed; it should be soft but not mushy. The color lightens as the fruit ripens, but the best test for ripeness is its aroma, which some people describe as rose-like. Avoid fruit with solid dark green skin and no aroma. It will often  rot before it ripens. Season: January through March and June through October for Florida and Caribbean guavas. March through June and September through January for all others.

Haws — Fruit of the hawthorn tree, haws come in many species and varieties throughout the world. The round ones resemble miniature apples; others are pear-shaped. They range in size up to an inch in diameter, and their flesh may be juicy or dry and mealy. Do not use fruit from trees that have been sprayed. Season: Late summer, early fall.

Herbs, dried — They should have distinctive aromas and good color for their varieties. If green herbs have darkened appreciably, turned gray, or lost their characteristic scent, they will lack flavor, and should be discarded. Old herbs and spices will not spoil preserves and pickles, but they will make less flavorful products. Dried whole-leaf herbs such as tarragon, thyme, and oregano release their full scent and flavor only when crushed. To test, place about 1/4 teaspoon of the herb in the palm of one hand, crumble the leaves between two fingers of your other hand, and smell the powder. Season: All year.

Herbs, fresh — Color varies from pale to dark green or grayish green, according to variety. Choose plants or branches with no signs of wilting. Refrigerate cut parsley in a jar or glass of water, and cover lightly with plastic. Fresh coriander with roots still attached keeps better and longer than cut stems; wrapped lightly in paper towels and enclosed in a sealed plastic bag, it will remain fresh and green for about a week in a refrigerator vegetable crisper. Season: All year (includes greenhouse-grown herbs).

Honeydew melons — Rind color, white to creamy white; blossom end should be springy to soft, with a fruity, spicy aroma when cut. Fully mature but unripe melons, the best type for preserving and pickling, have white rind with only traces of green, blossom ends that are hard to springy, and aroma is lacking. Season: All year.

Kiwifruit — Ripen kiwis at room temperature until they feel as soft as a ripe pear. Once ripe, refrigerate. Season: All year (includes imports).

Lemons — For a recipe calling for juice and grated peel, choose smooth-skinned fruit that gives easily to hand pressure, indicating thin peel and much juice. For marmalades and recipes using sliced whole fruit, select rough-skinned ones that are quite firm, indicating thick peel and less juice. Season: All year.

Limes — The familiar Persian limes have a bright green skin with no soft, yellowish spots indicating overripeness. Key limes are pale green-skinned when mature but unripe, and golden when ripe. Season: All year for both Persian limes and Key limes imported from Haiti.

Mangoes — Choose fruit that are firm, fresh-looking, and plump. Ripen at room temperature until they give slightly to the touch and have a fruity, spicy aroma. Skin color doesn't matter. To cut them up easily for cooking, cut straight across the flat seed on both sides; score to but not through the leathery skin, flex the fruit toward the skin side, and slice off the cubes, working over a bowl to catch all the juice. Then slice off the remaining flesh from the seed, and dice it the same way. Season: February through September.

Mulberries — If you can beat the birds to the semiripe ones (reddish purple), these berries make a pleasant jam. Old recipes generally indicate sufficient natural pectin content, but the only berries I have been able to obtain did not. If you plan to make Mulberry Jam (page 60) test for pectin and acidity before adding sugar, and adjust with liquid pectin and lemon juice if necessary.

> *The woman who is fortunate enough to have a garden as well as a home takes especial pleasure in thus making provision for winter at a minimum cost, while the woman who has a motor car makes use of it to get fresh [preserving] supplies from other people's gardens.*
>
> Janet McKenzie Hill, in her preface to
> the 1927 edition of *Canning, Preserving and
> Jelly Making,* first published in 1917

Nectarines — Rich reddish cheeks on orange-yellow ground or, for some varieties, greenish ground color. A slight softening can be felt with gentle hand pressure along the seam when fruit is ripe. Season: Mid-May through September.

Onions — Brittle, papery skin and no soft or moldy spots. Sprouting or hollow, woody centers indicate spoilage. Season: All year.

Oranges — Navel, temple, and sour (also called Seville) oranges, which have thick peel, are best for marmalades and conserves for which pectin content is a primary consideration. The white pith just beneath the colored peel contains a lot of pectin. Thin-skinned varieties such as Valencias, Hamlins, and Pineapples, and red-fleshed blood oranges may have lower pectin content. Like all citrus fruit, they should be heavy for their size. Russet spots and greening on the skin do not affect flavor or juice content. Regreening is caused by weather changes and has no effect on the sweetness or acidity of the fruit. Blood oranges tend to be about the size of tangerines. They have red-blushed peel and reddish orange or dark red flesh, and they make a beautiful red marmalade. Season: All year for most sweet oranges; December through June for blood oranges; January and February for sour, or Seville, oranges.

Papayas—Choose medium-size (about 1¼ to 1½ pounds) fruit, let ripen at room temperature 3 to 5 days, until the skin is speckled with gold, the best stage for preserving; fruit with completely golden skin is preferred for eating raw. Avoid fruit with bruises or soft spots. Season: All year.

Peaches—Ground color, or background, is yellowish to creamy, and texture is firm, or fairly firm. A red color, called blush, also indicates ripeness, but the blush alone is not a reliable test. Avoid peaches with bruise marks, indicating spoilage. Season: April through October.

Pears—Color depends on variety. Bartletts and comice are pale golden yellow when ripe. Anjous are pale green, sometimes tinged with yellow. Ripe seckel pears are dull brownish yellow blushed with dull red. Ripe forelle pears are highly colored with bright red blush and red freckles on golden yellow ground. Ripen pears in closed paper (not plastic) bags at room temperature out of direct sunlight. Season: All year.

Peas, snap—These edible podded peas are at their sweetest when the pods are plump and well filled with peas and a pale green color. Season: February through September.

Peppers, sweet and hot—Fully ripe sweet bell peppers come in a variety of colors: yellow, orange, scarlet, deep red, dark brown. Partly ripe ones streaked with pink or pale green ripen easily within a few days if enclosed in a paper bag out of direct sunlight. The bag traps gas given off naturally by the vegetable to make it ripen. Hot peppers—chiles—range in color from pale to dark green to red. Season: All year for bell peppers; late summer through early fall for hot chiles. I have had great success freezing whole chiles (trim the stems to ¼ inch). They should be prepared for use (stemmed, seeded, deveined, and chopped or sliced) while still frozen.

> To avoid a painful burning sensation, always wear rubber or plastic gloves when you handle raw chiles and do not touch your face or eyes.

Pineapples—Forget the old saw about pulling a leaf from the prickly crown. That is more a test of your strength than the fruit's ripeness. A fully ripe pineapple has a fresh-looking deep green crown and a fruity aroma that is diminished by chilling. Shell or skin color does not indicate ripeness. Ripe fruit gives slightly to finger pressure. Avoid fruit with signs of spoilage such as an old, dry, brownish crown, an unpleasant odor, and traces of mold that tend to start at the stem end. Large fruits are the best buys. A 2- to 3-pound pineapple contains less than 30 percent edible flesh; half of a 5-pound fruit has more flesh than a whole pineapple weighing 3 to 3½ pounds. Season: All year.

Plums, beach—*Prunus maritime* crops are sporadic, because the blossoms depend on cross-pollination to set fruit, and bad weather during the blossom stage may reduce transference of pollen by insects. Fruit varies in size from a half to one inch in diameter, and in color from red to deep purple or blue. Season: Fall.

Plums, Italian or prune variety—Deep purplish blue with whitish bloom, nature's protective coating; fruit gives slightly when pressed with fingers. Mature but unripe fruit are reddish blue. Italian plums and damsons are best for preserving, although other varieties may be substituted. If you substitute other varieties, test for pectin and acid content, and make adjustments accordingly. Season: January and February for imports; May through October for American crops, except for damsons, which are found largely at farmstands and farmers' markets in the fall.

Prickly pears—The edible fruit of a cactus variety, prickly pears are also called cactus pears. Ripe fruit has darkish red skin; the pulp may be yellow or deep red. Although the spines have been removed from the fruit before packing and shipping, it is a good idea to handle them cautiously. If you cut off both ends, and spear the fruit with a fork, it is relatively easy to slice through the thick skin and use the knife to pry the skin away from the pulp. Season: September through May.

Pummelos—The grandfather of our contemporary grapefruit, pummelo is often called Chinese grapefruit because it is traditionally part of the Chinese New Year's celebration in midwinter. The low-acid pulp may be pink or white. It is milder in flavor than today's grapefruit, and its juice cells are firmer. Pummelos are grown in both California and Florida, as well as China. The American varieties may reach 1½ to 2 pounds each. Like all good citrus fruit, pummelos should feel heavy for their size. Season: October through February for Florida fruit; November through March for the California varieties.

Quinces—Pale golden yellow but hard when ripe, and knobby in shape. The gray fuzz that appears naturally on the skins should be rubbed off with a dry towel. Shippers generally do this before packing the fruit, but farmstand, farmers' market, and homegrown fruit is usually fuzzy. Ripe quince also has a delightfully spicy scent. Avoid green fruit with no traces of yellow; it often shrivels or rots before it ripens. Season: August through February for California quince; fall into early winter for New York State fruit.

Raspberries, red or black—Perhaps the most perishable berries of all, they mold rapidly and crush easily. If you cannot prepare them the day they are picked (or purchased), gently turn them out into single layers on plates, refrigerate with a light covering of waxed paper or paper towel, and use within 24 hours. Season: May through January.

Raspberry jam tarts

¼ *pound pot cheese or cream cheese*
¼ *pound butter*
¼ *pound flour*

Mix into a dough, then cut into very thin squares. Fill the center of each square with raspberry jam and then turn up the corners in envelope fashion. Bake in a moderate oven until nicely browned.

They are so simple to make that I often do them myself,
Sincerely, Mary Pickford

From *Celebrated Actor Folks' Cookeries,* a collection of
favorite foods of famous players, published in 1916 to
benefit the American Red Cross and the Actors Fund

Rhubarb — For preserving, the palest pink varieties are best, even pale pink tinged with green. Avoid stalks that are too thin or too thick, indicating stringiness and toughness. Also avoid wilted stalks. Deep red varieties produce a less appetizing color in jam than lighter-colored ones. Season: January through June.

Rose hips — Cherry-size fruit of wild rosebushes, they make a slightly herbal-tasting jelly when combined with apple juice or Apple Pectin Extract (page 20). Season: They should be picked after first frost, when the fruit are bright red.

> Never use rose hips from bushes that have been sprayed or that grow beside a heavily traveled road where automotive fumes can leave deposits on them.

Shallots — Brown, papery outer skin, no signs of softness, sprouting, or mold. Season: All year.

Strawberries — Deep, bright red and fresh-looking, with bright green caps. The best for preserving are mature but not fully ripe. They are lighter in color than fully ripe berries. Season: All year.

Tangerines — Bright orange skin, relatively free from blemishes, and fruit heavy for its size. The old-fashioned Dancy variety makes a distinctive-tasting marmalade. Dancys have looser peel than Clementines and Mandarines, and a flattish shape instead of round. Season: October through May.

Tomatillos — Also known as Mexican green tomatoes and husk tomatoes, tomatillos range in size from about an inch in diameter to plum size. They are widely used in Mexican cookery for sauces and stews. They grow in papery husks, and are at their best when pale green in color. Look for them at fancy food shops, some farmstands and farmers' markets, and in shops catering to Hispanic customers. Season: All year.

Tomatoes, mature green—Glossy skin that resists puncturing when scraped with a fingernail or a knife; seeds that are pushed aside rather than cut when tomatoes are sliced, and well-formed jellylike substance in the seed chambers. Color ranges from medium to pale green, sometimes lightly streaked with pink. Season: All year, but supplies are heaviest and best in the fall, just before first frost.

Tomatoes, ripe—Color depends on varieties, ranging from yellow to orange to deep orange-red. The best are firm, plump, fairly well shaped, smooth and free from blemishes. Scars at the blossom end do not affect flavor, but tomatoes with growth cracks should be avoided for preserving and pickling because they spoil faster than unblemished fruit. Season: All year.

Watermelon—The only true test for ripeness is cutting and tasting. As the amount needed for my watermelon pickle recipe is small, your best buy is a quarter or half melon with characteristic deep pink or yellow flesh and the thickest skin you can find. Season: February through November.

MICROWAVE PRESERVING: WHAT WORKS, WHAT DOESN'T

About microwaving

Throughout this book you will find microwave directions for individual recipes only if the results are equal or superior to old-fashioned range top cooking methods. When range top cooking is too much trouble for a recipe (Quince Paste, page 193, for example), I tell you why, and give directions only for microwaving.

All the microwave recipes in this book were tested in a 700-watt variable power oven with one cubic foot interior. If your microwave oven is more or less powerful or spacious, you will have to make adjustments accordingly. By the end of summer 1991, several manufacturers were offering microwave ovens with power levels of 800 and 900 watts. It is always better to err on the side of undercooking, and to continue cooking in one- or two-minute increments, always remembering that cooking will continue for a couple of minutes or more after the power has been shut off, and that each mixture will continue to thicken as it cools.

- Contrary to popular opinion, microwaves cook from the outside in, just like conventional baking. They also cook some foods unevenly. That is why my recipes often call for setting an open canning jar upside down in the center of the cooking vessel, and distributing the food around it. This encourages even cooking, and shortens cooking time. It also spares you the need to stir at intervals.
- Food can stick and burn in a microwave oven if it is cooked with too little liquid or if you fail to stir at the intervals specified in individual recipes. This is more likely to occur after sugar and other sweeteners have been added.

Heavily sweetened spreads tend to caramelize and burn at the outer edges during the final stages of cooking if they are not stirred at frequent intervals.

- If your microwave oven lacks a fixed carousel (turntable), use a wind-up model for more even cooking.

- Sweet spreads, chutneys, sauces, etc., that come out too stiff can be salvaged by remelting them in a saucepan on a range top with a spoonful or two of water or other appropriate liquid (fruit juice or juice concentrate, for example) unless the condiment was so overcooked that the sugar has caramelized.

- A microwave oven does a great job with the initial cooking of many fruits and berries, and there is no need to add liquid if you crush the bottom layer to create some juice for the start-up. But because the microwave is an inefficient evaporator of the juices that will seep out as the fruits or berries cook, the final stage of the cooking called for in most preserving recipes is done faster and better in a pan on a range top. The best candidates for final cooking in a microwave oven are those that should thicken to spreading consistency without jelling. Chutneys, conserves, and preserves made with dried fruit fall into this category. So do citrus marmalades made with puréed peel and pulp.

- Most berries and some fruit with pits, such as peaches and sour cherries, contain so much juice that they cook faster and better on a range top. Pulpy fruit such as damson or Italian prune plums do well in a microwave.

- Citrus peels for candying and marmalade can be partially cooked in a microwave oven successfully if, after the initial boiling, you allow half an hour's standing time for the peel to soften. I find this method more trouble than it's worth, considering the insignificant difference in time between bringing water to a boil in a microwave oven and on a range top.

- The best quantities for microwaving are one to two cupfuls of fruit at a time; larger quantities take longer, and often will cook just as fast on a stove burner. Larger amounts also tend to boil over, so you not only mess up the oven, but lose some of the fruit.

- Fruit to be microwaved should be cut, chopped, or ground to an even texture, for uniform cooking. Damson plums or any other small fruit to be microwaved whole should first have the skins pricked in several places to keep them from exploding in the oven.

- Add fresh or dried herbs during the final cooking with sugar or other natural sweeteners. Taste the spread before packing it, and adjust the seasoning if you wish.

- Most pickles and relishes are best done on the range top, since crispness is what you want, and overcooking is far too easy in a microwave oven.

- The best containers for microwaving should have straight rather than sloping sides to allow for even penetration of microwave energy and handles that can be easily gripped with potholders. A pouring spout is also useful. The capacity should be at least four to five times as great as the amount of food to be microwaved at one time. More headroom is needed because liquids—particularly sweet ones—can boil up more than they do in range top cooking.

- Although some plastic containers are designed for microwave cooking, glass is preferable for heavily sweetened mixtures that can reach temperatures high enough to warp some plastics.

- Almost all the microwave recipes in this book were cooked in either a 2-quart ovenproof glass measure with straight sides, an open handle, and a pouring lip, or 2- or 3-quart Pyroceram (Corning Ware) casseroles with rounded corners and glass lids. Microwavable plastic wrap is safe to use if you vent it by turning back one corner to let steam escape during the cooking. But I much prefer to use either an ovenproof glass lid if available, or a microwave-safe plate as a makeshift cover.

- To avoid steam burns from microwaved food, always remove the cover away from you, and avoid leaning over the dish as the steam rises. If you use plastic wrap, be sure it is labeled for microwave use, and turn back one corner to allow steam to escape during cooking.

- Do not try to melt paraffin in a microwave oven. Paraffin is transparent to the microwave energy that cooks food, and will remain solid.

- Don't expect a recipe to need exactly the same cooking time and produce the same yield each time you make it. Among other things, seasonal variations in rainfall (and the amount of watering you do if the fruit is from your own garden or orchard) influence the juiciness and pectin content of fruit and berries.

JAMS, JELLIES, PRESERVES, AND MARMALADES

Ephraim Bull tames a wild grape

Ephraim Wales Bull's home in Concord, Massachusetts, is called Grapevine Cottage in recognition of his role in developing a grape hardy enough to survive New England's severe winters. Bull named his hybrid the Concord grape and sold seedlings throughout the country. He cultivated America's best-known native grape from a wild vine that grew on his own land. "Mr. Bull's important contribution brought him fame but little money," Imogene Wolcott wrote in The Yankee Cook Book *(1963 edition). "On the bronze tablet over his grave in Sleepy Hollow Cemetery in Concord are the words 'He sowed—others reaped.'"*

 ike Maria in *The Sound of Music,* I count jam and bread among "a few of my favorite things." Along with jellies, preserves, and marmalades. And not just on bread. In fact, I probably use more of these homemade spreads as ingredients in other dishes than I do on breakfast toast. For specific recipes, see Baking and Dessert-making With Home-preserved Foods. But don't stop there. Throughout this chapter you will find suggestions for using jams, jellies, preserves, and marmalades as important components in sauces, cakes, and sandwich-cookie fillings, and I hope my use of them will stimulate your own imagination.

If you are tasting homemade spreads for the first time, be prepared for a pleasant surprise. In many instances, the aroma of the fresh fruit will waft upward when you open the jar. The texture may be looser than you are accustomed to—more easily spreadable. The flavors are more intense because in each recipe I have used the least amount of sugar necessary instead of diluting the fruit flavor with excess sugar or a combination of juices from other types of fruit.

To the rescue

Stiff, overcooked jams and marmalades can easily be fixed. Either melt them down with a little water or fruit juice, or combine the stiff jam with an uncooked batch, and boil until it thickens to the proper consistency when tested.

Concord grape jam

MAKES ABOUT 4 CUPS

This may be my easiest recipe, and one of the freshest tasting. Melted down with a little water, the jam makes a good sauce for sherbet or ice cream.

If you're using homegrown grapes, and as many as a quarter of them are unripe (deep red instead of purple), test the cooked, unsweetened juice for pectin to see if you'll need equal quantities of purée and sugar.

> **3 pounds ripe Concord grapes, or a
> 2-quart basket containing about 3 to
> 3¼ pounds
> 3 cups sugar**

Place washed, drained, and stemmed grapes in a wide 4-quart saucepan. Crush them with a potato masher to release some juice. Bring to boil quickly, stirring to prevent sticking. Boil about 10 minutes, or until pulp whitens and skins are tender.

Remove from heat and push through a strainer, until you have 4 cups. Use a wooden spoon so that you don't scrape or crack the seeds.

At this point, you may let the purée stand up to 24 hours at room temperature, or pack it in freezer containers, seal, label, and freeze up to 12 months.

When you are ready to make the jam, bring the purée to a boil quickly in a wide 4-quart saucepan, stir in sugar all at once, and continue stirring until it dissolves. Boil rapidly about 20 minutes, or until gel tests almost done. This variety of grape is so rich in pectin that it is easy to overcook. If that should occur, return it to the saucepan, add a spoonful or two of water, reheat to a boil, and retest. Ladle at once into hot, sterilized jars, seal, cool, label, and store.

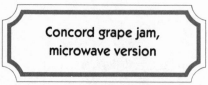

Concord grape jam, microwave version

MAKES ABOUT 2 CUPS

> **1 quart basket Concord grapes (about
> 1½ pounds)
> Sugar equal in volume to cooked,
> sieved grapes**

Wash, drain, and stem the grapes; place a single layer of them in a 2-quart microwavable glass measure or 2-quart casserole, and crush with a potato masher or pastry blender to release juice. Add remaining stemmed grapes, cover (vent if using plastic wrap), and microwave on high for 3 minutes; uncover, stir, and microwave 4 minutes more. Let stand 2 minutes, then push through strainer to remove seeds. Because this jam is so easy to overcook, I prefer to finish it on the range top. If you have used a microwavable casserole that is also flameproof, simply return the purée to it, add sugar, and cook as previously described. Or transfer the purée to 1½-quart saucepan, add sugar, and boil rapidly about 15 minutes, or until gel tests done. Ladle into hot, sterilized jars, seal, cool, label, and store.

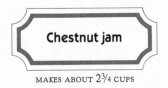

Chestnut jam

MAKES ABOUT 2¾ CUPS

Recipes for chestnut jam were still appearing in early-twentieth-century cookbooks, but disappeared soon after a blight wiped out native American chestnut trees in the first three decades of the century. Raw chestnuts today come largely from Italy and France. The early American chestnut jams were very heavily sweetened. My recipe uses less sugar, and makes a delicious filling for homemade sandwich cookies. If preparing raw chestnuts is too much trouble, you can make the jam with canned unsweetened chestnuts or chestnut purée available in specialty shops and some supermarkets. The jam will be darker, and somewhat smoky in flavor (directions follow).

> **1 to 1¼ pounds large chestnuts (about**
> **24 per pound)**
> **2 cups water**
> **¾ to 1 cup sugar, or to taste**
> **1 teaspoon vanilla extract, or 2 table-**
> **spoons armagnac, cognac, or dark**
> **rum**

Shell and peel the chestnuts as described on page 42. Place prepared chestnuts on a rack in a 4-quart or larger pressure cooker. Add water, cover, and cook at 15 pounds pressure for 15 minutes. Or place in a large saucepan, cover with water and a tight lid, and boil until the nuts are soft and falling apart. Strain and reserve the cooking liquid. Let the nuts cool slightly, then put them through food mill, using as much strained cooking liquid as necessary to make a spreadable purée. Return it to the pressure cooker or saucepan, add sugar, and cook,

Chestnut jam (continued)

uncovered over low heat, stirring often, until sugar crystals have dissolved. Off heat, stir in the vanilla or brandy or rum, and pack into freezer containers or hot, sterilized jars, seal, cool, label, and refrigerate or freeze.

Chestnut peeling made easy

Buy the largest chestnuts you can find; the edible yield will be greater, and you will have fewer nuts to peel. If you cannot prepare them within 24 hours of purchase, bag and freeze them to retard spoilage. To prepare them for cooking, use a chestnut knife (it has a 1-inch-long curved blade) or a small, sharp paring knife to cut an X in the flat side of each shell. Place no more than half a pound of chestnuts at a time, X side up, in a circle around the outer edge of a shallow microwavable dish and set it on a turntable, if available. Cover with a plastic dinner plate or vented microwavable plastic wrap, and microwave on high for 1½ minutes.

Protecting your hand with a glove or a paper towel folded twice to make four thicknesses, remove 3 or 4 nuts at a time, and peel off the shells and inner skin. Watch carefully for moldy spots, and cut them out if they are small. If they have spread throughout the nut, discard it. Set aside any nuts that resist peeling or whose meat is almost totally black. Return those that resist peeling to the microwave, cover, and zap on reheat power level for 1 minute. If they still resist peeling, discard them.

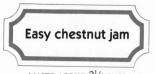

Easy chestnut jam

MAKES ABOUT 2¼ CUPS

1 (15.5-ounce) can unsweetened
    chestnut purée or canned whole
    chestnuts in water
¾ cup sugar
1 teaspoon vanilla extract, or 2 table-
    spoons armagnac, cognac, or
    dark rum

Place all ingredients in a food processor with steel blade, and pulse/chop until the purée begins to soften and absorb sugar. Then, process continuously until a smooth purée forms, stopping to scrape down sides of processor bowl. Scrape into a 1-quart microwavable glass measure, and microwave, uncovered, on high for 3 minutes. Stir and taste to make sure all sugar crystals have dissolved. Pack into hot, sterilized glass or plastic containers, cool, cover, label, and refrigerate or freeze.

If you use canned whole chestnuts, purée them in a food processor with enough of the canning liquid to form a smooth purée, before proceeding with the recipe. If the chestnuts are packed without water, prechop them in a food processor, then add water by the tablespoonful until a smooth purée forms, and continue as above.

NOTE

If jam should recrystallize, reheat it in the microwave, stir, and taste to make sure all sugar crystals have dissolved. This jam is best packed in small containers because it molds more easily than fruit jams.

> *It's too important a question to be settled by Amateurs! I can give you the views of a* Professional *— perhaps the most experienced jam-taster now living. Why, I've known him fix the age of strawberry-jam, to a day — and we all know what a difficult jam that is to give a date to — on a single tasting!*
>
> Lewis Carroll, *Sylvie and Bruno Concluded,* 1889

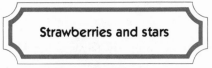

Strawberries and stars

MAKES ABOUT 2 CUPS

Strawberries are the dominant flavor in this jam; they also dye the carambola slices a deep rose-red. As a topping for cheesecake, this jam adds both flavor and beauty.

1 pint basket strawberries (about 10 ounces)
10 to 12 ounces ripe yellow carambolas (4 small)
1 cup sugar
¼ cup light corn syrup
¼ cup fresh lemon juice

Hull the strawberries and cut any large ones into halves or quarters. Trim brown edges from carambolas, and slice a scant ³/₈ inch thick with a sharp knife or a mandoline. A food processor mangles them. Layer the strawberries and carambola slices with sugar and corn syrup in a wide 4-quart saucepan, and let

Strawberries and stars (continued)

stand about 3 hours, or until sugar has dissolved and formed a syrup. Bring to a boil over high heat, and boil rapidly 10 minutes, stirring occasionally. Remove from heat, stir in lemon juice, and pour at once into a shallow 2-quart heatproof dish to cool. Cover lightly with waxed paper or a paper towel, and let stand overnight for fruit to plump.

The next day, place the jam in a 2½-quart saucepan, bring to full boil over high heat, and boil rapidly 5 to 8 minutes, stirring often to prevent sticking. The jam should be thick, but need not reach the gel stage. Fill hot, sterilized jars, seal, invert for 5 minutes, then set upright to cool. Label and refrigerate.

> *Well, I put to him the very question you are discussing.*
> *His words were cherry-jam is best, for mere chiaroscuro of*
> *flavour; raspberry-jam lends itself best to those resolved*
> *discords that linger so lovingly on the tongue; but for*
> *rapturous utterness of saccharine perfection, it's apricot-*
> jam first and the rest nowhere!
>
> Lewis Carroll, *Sylvie and Bruno Concluded,* 1889

Apricot jam

MAKES ABOUT 2 CUPS

Dried apricots make a more intensely flavored jam than fresh apricots, and microwaved jam is superior to the range top version in terms of color and flavor.

1 (6-ounce) package dried apricots
1 cup water
1 cup sugar, or to taste

Cut apricots into ¼-inch-wide strips. Set an open 8-ounce canning jar upside down in the center of a 2-quart microwavable glass measure or casserole, distribute the prepared apricots evenly around it, and add the water. Cover with vented lid, and microwave on high for 5 minutes. Remove from oven, remove jar with a jar lifter, and spread the fruit out to soften and plump up. Stir in the sugar, and microwave, uncovered, for 5 minutes, stirring after first 3 minutes so jam will cook evenly. It is done when no sugar crystals remain and the jam holds its shape when stirred. Stir immediately after removing it from the microwave to stop the cooking. Ladle at once into hot, sterilized jars, seal, cool, label, and refrigerate.

Variation　To make apricot butter, purée the precooked fruit in a food processor.

. . . every summer in Texas there is a three-way race among the small fry, the mockingbirds, and the housewives to see who will get to the figs first. The kids and the mockingbirds, having more time, almost always do all right for themselves; and in normal years, the womenfolks get theirs, too.

Arthur and Bobbie Coleman, *The Texas Cookbook,* 1949

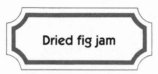

Dried fig jam

MAKES ABOUT 2½ TO 2¾ CUPS

Unless you have access to wild figs or grow your own or are willing to pay top dollar at the store, you'd best make jam from dried fruit. In fact, I prefer dried figs because they make luscious jams with little or no added sugar, since drying concentrates the fructose naturally present in all fruit. One of my tasters recommends using this as filling for homemade fig newtons made with a shortbread-type dough. Even easier are sandwich cookies made with good quality store-bought cookies.

> **8 ounces dried figs***
> **1 cup water**
> **¼ cup sugar**
> **¼ cup fresh orange juice**
> **2 tablespoons cognac-based orange-**
>   **flavored liqueur**

*Mission and calimyrna figs are my first and second choices.

Stem and quarter the figs with scissors. Place figs and water in a 2-quart microwavable glass measure or lidded casserole, cover (vent if using plastic wrap), and microwave on high for 3 minutes; let stand 2 minutes. Put the figs with their syrup and the remaining ingredients in a food processor, and chop medium fine. Fill hot, sterilized jars or freezer containers, seal, and cool. Label and refrigerate or freeze.

Kiwi-lemon preserves

MAKES ABOUT 1 CUP

Kiwis have been praised and vilified by the food-writing community as beautiful to the eye, but bland to the palate. Their color, like that of some other green fruits and some green vegetables, usually turns an unappetizing olive drab when heated. Adding lemon juice and peel prevents that problem, while adding a pleasant flavor.

About 1 pound kiwis (4 to 6)
Peel of half a small lemon
¾ cup sugar, divided
2 tablespoons fresh lemon juice

Peel and slice kiwis as thin as possible with a sharp knife or a mandoline; a food processor does a very uneven job. Pulse/chop the lemon peel in a small food processor with 2 tablespoons of the sugar (it acts as an abrasive). Add lemon juice and mix all the ingredients in a 1½-quart saucepan. Let stand, stirring occasionally, until sugar has dissolved, about 20 minutes or more. Bring to full boil on high heat, and boil rapidly about 15 minutes, or until gel tests done. Fill a hot, sterilized half-pint jar or two 4-ounce jars, seal, invert for 5 minutes, then set upright to cool. Label and refrigerate.

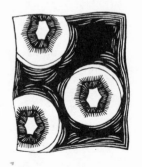

To a pound of Cherrys, half a pound of currant juice, let it boil half an hour, then put in a pound and a half of sugar, let it boil (til) it is a thick jam, scum it well. The Cherrys may be stoned or not, as you like.

From the manuscript receipt book of Elizabeth Duncumb,
Sutton Coldfield, Warwickshire, England, 1791

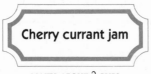

Cherry currant jam

MAKES ABOUT 2 CUPS

Don't attempt this recipe unless you can get fresh currants to make the juice. Commercially bottled currant juice doesn't work because it lacks the pectin of home-cooked juice prepared with raw currants.

> 1 pint basket tart red cherries (about
>   2 cups)
> 1 cup stemmed red or white currants,
>   or a mixture, or the same amount of
>   cooked currant juice*
> ½ cup sugar per cup of cooked fruit

*See Penny Pincher's Red Currant Jelly recipe (page 74) for currant juice directions.

Stem and pit the cherries. Pulse/chop the cherries and currants coarsely in a food processor. Place in a 2-quart glass microwave measure or 2-quart casserole with vented cover, and microwave on high for 5 minutes; let stand 2 minutes. At this stage you may refrigerate or freeze the stock for later use.

To complete the jam, in one or two batches, allow ½ cup sugar for each cup juice. Boil in a 1½-quart saucepan for 1 cup of jelly, or a 2- to 2½-quart saucepan for 2 cups of jelly, until gel tests done. Pack in hot, sterilized jars, seal, invert for 5 minutes, then set upright to cool. Label and refrigerate unless you plan to use it within a week or two.

Blackberry jam

MAKES ABOUT 1½ CUPS

> 1 pint basket blackberries (about
>   2 cups)
> 4 teaspoons fresh lemon juice
> 1 cup sugar

Mash berries with potato masher or pastry blender in a 2½-quart saucepan. Bring to boil over high heat, and boil rapidly 5 minutes. Remove from heat, and

Blackberry jam (continued)

stir in lemon juice. Either freeze in a tightly covered container to use later or add the sugar, and boil rapidly until gel tests done. Pack in hot, sterilized jars, seal, invert for 5 minutes, then set upright to cool. Label and refrigerate unless you plan to use it within 1 or 2 weeks.

> *I like picking blackberries. I enjoy the sights and sounds, the feeling of freedom and isolation it affords. I like the luxury of this delicious wild fruit to freeze, bake into pies and cobblers, and make into jelly and jam.*
>
> Rachel Peden, *Rural Free, A Farmwife's Almanac of Country Living*, 1969

Variation   For preserves, mix the sugar with the blackberries in a 4-quart saucepan, lightly cover with waxed paper, and let stand about 24 hours, stirring occasionally, until syrup forms. Add lemon juice, bring quickly to a boil, and boil rapidly about 4 minutes, or until gel tests done. Pack as directed for the jam above.

> *Collect rose hips preferably after the first frost, when they are red and ripe but still firm, and prepare as soon as convenient. Wash, remove the "brushes" [blossom ends], barely cover with water, and simmer for 15 minutes. Extract the juice and use it for jelly or syrup. Sieve the pulp and use it for jams, fruit catsup and so forth. The flavor needs a lift from some tart fruit such as lingenberry [lowbush cranberry].*
>
> Robert A. Henning, editor and publisher, *The Alaskan Camp Cook*, 1962

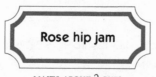

Rose hip jam

MAKES ABOUT 2 CUPS

Without the assistance of my niece, Carol Karcher Lesem, a friend, Kathy Cardlin, and Kathy's mother, there would have been no fruit for this old-fashioned jam. As all three women can attest, picking the rose hips—the seed pods remaining on wild or domestic rosebushes after the flowers have dropped their petals—is a thorny job, requiring heavy gardening gloves, pruning shears, and persistence. The results, I think, are worth it. The jam is an orangy pink, and has a mild herbal flavor.

In Alaska, where fruit with high vitamin C content (oranges and tomatoes) are expensive, rose hips are used as a readily available alternative for making jelly, jam, or fruit syrup.

CAUTION

Do not use rose hips from bushes that have been sprayed or that grow beside a busy roadway, where automotive emissions could deposit toxic materials on the bushes.

> 1 quart rose hips the size of
>   small cherries
> 2 tablespoons fresh lemon juice
> Water
> Apple Pectin Extract (page 20)
> Sugar

Try to have ¾ of the rose hips bright red, and the remainder, mature but unripe—green tinged with red; protect your hands with rubber gloves and use scissors to remove blossom ends and release the hips from their thorny branches. Place rose hips, lemon juice, and water to cover in a 2-quart saucepan, cover, and boil 20 minutes. Push through a strainer with mesh fine enough to trap all the little seeds; use a rubber scraper to salvage as much purée as you can from the underside of the strainer. You should have about 1¾ cups of thin purée; at this point you may freeze the purée for later use.

To make jam, measure half the purée into a 1½-quart saucepan, stir in an equal volume of apple pectin extract, and ⅔ cup sugar. Bring quickly to boil, and boil about 25 minutes, stirring occasionally to prevent sticking, until gel tests done. Pour into hot, sterilized jars, seal, invert for 5 minutes, then set upright to cool. Label and refrigerate.

The first thing I remember tasting and then wanting to taste again is the grayish-pink fuzz my grandmother skimmed from a spitting kettle of strawberry jam. I was about four.

M. F. K. Fisher, *The Gastronomical Me*, 1943

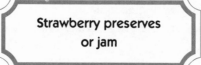

Strawberry preserves or jam

MAKES ABOUT 3½ CUPS

This is my favorite strawberry preserve: not too sweet, not too stiff. If you make it regularly, you'll find no two batches exactly alike, because the pectin content of berries varies widely. Sometimes the jelly will set, with the ruby berries suspended in it like jewels. Other times it will be no thicker than a good dessert sauce—a use for which I heartily recommend it—with coeur à la crème, crêpes, ice cream, even toasted pound cake.

> **2 pint boxes (about 20 ounces) firm strawberries (preferably a third of them underripe)**
> **3 cups sugar**
> **3 to 4 tablespoons fresh lemon juice**

Gently dump the berries into a large bowl or sink full of cold water. Remove them at once by handfuls to a colander or large strainer to drain well. Pinch off caps, layer berries with sugar in a wide 4-quart saucepan, and let stand about an hour or more, until juice begins to form, if making preserves. For jam, crush the berries with the sugar, using a potato masher.

For either spread, place pan over low heat and stir occasionally and gently until sugar melts. Raise heat and boil rapidly 10 minutes, counting from the time when mixture reaches full, rolling boil. Then, remove from heat and stir in lemon juice at once. Use the larger amount of juice if few of the berries were underripe.

Pour mixture into one or more shallow, heatproof dishes. The quicker it cools, the better its color will be. After it cools, I like to cover the dishes lightly with a clean dishtowel or double thickness of cheesecloth to keep out dust, insects, and passers-by, who may be tempted by the lovely fragrance and color.

About 24 hours later, use a rubber scraper to return all the mixture to the pan. Bring quickly to boil, and boil rapidly 10 to 15 minutes more, timing after the mixture reaches full boil. Unless you have homegrown berries, it probably won't pass the gel test, but will fall in thick drops from a metal spoon held above the steam.

Remove from heat, and stir and skim about 5 minutes to prevent floating fruit. Pour into hot, sterilized jars or glasses, seal, invert for 5 minutes, then set upright to cool. It thickens as it cools. Label and store.

Rhubarb: probably a Russian immigrant

The Russians probably introduced rhubarb to America when they were consolidating their fur trade in Alaska in the 1770s. During the same decade, Benjamin Franklin tasted fresh rhubarb while visiting Scotland, and sent seeds home to John Bartram, whose botanical garden was the first in the colonies, Claire Shaver Haughton writes in Green Immigrants, The Plants That Transformed America *(1978). But rhubarb remained a curiosity to most Americans until about 1809, when a traveler from Maine brought some roots home to share with other gardeners. Within twenty years rhubarb roots were being sold commercially. The plant that we make into pie fillings, sauces, and jams has been a popular perennial in American gardens since the end of the Civil War.*

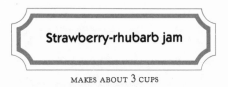

Strawberry-rhubarb jam

MAKES ABOUT 3 CUPS

Surprisingly, the paler the rhubarb and the strawberries, the prettier the deep, rosy color of the jam. I like this jam best when cooked to the consistency of a thick sauce because I like to serve it as a sauce on fresh strawberries or strawberry ice cream or frozen strawberry yogurt.

> ½ pound rhubarb
> 1 quart strawberries (about
>   1¼ pounds), hulled, or 1 (20-ounce)
>   bag frozen unsweetened
>   strawberries
> 2½ cups sugar

Trim rhubarb and cut into ½-inch pieces. Layer the strawberries and rhubarb with the sugar in a 2-quart saucepan, and let stand at least 6 hours at room temperature; stir occasionally, until all the sugar has dissolved and the mixture is very syrupy.

Transfer to a deep 12-inch skillet or wok,* and boil rapidly for 4 minutes. Ladle immediately into a shallow 2-quart ovenproof glass dish, and let stand overnight

*You may also prepare this jam in a 3-quart saucepan, but the cooking may take longer.

Strawberry-rhubard jam (continued)

for the fruit to plump up. Cover lightly after the mixture reaches room temperature.

To prepare the jam, drain syrup into a wide, deep saucepan or a 10-inch skillet at least 3 inches deep, and boil rapidly 4 minutes; add the fruit, and boil rapidly for 2 minutes more, or until jam is thick and syrupy. Ladle into hot, sterilized jars, seal, invert for 5 minutes, then set upright to cool. Label and store.

Peeling fruit

Ripe tomatoes, ripe peaches, and most plums usually peel easily if they are immersed in boiling water for a few seconds. If you have a wire salad basket with a bucket handle, fill it with a single layer of fruit and dip it first into a pan of boiling water and then into a large bowl of cold tap water until the fruit can be handled easily. The skins should lift off without difficulty. If not, dip the fruit into the boiling water a few seconds longer. Unripe tomatoes, peaches, plums, apples, and pears require a swivel-blade peeler or a small sharp knife. Some ripe nectarines can be peeled like ripe peaches, but others need a peeler.

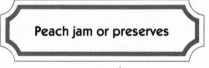

Peach jam or preserves

MAKES ABOUT 6½ CUPS

The peachy flavor and color of this jam (or preserve) are the first of its advantages. Another is that you don't have to use fully ripened fruit, often so difficult to find today. Mature but unripe peaches make a much more flavorful jam. I like it on toast or mixed into plain yogurt or spooned straight from the jar, to satisfy a desire for a little something sweet at the end of a meal.

> 4 to 6 pounds peaches
> 5⅓ cups sugar
> ½ cup fresh lemon juice (about 2½ to
>   3 medium lemons)
> 1½ teaspoons ascorbic acid mixture
>   (optional, page 245)
> 6 tablespoons brandy or
>   sherry (optional)

Peel and pit the peaches, and slice thinly; you should have about 2 quarts.

Mix prepared peaches with sugar in wide 4-quart saucepan. Heat, stirring, until sugar dissolves completely. For jam, crush fruit with potato masher as it softens. Leave slices whole for preserves. When mixture reaches a full, rolling boil that cannot be stirred down, boil rapidly 10 minutes, stirring occasionally.

Remove from heat and stir in lemon juice and ascorbic acid mixture, if desired, at once. Pour into a large, deep platter or several shallow, heatproof glass dishes and let stand until cool. (Shallow containers permit contents to cool quickly, which helps retain jam color.) When cool, cover lightly with waxed paper to protect from dust but permit evaporation. Let stand 24 hours.

The next day, measure the jam or preserves; you should have about 8 cups. Place half of it in a wide 2½-quart saucepan, and bring to boil quickly, stirring to prevent sticking. Boil rapidly, continuing to stir often to prevent sticking, about 10 minutes for jam, or until gel tests done for preserves. The preserves can take as long as 15 minutes if fruit is very juicy as a result of a rainy growing season.

Remove from heat, stir in half the brandy or sherry, if desired, and skim and stir about 5 minutes to prevent floating fruit if you're making preserves. The stirring is not necessary for jam. Ladle the mixture into hot, sterilized jars, seal, invert, then set upright to cool. Label and store. Repeat the process with remaining fruit mixture, or freeze it for later use.

And the canning went on: early apples from our trees—
magnificent Gravensteins—for jelly and applesauce; corn
on and off the cob; prunes, petite prunes and red plums,
whole and in conserve; damsons for jam and damson
cheese . . .

James Beard, *Delights and Prejudices,* 1964

Damson plum jam

MAKES ABOUT 2 CUPS

Damsons are clingstone fruit—hence, messier to prepare than our modern hybrids that separate more easily from their pits. But I think their flavor is superior and, of course, the natural pectin content is so high it needs no boosting. I prefer to finish the microwave version on the range top, making one cup at a time.

Damson plum jam (continued)

1 pound damson plums
½ cup water, or 6 tablespoons water
**   and 2 tablespoons tawny port,**
**   cognac-based orange-flavored**
**   liqueur, or dark rum**
¾ cup sugar for each cup of cooked
**   fruit**

Stem, wash, and drain the plums, and prick them with a sharp-tined fork to prevent their exploding during cooking. Place plums and water or water and wine, liqueur, or spirit of your choice in a 2-quart microwavable glass measure or casserole. Cover (vent if using plastic wrap), and microwave on high for 4 minutes. Let stand 2 minutes. For a smooth jam, put mixture through a food mill to remove pits. Although it's messier to do, I prefer to remove the pits with a small fork. Transfer the pulp and skins to a colander set over a deep bowl. Remove pits with a small fork, then scrape pulp and skins into the juice. If necessary, add water to reach the 2-cup mark. At this point you may freeze the jam stock for future use.

To make jam: For 1 cup, combine 1 cup of the stock with ¾ cup of sugar in a 1½-quart saucepan. Bring quickly to boil, and boil 7 or 8 minutes, or until jam passes freezer test. To make 2 cups, use all the stock and 1½ cups sugar in a 3-quart or larger saucepan, and increase cooking time as necessary. Fill hot, sterilized jars, seal, invert for 5 minutes, then set upright to cool. Label and store.

> *"This is the nicest pahty I evah was at,"* remarked the
> Little Colonel, as Walker helped her to jam the third time.
>
> Annie Fellows Johnston, *The Little Colonel,* 1904

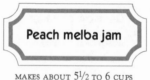

Peach melba jam

MAKES ABOUT 5½ TO 6 CUPS

Fresh raspberries were not widely available in markets, and they cost the earth when I first developed this recipe in the 1970s. It represented my attempt to have the glorious flavor of the berries without utterly destroying my budget. The jam became so popular with my friends that I decided to add two other spreads that combine the berries with either currant juice (see Penny Pincher's Red Currant Jelly, page 74) or crabapple juice (see Crabapple Jelly, page 81). And when fresh raspberries are out of season or especially pricey, I substitute a 12-ounce package of frozen unsweetened raspberries for each pint of fresh.

> 3 pounds mature but unripe peaches
> 1 pint basket ripe red raspberries (12 ounces)
> 1/2 cup fresh lemon juice (reserve seeds)
> 4 cups sugar
> 1/4 teaspoon almond extract

Method for unstrained jam Peel, pit, and slice the peaches. Rinse and drain the raspberries. Place peaches and 1/2 cup of water in wide 4-quart saucepan. Place lemon seeds in metal tea ball or tie loosely in a double thickness of dampened cheesecloth. Add seed packet to pan, bring quickly to boil, and boil rapidly 5 minutes, mashing fruit. Add berries all at once, and continue to boil and mash mixture 5 minutes more.

Remove from heat, stir in lemon juice, and pour into a heatproof bowl of at least 2-quart capacity. Let stand, uncovered or lightly covered with a clean cloth, about 24 hours.

The next day, remove and discard lemon seeds, and measure fruit. You should have about 6 cups. At this stage, you may freeze the fruit mixture for later use. To make jam, place half of fruit in a wide 2½-quart saucepan and bring to boil over medium heat, stirring often to prevent sticking. When it boils, add 2 cups of sugar all at once and stir until mixture returns to boil and sugar dissolves. Boil rapidly 20 to 25 minutes, or until jam holds its shape when about 1/2 teaspoon is dropped on a chilled saucer. Stir often during the last 10 minutes to prevent sticking and reduce splattering.

Remove from heat, stir in 1/8 teaspoon of almond extract, and stir and skim for 2 or 3 minutes. Pour into hot, sterilized jars or glasses, seal, invert for 5 minutes, then set upright to cool. Label and store. Repeat process, using remaining ingredients.

Method for seedless jam Place peaches and 1/2 cup of water in a wide 4-quart saucepan. Place lemon seeds in metal tea ball or tie loosely in a double thickness of dampened cheesecloth and add to pan. Bring quickly to boil, stirring and mashing to crush fruit. Boil rapidly 10 minutes, continuing to mash fruit. Remove from heat, stir in lemon juice, and pour mixture into a heatproof bowl of at least 2-quart capacity.

Place raspberries and 1/4 cup of water in a 1½-quart saucepan and boil, uncovered, about 5 minutes, or until berries are soft. Remove from heat and

Peach melba jam (continued)

force through a strainer into the peach mixture. Discard berry seeds. Let jam mixture stand, uncovered, about 24 hours.

The next day, discard lemon seeds and measure fruit. You should have about 5½ cups. At this stage you may freeze the stock for later use. To make jam, place half the stock in a wide 2½-quart saucepan and bring to boil over medium heat, stirring often to prevent sticking. When it boils, add 2 cups of the sugar all at once and stir until mixture returns to boil and sugar has dissolved. Boil rapidly 20 to 25 minutes, or until jam holds its shape when about ½ teaspoon is dropped on a chilled saucer. Remove from heat, stir in ⅛ teaspoon almond extract, and stir and skim for 2 or 3 minutes. It will thicken more as it cools.

Pour at once into hot, sterilized jars or glasses and continue as above. Repeat with remaining fruit mixture and sugar.

> *Jellies and jams made with added pectin do not have as strong flavor as those made without added pectin.*
>
> Fannie Merritt Farmer, *The Boston Cooking School Cook Book,* seventh edition, 1945

Raspberry jam

MAKES ABOUT 2 CUPS

If you grow your own raspberries or buy them at farmers' markets, you'll need 1½-pint baskets of berries—about 18 ounces.

**3 (6-ounce) trays raspberries, or 1½
  (12-ounce) bags frozen
  unsweetened raspberries
2 tablespoons fresh lemon juice
Sugar**

Set an open 8-ounce canning jar upside down in the center of a 2-quart microwavable glass measure or casserole. Distribute the berries around it, add the lemon juice, cover (vent if using plastic wrap), and microwave on high for 2 minutes; let stand 2 minutes. If the berries are frozen, you may need to microwave them 30 to 45 seconds longer. Transfer berries and juice to a 1½-quart saucepan, add ¾ cup of sugar, bring to boil quickly, and boil rapidly until slightly thickened. It will thicken more as it cools. Pack into a hot, sterilized 12-ounce jar, seal, invert for 5 minutes, then set upright to cool. Label and store a few days for flavors to mellow.

Raspberry currant or crabapple jam

MAKES 1 CUP

If you keep juice for Crabapple Jelly (page 81) or Penny Pincher's Red Currant Jelly (page 74) in your freezer, you can make this jam in about 20 minutes, including the time for defrosting half a cup of the juice of your choice.

½ cup currant or crabapple
   juice, defrosted
1 half-pint tray red raspberries
   (6 ounces)
1 tablespoon fresh lemon juice
¾ cup sugar

Place the juice in a 1½-quart saucepan over medium heat to defrost while you pick over the berries; rinse under running water and drain well. Add the berries, lemon juice, and sugar to the saucepan, and boil rapidly about 15 minutes, or until jam thickens; drop about ½ teaspoon of the jam on a chilled saucer in the freezer. If after a minute or two the jam wrinkles when pushed with a finger, it is thick enough. Pour into a hot, sterilized 8-ounce canning jar, seal, and cool. Label and refrigerate.

If you double the recipe, cook it in a 3-quart or larger saucepan. You may also substitute frozen raspberries for the fresh, using half a 12-ounce package for each cup of jam desired.

Warning: Do not substitute bottled currant or apple juice. Their pectin content is destroyed by processing.

The West Indian connection

The big boost for preserves came in the 16th century, when the Spanish began growing sugar cane in the West Indies. By 1800, sugar was cheap and plentiful enough for the middle classes to use it in preserves, and cookbooks of the period regularly include instructions for putting up fruit with pounds and pounds of sugar.

Harold McGee, *On Food and Cooking*, 1984

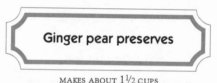

Ginger pear preserves

MAKES ABOUT 1½ CUPS

This very sweet, spicy preserve was a favorite in the late nineteenth and early twentieth centuries, when candied or crystallized gingerroot was imported from the southern Chinese city of Canton.

Half a 5-ounce lemon
1 pound mature but unripe pears
1 ounce crystallized ginger or drained
    preserved stem ginger
1½ cups sugar

Slice lemon as thinly as possible; discard the end and any seeds. Peel and core the pears, and slice about ¼ inch thick. Slice the ginger into thin strips. Mix all the ingredients in a wide 3- or 4-quart saucepan, and let stand at least 12 hours, stirring occasionally, until sugar has dissolved completely into a syrup. Bring to a boil quickly, and boil steadily about 35 to 38 minutes, or until preserve is thick and a light amber color. Watch closely and stir often during the final 10 to 15 minutes, to prevent sticking and burning. Ladle into a hot, sterilized 12-ounce jar, seal, cool, label, and store at least 2 weeks before serving.

Preserving grape leaves

Every time I buy Concord grapes at a market, I remember the joy of having a seemingly endless supply along the back fence of our yard in Harrisburg, Arkansas, in the 1920s. Nowadays the sight of a grapevine sets me to thinking instead of that popular Greek and Middle Eastern appetizer, stuffed grape leaves. Although you can buy brined leaves in specialty shops and supermarkets to stuff with rice filling, you can also easily preserve your own. Pick leaves in the spring when they are light in color, medium in size, and still tender. Blanch them in boiling water in stacks of a dozen each just until they go limp and change color. Drain well, wrap in freezer paper, and freeze for 6 months or more. One advantage of this method is the low sodium content.

Grape preserves

MAKES ABOUT 3½ CUPS

This was my number one comfort food in childhood. Number two was Concord Grape Jam (page 40), which has the same tart/sweet flavor, but lacks the chewiness of the whole grape skins in the preserves. A slice of Wonder Bread slathered with sweet cream butter and the preserves or jam made every real or imagined problem easier to bear. Now in my seventh decade of life, only one thing in the formula has changed: I prefer French or Italian white bread or my own oatmeal–whole wheat loaf as the base. Because the grapes have an extremely high pectin content even when fully ripe, they are easy to overcook. If the preserves are too stiff after cooling, melt them down with a little water and repack.

2 pounds ripe Concord grapes
½ cup water
2¼ cups sugar

Reserving skins, squeeze pulp from grapes. Place pulp in a 1- or 1½-quart saucepan, bring quickly to boil, and boil rapidly about 4 to 5 minutes, or until pulp loses its translucency. Stir occasionally. Force through strainer to remove seeds. Push with a wooden spoon to extract as much pulp as possible.

Place pulp, skins, and water in a wide 1½-quart saucepan, bring quickly to boil, and boil steadily about 15 minutes, until skins are tender. Taste one to be sure. Remove from heat. At this point you may let the mixture stand, uncovered, up to 24 hours, or freeze it for later use, or finish the cooking at once.

To complete the preserves, measure the cooked fruit. You should have about 3 cups. Add sugar, bring quickly to boil, stirring, and boil rapidly about 10 minutes, or until preserves are almost at gel stage. Remove from heat, stir, and skim if necessary. Ladle into hot, sterilized jars, seal, and cool. Label and store in a cool, dry spot. I usually let it stand a week before using.

A jam worth fighting for

Birds love mulberries, so you may have to fight for your share if you are lucky enough to have mulberry trees on your property. On the other hand, you may share the feeling of a friend who has two of the trees overhanging her driveway in Danbury, Connecticut. She keeps threatening to have them cut down because the windfall berries get tracked into the house on the soles of one's shoes. In Artemas Ward's The Encyclopedia of Food *(1923) the berry is described as being "both wholesome and agreeable eaten raw, and is excellent for cooking, especially when mixed with some more acid fruit as apples or rhubarb in pies and puddings."*

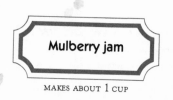

Mulberry jam

MAKES ABOUT 1 CUP

Make the acid and pectin tests (page 19) before adding sugar to this jam, and fortify with liquid pectin if necessary. The berries I used contained a negligible amount of pectin, and were not very juicy—hence, the low yield. If you can obtain larger and juicier berries, the yield should be higher.

> **4 cups half-ripe (red to purple) mulberries**
> **¼ cup water**
> **Fresh lime juice**
> **Sugar**

Place berries and water in a 1½-quart saucepan, cover, and cook about 5 minutes, until berries are soft. Remove from heat, and taste for acidity, adding lime juice as necessary. Cool a teaspoonful of the juice to room temperature, and test for pectin. Discard test mixture without tasting. Add liquid pectin, 1 tablespoon at a time, retesting until you have the desired pectin level, and add sugar accordingly (see page 19) before boiling the jam until it is thick. It need not set like jelly. Ladle into a hot, sterilized 8-ounce jar, seal, cool, label, and refrigerate.

Microwave directions　Reduce the water in the first step to 2 tablespoons. Microwave jam (see pages 33~35 for details) on high in a 2-quart microwavable glass measure or casserole with vented cover about 5 minutes. Test for acidity and pectin, and discard test mixture without tasting. Add lime juice and sugar, and transfer to a range top pot for final cooking because microwaving does a poor job of evaporating liquid rapidly. Pack as above.

A gourmand at breakfast

Archie Goodwin, "gofer" for the famous fictional detective Nero Wolfe, describes his boss at breakfast: "He was a sight, as he always was when propped up in bed with his breakfast tray. Already down the gullet were the peaches and cream, most of the unrationed bacon, and two-thirds of the eggs, not to mention coffee and the green-tomato jam."

Rex Stout, *Nero Wolfe Cook Book,* 1973

Green tomato jam

MAKES ABOUT 3 CUPS

2 pounds green tomatoes
½ cup packed, thinly sliced (⅛ inch)
　　unpeeled lemon (about 2 medium);
　　reserve seeds
1 tablespoon grated crystallized ginger
½ cup water
2½ cups sugar

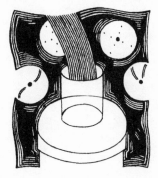

The paler the tomatoes, the better the color of the jam will be. Even those lightly streaked with pink will do. Core tomatoes and chop in a food processor. Place prepared tomatoes, lemon slices, ginger, and water in a wide 2½-quart saucepan. Place lemon seeds in a metal tea ball or tie loosely in two thicknesses of dampened cheesecloth and add to pan. Bring to boil quickly. Adjust heat to boil steadily about 15 minutes, until tomatoes and lemon peel are tender. Cool, cover, and let stand about 24 hours.

Green tomato jam (continued)

The next day, measure; you should have about 3¾ cups. Measure sugar into a bowl, and place tomato mixture in the saucepan. Bring to boil quickly, stirring to prevent sticking. Add sugar all at once, and continue stirring until jam boils again. Boil rapidly, stirring often during the last 10 to 15 minutes of cooking to prevent sticking. It should take 30 to 35 minutes for the jam to thicken enough so ¼ teaspoon of it holds its shape after a minute or two on a chilled plate in the coldest part of the refrigerator. Remove from heat while testing. Ladle into hot, sterilized jars, seal, cool, and label. Let stand 1 week for peel to mellow.

Variation   You can also make this jam with 2 pounds of cherry tomatoes, cored and cooked whole. If you use cherry tomatoes, increase the water to 1 cup, cook the tomatoes and lemon slices, ginger, and water, covered, about 20 minutes in the first step, until the tomatoes and the lemon peel are tender, then proceed as in Green Tomato Jam. The yield runs closer to 4 or 5 cups. If that is too much for your household, simply halve all the ingredients.

Clipper ship cargo

Early America's love affair with crystallized ginger very likely began with the China trade, when clipper ships sailed back and forth between New England ports and the Far East, laden with American goods on the way out, and oriental food and merchandise on their return.

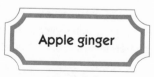

Apple ginger

MAKES ABOUT 4 CUPS

Dozens of nineteenth- and early-twentieth-century cookbooks have recipes for this ultrasweet, spicy preserve. It's more confection than spread—something for people with a real sweet tooth. It makes a good substitute for sugar in cheese-cake batter, or for brown sugar syrup in apple Upside-Down Cake (page 230).

2 pounds firm, ripe, tart apples
¼ cup coarsely chopped crystallized
    ginger or drained preserved stem
    ginger
4 cups sugar
½ cup water
1 tablespoon grated lemon peel
3 tablespoons fresh lemon juice

Peel and core the apples and chop them coarsely in a food processor; you should have about 5 cups.

Place apples and the remaining ingredients in a 3-quart saucepan. Bring to a boil, stirring until sugar has dissolved and mixture again boils. Simmer an hour or more, until apples are tender and preserve is thick. Ladle into hot, sterilized jars, seal, and cool. Label and store.

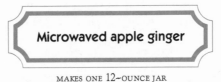

Microwaved apple ginger

MAKES ONE 12~OUNCE JAR

1 pound firm, ripe, tart apples
1 to 2 tablespoons coarsely chopped
    ginger — crystallized, drained
    preserved, or raw
1½ tablespoons fresh lemon juice
1¼ cups sugar

Peel and core the apples, and pulse/chop them coarsely in a food processor. Place the apples and remaining ingredients in a 3-quart microwavable nonplastic casserole, and stir occasionally until sugar forms a syrup. This takes about 5 minutes. With a wooden spoon, push the solids into a ring around the outside of the casserole. Microwave, uncovered (see pages 33~35 for details), on high for 4 minutes; stir, and microwave about 15 minutes longer, stirring every 5 minutes, or until apples are translucent (glassy looking) and a pale golden color, and very little syrup remains. Ladle into a hot, sterilized 12-ounce jar, seal, and cool. Label and store at least a week before using.

Wild pineapples among the sugarcane

Pineapples today are almost synonymous with Hawaii, but they were well known for three centuries before the first white settlers found wild plants growing among the sugarcane plants the Polynesians had introduced from their native islands.

Columbus found pineapple growing on what is now Guadeloupe when he anchored there in 1493. They probably had been planted by the native Carib Indians, who found them during raids along the Amazon in South America, where pineapples had been cultivated for centuries. When or how the fruit first reached Hawaii remains a mystery. "The most generally accepted theory is that they either floated in from a wrecked Spanish or Portuguese ship or were brought ashore by sailors, and discarded," Claire Shaver Haughton *writes in* Green Immigrants, The Plants That Transformed America.

Fresh Hawaiian pineapples were shipped to California during the Gold Rush years of 1849 and 1850, and both fresh and canned pineapple were exhibited at America's first World's Fair, the Philadelphia Centennial Exposition of 1876. J. D. Dole, a Yankee who settled in Hawaii in 1898, persuaded fellow homesteaders to plant pineapples, while he developed commercial canning and shipping. Today pineapples are grown commercially not just in Hawaii, but also Africa, Australia, Malaysia, Mexico, and the East and West Indies.

Pineapple-blueberry jam

MAKES ABOUT 3 CUPS

Both flavors stand on their own in this rich, dark red jam. (The color surprised me the first time I made the jam; I'd always been told that blue mixed with yellow yields green. Obviously not in the world of fruit.) Pineapple-blueberry jam is great on toasted pound cake, sponge cake, or angel food cake. I sometimes swirl it into softened vanilla ice cream and refreeze it, or layer the jam with vanilla ice cream to make parfaits.

> 1 fresh ripe pineapple (3½ pounds)
> 1 pint basket blueberries, or
>   1 (12-ounce) package frozen
>   unsweetened blueberries
> 2¼ cups sugar

Peel and shred the pineapple in a food grinder or food processor using a medium or larger disc to obtain 2 cups. Wash, stem, and sort the blueberries. Place both fruits in a wide 2½-quart saucepan. Bring to boil over medium heat, stirring occasionally. Boil steadily about 10 minutes, stirring occasionally.

Add sugar all at once, and stir until it dissolves and mixture again boils steadily. Adjust heat as necessary to keep jam boiling about 20 minutes, but start testing for gel after the first 10 minutes in case the berries have especially high pectin content. Stir often, as this jam tends to stick. It's done when about 1/2 teaspoon holds its shape in a metal spoon after it rests a couple of minutes on a cool saucer. Ladle into hot, sterilized jars, seal, and cool. Label and store.

> *Our ancestors satisfied a hunger for companionship with, among other things, day-long visits with friends and relatives. While the children played, the ladies cooked dinner, talked to their heart's content, sewed, quilted, embroidered, and made pickles and preserves.*
>
> Olivia Solomon, *Cracklin Bread and Asfidity,* 1979

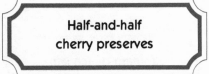

Half-and-half cherry preserves

MAKES ABOUT 4 CUPS

Sheer improvisation, this. The natural spiciness of the sour pie cherries makes a splendid foil for the blander, dark sweet variety. The fruit in tender jelly is tart enough to serve as a relish with meat and poultry. But I also like it on cream cheese sandwiches, buttered toast, and cottage cheese.

1 pound ripe dark sweet cherries
1 pound ripe sour cherries
1/2 cup water
1 1/4 cups Lemon Pectin Extract
  (page 20)
Sugar
4 drops almond extract

Stem and pit the cherries. Place cherries and water in a 3-quart saucepan, bring to a boil quickly, and adjust heat to boil rapidly for about 10 minutes, or until dark cherries are tender and juice is blue-red.

Measure. You should have a scant 3 cups. Stir in pectin extract. Make pectin test (page 19). *Discard test mixture without tasting.*

Half-and-half cherry preserves (continued)

Return fruit mixture to saucepan, and measure sugar into a bowl while you bring the fruit mixture to a boil quickly. Add the sugar all at once, and stir until it dissolves and mixture boils again. Adjust heat to retain a steady boil. Stir occasionally while cooking 20 to 30 minutes, or until gel tests done.

When it's done, remove from heat, stir in almond extract, and stir and skim, if necessary, for about 10 minutes to cool and prevent floating fruit. Pour into hot, sterilized jars. Seal. Let stand undisturbed until cool and set (about 24 hours). Label and store.

Tomato-peach jam

MAKES 2½ TO 3 CUPS

An unlikely sounding combination—tomatoes and peaches—actually makes a beautiful sweet red jam. My recipe was inspired by an old one that called for yellow tomatoes.

> 2 pounds firm ripe tomatoes
> 2 pounds mature but unripe peaches
> Sugar equal in volume to prepared
>   cooked fruit
> 2 tablespoons Vanilla Brandy
>   (opposite page), or ½ teaspoon
>   vanilla extract

Peel, core, and slice tomatoes. Peel and pit peaches, and cut into chunks. Place prepared tomatoes and peaches in a 4-quart saucepan. Bring quickly to a boil, reduce heat, cover, and simmer, stirring occasionally, until fruit is tender, about 15 to 20 minutes. Remove from heat and purée in a food mill or force through a coarse strainer to remove the tomato seeds.

Measure. You should have about 6 cups. At this stage, you may freeze the jam stock for later use, or finish cooking the jam.

To make half the recipe, measure 3 cups of the fruit mixture into a 3-quart saucepan; bring quickly to a boil, stirring often to prevent sticking. Add the sugar, and continue stirring until sugar has dissolved and jam has returned to a boil.

Boil rapidly, stirring often, for about 40 minutes, or until mixture thickens enough so that a little of it holds its shape when chilled for a minute or two on a prechilled saucer in the freezer or coldest part of the refrigerator.

Then, stir in 1 tablespoon of the Vanilla Brandy or ¼ teaspoon of the vanilla extract. Ladle into hot, sterilized jars, seal, invert for 5 minutes, then set upright to cool. Label and store at least a week before using.

If desired, repeat process with remaining jam stock.

MAKES 1 PINT

This flavoring is called for in several recipes in my book, and it also can be used instead of vanilla in baking and in puddings. A spoonful or two is delicious on fresh, frozen, or canned fruit, with or without syrup.

1 or 2 whole vanilla beans
1 pint brandy

Drop the beans into the bottle, reseal it, and let stand at least 2 weeks. It keeps indefinitely, and the beans can be reused until they lose their strength.

A plant world "Typhoid Mary"

Gooseberries have been called "one of the Typhoid Marys of the plant world" because their bushes are host to blister rust, a disease fatal to white pine trees. As if that weren't bad enough, "Lots of Americans still regard rhubarb and gooseberries as hayseed food, suitable only for low country humor rather than the healthful delicacies they really are,"

Lewis Hill wrote in Fruits and Berries for the Home Garden *(1977).*

"Laws in most states require that all Ribes (the botanical family to which gooseberries belong) be planted at least 900 feet from any member of the pine family, and even farther from a nursery where white pine seedlings are grown," Hill adds.

I buy most of my gooseberries at the Union Square Greenmarket, a three-times-a-week farmers' market about half a mile from my New York apartment—but they are also sold in specialty shops and upscale supermarkets.

Gooseberry jam

MAKES ABOUT 1¼ CUPS

Thinned with water, this tart jam may be used to glaze a ham or pork roast. Although the flavor is the same, pink-tinted berries make a more appetizing-looking spread than the big green ones. Because this berry is so high in natural pectin content, it is a natural for the microwave.

> **1 pint basket (12 ounces) gooseberries**
> **2 tablespoons water**
> **Sugar equal in volume to the cooked**
>   **fruit**

Remove stem and blossom ends of gooseberries with scissors. Set an open 8-ounce canning jar upside down in the center of a 2-quart microwavable glass measure or casserole. Pour berries in an even layer around the edge; add water, and a vented cover, and microwave (see pages 33–35 for details) on high for 3 minutes; let stand 2 minutes. Carefully remove the jar with your jar lifter; it will be too hot to handle any other way. Let berries cool slightly, then measure. You should have 1¼ to 1⅓ cups. Return it to the glass measure or casserole. Add an equal volume of sugar, and stir until crystals have dissolved. Microwave, uncovered, on high for 5 minutes; stir, then microwave 5 to 7 minutes longer, or until gel tests done. Fill hot, sterilized jars, seal, invert for 5 minutes, then set upright to cool. Label and refrigerate.

Alternative directions If you cook this on a range top, use a 1½- or 2-quart saucepan, and increase the water to ½ cup to allow for greater evaporation.

Spicy blueberry jam

MAKES ABOUT 5 CUPS

Blueberries have so much natural sweetness that lemon juice, vinegar, or some other acid must be added to make them jell quickly in any recipe without added pectin. Red wine vinegar adds just the right tartness, and the spices make it a much more interesting spread than anything you can buy.

I like this jam particularly on cream cheese or cottage cheese or mixed into plain yogurt. Instead of serving it with plain muffins, I sometimes put a small dollop of jam on each one before the batter goes into the oven.

> 2 pint baskets ripe blueberries, or
>   2 (12-ounce) bags frozen
>   unsweetened blueberries
> 1/2 cup red wine vinegar
> 3 cups sugar
> 1/4 teaspoon each of ground nutmeg,
>   cinnamon, and mace
> 1/8 teaspoon ground cloves

Wash, drain, and stem the ripe blueberries. Place the berries and vinegar in a 4-quart saucepan over medium heat. If you use frozen berries instead, there's no need to defrost them first. When juice starts to form, increase heat slightly, and stir often until mixture boils. Boil steadily about 10 minutes, stirring occasionally to prevent sticking.

Remove from heat and measure. You should have about 3¾ cups. If necessary, add water to fill to 4-cup mark. Return mixture to pan.

Combine sugar and spices in a bowl.

Bring fruit mixture to a boil over medium heat. Add sugar and spices all at once, and stir until jam boils again. Adjust heat so jam boils steadily for 5 to 15 minutes, or until gel tests done; stir often to prevent sticking. When gel tests done, remove from heat, and quickly skim any foam from the surface before ladling the jam into hot, sterilized jars. Seal, invert for 5 minutes, then set upright to cool. Label and store a week or so for flavors to meld.

Beet preserves: a Passover holiday tradition

Eva Lubetkin Cantor, a New Yorker who grew up in the city around the turn of the century, recalls that her mother put up so much beet eingemachts for the spring holiday of Passover that she stored the preserves in ten-gallon crocks. The preserves were a long-standing Passover tradition in Mrs. Cantor's family, Joan Nathan writes in The Jewish Holiday Kitchen *(1979). They were eaten with a spoon and accompanied by tea in a glass.*

Beet eingemachts

MAKES ABOUT 1 PINT

Preserves made from beets, black radishes, and carrots are a tradition begun in Eastern Europe, especially among Jewish families who serve them during the early spring festival of Passover. The custom apparently began because fresh fruit was rare and costly at that season, so plentiful and inexpensive root vegetables were used instead. I usually prepare only one jar at a time because the ingredients are available the year round.

> 1 (4- or 5-ounce) lemon
> ½ pound beets
> 1½ cups water
> 1 cup sugar
> 2 teaspoons packed, grated,
>   fresh gingerroot
> ½ cup blanched, slivered,
>   toasted almonds*

Halve the lemon, discard seeds and ends, and cut into small chunks. In a food processor pulse/chop the lemon to medium texture, stopping to scrape down the sides of the bowl as necessary. Peel beets, and cut to fit processor feed tube if necessary. Replace the chopping blade with a fine shredding disc, and shred the beets. Transfer mixture to a 3-quart saucepan, add the water, bring quickly to a

*To toast the slivered almonds, arrange them in a ring around the outer edge of an 8- or 9-inch microwavable glass pie plate, and microwave (see page 33 for details), uncovered, on high 3 to 3½ minutes, stirring once, until they are aromatic and a very pale tan; they will darken more as they stand. The almonds may also be toasted in a conventional oven; place them in a single layer in an ungreased shallow ovenproof pan or dish, set it on the lowest rack in a preheated 350-degree Fahrenheit oven, and toast 6 minutes or more, until the nuts are a very pale tan. Stir at least once.

boil, and boil about 15 minutes, until beets are tender; stir occasionally. You should have a scant 2 cups of beet-lemon stock. At this stage, you may refrigerate it, covered, for a few days, or freeze for a few months.

To complete the preserves, place the stock in a 3-quart saucepan, stir in the sugar and gingerroot, bring quickly to a boil, and boil rapidly for 15 to 20 minutes, or until mixture thickens somewhat; a little of the liquid should wrinkle when pushed with a finger after a minute or so on a chilled saucer in the freezer. Stir in the toasted almonds, pack in hot, sterilized jars or glasses, cover tightly, label, and refrigerate. This preserve keeps for months.

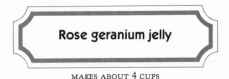

Rose geranium jelly

MAKES ABOUT 4 CUPS

A rose geranium is one of my favorite houseplants, with its spicy fragrance and beautiful blossoms. Our grandmothers used leaves from these plants to perfume and flavor their apple jelly. I like rose geraniums even better in this honey-sweetened spread, because the leaves seem to accentuate the natural spiciness of the honey. I never feel guilty about cutting a few leaves from my rose geranium, because careful pruning is actually good for it.

If this one is too sweet for your taste, take a shortcut. Melt down a jar of good quality apple jelly from the supermarket, add a couple of rose geranium leaves, and bring quickly to a boil. Remove from heat, let cool slightly, fish the leaves out with a fork, then place a fresh leaf in a hot, sterilized canning jar, fill, seal, cool, label, and refrigerate it for a week or so before serving. If you transfer it to a traditional canning jar, no one will know your guilty secret.

> 1½ cups clover honey
> 1 cup sugar
> 1¼ cups plus 1 tablespoon water
> 2 tablespoons strained lime juice
> 7 rose geranium leaves, washed and
>   dried
> 3 ounces (1 pouch) liquid pectin

Mix the honey, sugar, water, lime juice, and 3 of the leaves in a 4-quart saucepan.

Bring quickly to a full, rolling boil that cannot be stirred down. *Watch*

Rose geranium jelly (continued)

carefully, and remove from heat at once when the foam starts to rise. This jelly boils over very easily.

Stir in the pectin as boiling subsides. Use a slotted spoon to stir and skim jelly for about 5 minutes, removing leaves as you do so. Place a fresh leaf in each sterilized jar or glass, and fill with jelly. The leaves will rise to the top. Seal and label. Let stand a couple of weeks for flavor to develop.

Please don't squeeze the jelly bag

If you want to salvage the last drops of juice for jelly, it's okay to squeeze the jelly bag with clean hands—but the jelly may be cloudy, since minute particles of fruit can get through under pressure.

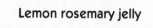

Lemon rosemary jelly

MAKES ABOUT 3 CUPS

Now that fresh herbs are routinely available at many supermarkets, herb jellies are a cinch to make. While dried herbs can be substituted in making the infusion, only fresh sprigs of herbs should be packed in the jars. This jelly is really more of a relish than a bread spread. It is good with roast meats, served on the side, or used as a glaze in the last 15 to 20 minutes of cooking. Try substituting it for the sugar when making applesauce or for sautéing apple slices to serve with meats.

3 lemons (4 ounces each)
4 1/2 cups water
2 tablespoons dried rosemary leaves,
    or about 1/4 cup fresh
Sugar
Fresh rosemary sprigs (optional)

Slice lemons crosswise as thin as possible with a sharp knife or a mandoline. A food processor does an uneven job. Discard the ends and seeds. Place lemon slices in the water in a large mixing bowl and let stand, uncovered, overnight, or for at least 12 hours.

The next day, transfer mixture to a 3-quart saucepan, and boil rapidly for 30 minutes. Crumble the dried rosemary or bruise the fresh. Add the rosemary leaves during the last 5 minutes of cooking. Remove from heat, cover tightly, and let stand 30 minutes.

Drip mixture through a dampened jelly bag or 4 thicknesses of dampened cheesecloth until you have about 3 cups of juice. At this stage, you may freeze the jelly stock for later use.

To make an 8-ounce jar of jelly, place 1 cup each of jelly stock and sugar in a 3-quart saucepan, bring to a boil, and boil rapidly 10 to 15 minutes, or until gel tests done. Remove from heat, and stir and skim 3 to 5 minutes.

If desired, place a fresh rosemary sprig in a hot, sterilized jar before filling it. Seal, invert for 5 minutes, then set upright to cool. Label and store.

To make a 12-ounce jar of jelly, use 1½ cups each of jelly stock and sugar; or for the entire recipe, 3 cups of jelly stock and 3 cups of sugar, and proceed as above.

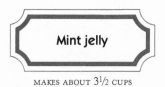

Mint jelly

MAKES ABOUT 3½ CUPS

Have you ever used mint jelly in chocolate jelly roll or between the layers of a chocolate cake? Ambrosial, that's what it is. So is a parfait of chocolate or vanilla ice cream layered with this mint jelly, melted down with a little water. The jelly recipe is a very old one, calling for fresh mint and cider vinegar; I've used white wine vinegar with equal success. But never dried mint: it tends to have a musty smell.

> 1 large bunch fresh mint (1 cup
>   packed)
> ½ cup white wine vinegar or cider
>   vinegar
> 1 cup water
> 3½ cups sugar
> Green vegetable coloring
> 3 ounces (1 pouch) liquid pectin

Wash and dry the mint in a salad basket (or roll it lightly in a terrycloth towel and refrigerate for an hour or so). Set aside four 2-inch sprigs from the mint tops.

When virtually no water remains on the mint, measure, and crush to bruise the leaves and release the oil that carries the flavor.

Place crushed mint, vinegar, water, and sugar in a deep 4-quart saucepan, and bring quickly to boil.

Mint jelly (continued)

While mixture is heating, add enough drops of vegetable coloring to tint jelly as green as you wish.

When mixture boils, add pectin, stirring constantly, and bring to full, rolling boil that cannot be stirred down. Boil 30 seconds and remove from heat at once.

Place mint sprigs in sterilized jars. Strain jelly into them. Seal. The mint will rise to the top. Let stand undisturbed until set. Label and store a week or two for full flavor to develop.

> *Fired with a housewifely wish to see her store-room stocked with home-made preserves, she undertook to put up her own currant jelly. [Meg] spent a long day picking, boiling, straining, and fussing over her jelly. She did her best; she asked advice of Mrs. Cornelius; she racked her brain to remember what Hannah did that she had left undone; she reboiled, resugared, and restrained, but . . . "The—the jelly won't jell and I don't know what to do!"*
>
> Louisa May Alcott, *Little Women,* Part II, 1892 edition

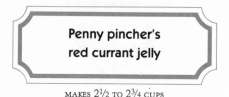

Penny pincher's red currant jelly

MAKES 2½ TO 2¾ CUPS

By using two juice extractions, you get almost three cups of jelly from only one quart of currants. My recipe appeared in slightly different form in the New York *Daily News* Good Living section several years ago.

> **1 heaped quart basket (1½ pounds)**
> **red currants**
> **2¼ cups water, divided**
> **Sugar equal in volume to the strained,**
> **cooked juice**

Stem, wash, and drain the currants; it does not matter if a few bits of stem remain on individual berries. Place the currants in a 4-quart saucepan, add ¾ cup of water, bring to boil over high heat, stirring; boil about 10 minutes, until mixture is very juicy. Drip through a jelly bag; return seedy pulp to pan, add the remaining 1½ cups of water, and repeat boiling and straining steps. Combine the two juice extractions, and measure. You should have about 2⅓ cups of juice. At this point you may refrigerate the juice or freeze it.

To make one 8-ounce jar or two 4-ounce jars of jelly at a time, measure 1 cup of juice into a 1½-quart saucepan. Stir in 1 cup of sugar, and bring to a boil over high heat, stirring; boil vigorously for 10 to 15 minutes, or until gel tests done. Fill jar(s), seal, invert for 5 minutes, then set upright to cool. Label and store.

To make one 12-ounce jar, use 1½ cups of jelly stock and 1½ cups of sugar; to prepare the entire batch, use as much sugar as you have jelly stock, and follow directions in preceding paragraph.

Avoid toxic pits

Many old recipes for cherries, peaches, and apricots suggest using a few kernels from the fruit pits to flavor jams and preserves. That is dangerous advice. The pits, or stones, of these fruits contain hydrocyanic acid, a highly toxic and life-threatening substance. In colonial times Northern Indians, who used wild chokecherries and their pits to make a dried paste to store for winter meals, leached out the acid during the drying process.

Pyramid jellies

Mould variously colored jellies, the more the better, in wineglasses pointed in shape. Warm a little of each enough to run, fill the glasses and cool. Turn out on an ornamental plate, arrange prettily and heap whipped cream about the base. Serve one pyramid to each person in a sauce dish with a portion of cream. Lemon and orange jellies may be moulded and served in the same way. A dainty dish for a company tea. Takes the place of fruits.

Emma Frances Voris, *The New Columbian White House Cookery*, 1893, a cookbook commemorating the World's Columbian Exposition in Chicago

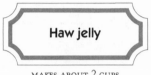

Haw jelly

MAKES ABOUT 2 CUPS

Haws are the fruit of the hawthorn tree, which is either a blessing or a curse, depending on whose yard the fruit falls in. I am indebted to my friends Cherna and Norman Weinstein, of Brooklyn, for supplying the fruit for my recipe testing. The fruit was from a tree in a neighbor's yard whose branches overhang the Weinsteins' property. Haws may be apple- or pear-shaped, range in size from

Haw jelly (continued)

tiny to an inch in diameter, and in flesh, from juicy to mealy-dry. The flavor is unique—only vaguely reminiscent of apples. The Chinese use the pulp to make candy wafers about the size and thickness of a dime. The fruit my friends pick is about the size of cranberries; if you have access to larger varieties, I urge you to use them: it will reduce preparation time.

> **2 pounds (2 quarts) haws**
> **4 cups water**
> **¼ cup strained fresh lemon juice**
> **Sugar equal in volume to cooked,**
> **strained juice**

Wash and drain haws. Remove blossom and stem ends. Place prepared haws and water in a 4- to 5-quart saucepan, cover, and boil about 20 minutes. Mash with potato masher, cover, and cook 10 minutes longer. Drip through a jelly bag (in two batches if necessary). You should have about 2 cups of cloudy pink juice; stir in the lemon juice, which will clarify the haw juice. At this point you may refrigerate or freeze the juice for later use.

To make jelly, add sugar equal in volume to the juice, and boil rapidly in a 3-quart saucepan (or a 1½-quart saucepan if you wish to make only half the recipe) until gel tests done. The fruit I have had was so high in pectin that it jelled in a scant 3 minutes of final cooking. Fill hot, sterilized jar(s), seal, invert for 5 minutes, then set upright to cool. Label and store. Because red jellies darken rapidly at room temperature, this is best kept in the refrigerator.

Chokecherry jelly

MAKES ABOUT 2 CUPS

Chokecherries (*Prunus virginiana*) and wild black cherries (*P. serotina*) are among the most widely distributed trees on our continent, Barrie Kavasch writes in *Native Harvests* (1979), adding that they "usually produce abundant red to black fruits, tart and tasty, about the size of large peas, excellent raw. Avoid eating the leaves and kernels, as they are toxic." Others, including an early colonist named William Wood, were less enthusiastic. In *New England's Prospect* (1634) Wood wrote " . . . they be much smaller than our English cherries; nothing neare so good if they be not very ripe; they so furre the mouth that the tongue will cleave to the roofe, and the throat was horse with swallowing those red berries . . . " Cooked, well, that's a different matter. In *The L.L. Bean Book of New New England Cookery* (1987) authors Judith and Evan Jones say these wild cherries are "benign and have an unusual and delectable flavor—just one more of nature's surprises." The chokecherry recipe and the beach plum recipe following are from their book.

2 quarts chokecherries
1 quart water
3 tablespoons liquid pectin
2 cups sugar

Boil the chokecherries gently in the water, covered, for 20 minutes. Mash the cooked fruit by hand or in a food processor, and put the mash in a jelly bag. Hang from a hook or a faucet with a bowl underneath and let drip for about 24 hours, or until all the juice is extracted. Measure the juice (you should have 1½ cups) and pour into a saucepan. Add the pectin to the juice, bring to a boil, then stir in the sugar and simmer until just dissolved. Pour into hot, sterilized jelly jars and seal.

> And then I thought, provided she keeps that homemade taste, what sort of person am I to deprive the rest of mankind of the pleasure of Mrs. Adams's jams and jellies? So here's the deal. The loan is yours. Provided that you guarantee to supply me one dozen jars of wild beach plum jelly every year. Okay?
>
> Banker John Norton in Douglas Kiker's *Murder on Clam Pond*, 1986

**Nancy Nagel's
beach plum jelly**

MAKES 7 CUPS

The beach plum—*Prunus maritime*—is a wild native plum that used to grow abundantly along beaches, coastal plains and among sand dunes from the Canadian maritime provinces of Nova Scotia and New Brunswick south to Virginia and thrived around the Great Lakes. They are less plentiful now because land development for vacation housing has to some extent taken over their land.

I have never been fortunate enough to find beach plums on my occasional visits to the south shore of Long Island, so I am particularly grateful to Judith and Evan Jones for allowing me to include Nancy Nagel's recipe from their book, *The L.L. Bean Book of New New England Cookery* (1987). If you can find beach plums that are not quite ripe, they should contain enough natural pectin to make the commercial kind unnecessary. Make the pectin test (page 19) to be sure.

Nancy Nagel's beach plum jelly (continued)

> 5 cups whole beach plums, washed
>   and cleaned of leaves (don't bother
>   about the stems)
> 1 cup water
> 6 cups sugar
> 3 ounces liquid pectin

Crush the plums with a potato masher in a big pot, add the water, and simmer, covered, for 20 minutes. Continue to mash them now and then during the cooking. Filter the mixture through a really fine jelly bag. Don't mash or try to force it through — just let it drip slowly if you want a clear jelly. If the plums were juicy, you will have about 3½ cups when finished.

Stir the 3½ cups juice (if you don't have quite that much cut down on the sugar and pectin accordingly) and sugar together in a large pot and bring to a rolling boil — it should be boiling so hard you can't stir down the bubbles. Add the pectin, stirring constantly, and boil for 1 minute. Remove from the heat and let sit for a minute, then skim off all the foam. Pour into hot, sterilized jars, and seal.

> *He dashed off and returned presently with a small package, very heavy for its size. It was, said the printing on the top, "Old Forester Jell." The contents, it stated further, were "sugar, water, whiskey, citrus pectin and citric acid." It was, in other words, jellied whiskey, or whiskied jelly, as you care to put it. You eat it on things.*
>
> *. . . You can see the multifold advantages of this. A lady traveling alone on a train, for instance, is sometimes sensitive about ordering a couple of slugs before breakfast, fearing that a false, or even worse, a true, impression may be given to the passers-by.*
>
> *But if she were just eating jelly on her biscuit, nobody would pay any particular attention, and she could be stiff as a mink by Philadelphia.*
>
> Joe H. Palmer, *This Was Racing,* 1953, a collection of the
> sportswriter's columns from the New York *Herald Tribune*

Wine jellies

Champagne jelly sounds glorious. It is, in fact, a great disappointment. The delicate flavor of champagne, like that of fine still wines, is overwhelmed by the amount of sugar needed in jellymaking. You'd be smarter to drink the champagne and put your preserving money into fortified or flavored wines whose more robust character will withstand dilution by sugar without sacrificing the essential flavor of the wine.

In my experience, the only grape wines that retain any of their true fruit flavor in jelly are those made from native American grapes—Concords, Catawbas, and Niagaras, for instance. If you like these wines, you may like jelly made from them. Pectin manufacturers usually suggest sangría and fortified wines such as port for jellymaking. Frankly, they're not to my taste.

But ginger-flavored currant wine—an English import—makes a superb jelly whose ginger flavor lasts a full year. It's marvelous on toast or on cream cheese sandwiches. I like it as a glaze for roast pork or ham and as flavoring for poached pears, baked apples, and applesauce.

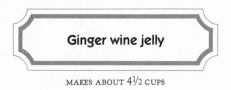

Ginger wine jelly

MAKES ABOUT 4½ CUPS

2 cups ginger-flavored currant wine
3 cups sugar
3 ounces (1 pouch) liquid pectin

Place wine and sugar in a wide 2½-quart saucepan, and stir until sugar dissolves. Bring quickly to a full, rolling boil that cannot be stirred down.

Remove from heat, and add pectin all at once, stirring constantly. Skim, if necessary. Pour into hot, sterilized jars, and seal. Let stand undisturbed until set—it may take 24 hours. Label and store.

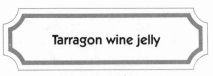

Tarragon wine jelly

MAKES ABOUT 5½ CUPS

Tarragon wine jelly, like the Ginger Wine Jelly (above), is a good relish to serve with or to use as a glaze on roasts. The scent and flavor of tarragon are not as long-lasting as ginger, so plan to use this one soon after the jar is opened. For this jelly I do like a grape wine, Gewürztraminer, because it is naturally spicy and fruity.

The recipe calls for tarragon, but you could just as well substitute basil, rosemary, thyme, chervil, or summer savory.

To make plain wine jelly, omit the herb and the step that produces the herb infusion, and use exactly 2 cups of wine.

Tarragon wine jelly (continued)

**Slightly more than 2 cups dry white
wine, preferably Gewürztraminer
2 tablespoons dried tarragon leaves
3 cups sugar
3 tablespoons fresh lemon juice
3 ounces (1 pouch) liquid pectin
4 or 5 fresh tarragon sprigs (optional)**

Bring 1 cup of the wine to full boil in a small saucepan. Remove from heat, stir in tarragon, cover tightly, and steep 15 minutes.

Strain tarragon "tea" into a 2-cup measure and add enough wine to reach the 2-cup level. Place wine, sugar, and lemon juice in a wide 2½-quart saucepan and bring to boil over medium heat, stirring constantly until sugar has dissolved and mixture reaches full, rolling boil that cannot be stirred down. Boil hard 1 minute, remove from heat, and stir in pectin all at once. Stir and skim, if necessary, for 5 minutes. Place a fresh sprig of tarragon in each hot, sterilized jar, pour in the jelly, seal, and label. The fresh herb will rise to the top. It should stand at least a week for flavor to mellow before serving.

> *Archie Goodwin, "gofer" for fictional detective Nero Wolfe, reflects on jellymaking: "As I sat in the kitchen at ten minutes past eight Monday morning, having brioches, grilled ham, and grape-thyme jelly, my mind was hopping around. First, why was Fritz so damn stubborn about the jelly: Why wouldn't he try it, just once, with half as much sugar and twice as much sauterne? I had been at him for years."*   Rex Stout, *Death of a Doxy,* 1966

Concord grape jelly

MAKES ABOUT 1 CUP

In some American cookbooks from the early part of this century you will find recipes for spiced grape jelly or venison jelly, so-called because it was served as a relish with venison. To convert this recipe to the spiced version, simply add a pinch each of ground cinnamon, cloves, and allspice—or more to taste—to the juice for the final cooking.

**1 quart basket (about 1½ pounds)
Concord grapes
Sugar equal in volume to cooked,
strained juice**

Wash, drain, and stem the grapes. Place a single layer of the grapes in a 2-quart nonplastic microwavable measure or casserole and crush with a potato masher or pastry blender to release juices. Add remaining grapes. Cover (vent if using plastic wrap), and microwave on high about 5 minutes, or until mixture boils. Let stand 2 minutes. Drip through a jelly bag. You should have about 1 cup of juice. At this stage you can refrigerate or freeze the juice for later use.

To complete the jelly, transfer it to a 1½-quart saucepan, stir in an equal measure of sugar, and boil rapidly about 10 minutes, or until gel tests done. Pour into a hot, sterilized jar, seal, invert for 5 minutes, then set upright to cool. Label and store.

> *"Oh, it's just like a pink story,"* she cried, clapping her hands. *"The shades on the can'les, the icin' on the cake, an' the posies in the bowl—why even the jelly is that colah, too."* Annie Fellows Johnston, *The Little Colonel,* 1904

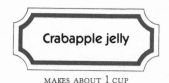

Crabapple jelly

MAKES ABOUT 1 CUP

This makes a beautiful deep pink jelly that tastes much the same as apple jelly. Because the juice has a very high pectin content, it may be substituted for currant juice in the Raspberry Currant Jam (page 57) and Cherry Currant Jam (page 47) recipes. Count on about 1 pound of crabapples for each cup of cooked juice.

1 pound crabapples
1½ cups water
1 tablespoon fresh lemon juice
Sugar

Wash and drain the crabapples. Remove stem and blossom ends, then quarter the fruit. You should have about 3 cups. Place prepared apples, water, and lemon juice in a 2-quart microwaveable glass measure or casserole; cover (vent if using plastic wrap), and microwave on high for 5 minutes, or until mixture boils. Stir, re-cover, and microwave (see pages 33–35 for details) on high 5 minutes longer. Let stand 3 minutes. Drip through a dampened jelly bag until dripping slows almost to a standstill. You should have a generous 1 cup of juice.

Crabapple jelly (continued)

If desired, freeze in a covered container for later use. Or, mix with 1 cup of sugar in a 1½-quart saucepan, and boil rapidly until gel tests done. Fill a hot, sterilized jar, seal, invert for 5 minutes, then set upright to cool. Label and store.

> *Europeans are not supposed to like jelly with meat, but perhaps there were enough Americans present to account for its all vanishing. Anyway, it was a Dane who asked for the rule [for Paradise Jelly] and who said he would get his mother to try it next time the quinces are ripe.*
>
> Louise Andrews Kent and Elizabeth Kent Gay, *The Winter Kitchen*, 1938

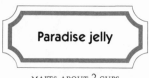

Paradise jelly

MAKES ABOUT 2 CUPS

Paradise jelly has been around at least since the 1930s, when it appeared in the first edition of *Joy of Cooking*. The origin of the name is less easily explained. Some historians think it refers to the quince, believed by some to have been the "apple" in the Garden of Eden.

> **1½ pounds ripe quinces**
> **¾ pound apples**
> **2 cups cranberries (about 8 ounces)**
> **4 cups water**
> **¾ cup sugar for each cup of cooked**
> **juice**

Peel and core the quinces and apples, and cut into chunks. Sort, wash, and drain the cranberries.

Place prepared quinces, apples, cranberries, and water in a 4- to 5-quart saucepan. Cover, bring quickly to boil; uncover, and boil rapidly about 45 minutes, or until apples are mushy and quince chunks are tender. Drip through jelly bag to obtain 2 cups of juice. Purée pulp in a food processor and save it to make Paradise Butter (page 113); at this point you may refrigerate or freeze the juice and purée for later use.

To make jelly, place the juice in a saucepan with sugar (use 1½-quart saucepan and ¾ cup sugar for 1 cup of juice or 2- to 3-quart saucepan and 1½ cups sugar for 2 cups juice). Bring quickly to boil, and boil 10 to 15 minutes, or until gel tests done. Fill hot, sterilized jars, seal, invert 5 minutes, then set upright to cool. Label and refrigerate.

A Navajo legend says that a hair must be plucked from the head of a gatherer of prickly pears so the plant will yield fruit without twisting its heart.

Carolyn Niethammer, *American Indian Food and Lore,* 1974

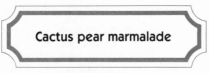

Cactus pear marmalade

MAKES ABOUT 2 CUPS

The orange version of this spread makes a tomato-red marmalade. The lime version is somewhat darker. I prefer the orange version, but true marmalade lovers tend to choose the lime version.

1 medium unpeeled orange (about 7 ounces)
¾ cup water
4 to 6 prickly (cactus) pears (total weight 1½ to 2 pounds)
1½ cups sugar

Slice the orange as thin as possible; discard end pieces and seeds. Soak orange slices in the water in a 4-quart covered saucepan for at least 3 hours; longer won't hurt. While orange soaks, peel the cactus pears (see Note), and put through a food mill with medium disc to remove seeds. You should have about 1½ cups of pulp.

Add cactus pear pulp to the oranges and water, and bring to boil quickly over high heat, stirring often. When entire surface is bubbling, continue to boil for 5 minutes. At this point you may pack, seal, cool, label, and refrigerate or freeze the stock.

To complete the marmalade, defrost (if frozen), bring to a boil in the 4-quart saucepan, add sugar all at once, and stir to dissolve. Return to full boil, and boil rapidly 15 to 18 minutes, or until it passes freezer jelling test. Pack into hot, sterilized jars, seal, cool, label, and store.

Variation Substitute one (4-ounce) lime for the orange, and reduce the final cooking time to 9 to 13 minutes, or until marmalade passes gel test.

NOTE

Although the spines are removed from the peel before marketing, the fruit should be handled cautiously. Place it on its side on a cutting board, spear with a fork, cut off both ends, and slash about ¼ inch deep from end to end. Steady the fruit with the fork as you pull off the peel.

To make marmalade

To two pounds of quinces put three quarters of a pound of sugar and a pint of spring water, then put them over the fire, and boil them until they are tender; then take them up and bruise them; then put them into the liquor, let it boil three quarters of an hour, and then put into your pots or saucers.
Jean McKibbin, editor and illustrator of *The Frugal Colonial Housewife,* the Dolphin Books 1976 edition of *The Frugal Housewife or Complete Woman Cookbook* by Susannah Carter (1772)

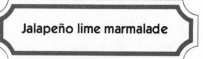

Jalapeño lime marmalade

MAKES ABOUT 2 CUPS

Use this as you would pepper jelly, as a relish with meat and poultry, or with cream cheese and crackers for a snack.

3 large limes (3½ to 4 ounces each)
1 small ripe, red jalapeño or other hot
chile
Water
Sugar

Slice limes in a food processor, using a 1-millimeter disc if available; if not, slice with a very sharp knife. Discard end pieces. Stem the jalapeño or other hot chile and pulse/chop fine in a food processor; for milder flavor, remove some of the seeds and veins before chopping. Place prepared limes and chile in a 2-quart measure and add water to reach the 2-cup level; let stand about 24 hours.

Transfer to a 3-quart saucepan, bring quickly to a boil, and boil 10 to 15 minutes, stirring occasionally, until peel is tender and translucent, and mixture appears milky. Measure; you should have about 1⅓ cups. Like all the other sweet spreads in this book, the cooked stock may be frozen for later use. But why bother, when limes are in good supply all year and jalapeños are increasingly available all year even in supermarkets.

To prepare the marmalade, return fruit mixture to pan, add an equal volume of sugar, and boil until gel tests done. It may take as little as 2½ minutes. Pack in hot, sterilized jars, seal, cool, label, and store at least 2 weeks before serving.

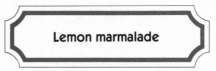

Lemon marmalade

MAKES ABOUT 10 OUNCES

With good quality lemons in markets the year round, why bother to make more than one jar at a time, as needed?

1 lemon (4 to 5 ounces)
1¹/₂ cups water
Sugar

Halve the lemon from stem to blossom end. With cut sides down, slice as thin as possible. Discard end pieces and seeds. You should have about ²/₃ cup, packed.

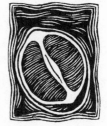

Place lemon slices and water in a small bowl, cover, and let stand 12 to 24 hours at room temperature. Transfer to a 1¹/₂-quart saucepan, and boil, uncovered, about 15 minutes, or until peel is tender and translucent, and pulp is breaking up. At this stage, you may refrigerate or freeze the stock for later use. When you are ready to make the marmalade, measure the stock and pour it into a 1¹/₂- or 2-quart saucepan. Stir in an equal volume of sugar, bring quickly to a boil, and boil rapidly 12 to 15 minutes, or until gel tests done. Skim, if necessary, and stir for 2 or 3 minutes to cool the mixture slightly and prevent the peel from floating to the top. Pour into a refrigerator storage container (hot and sterilized, if glass), seal, cool, label, and refrigerate a week or two for flavor to mellow.

The feijoa makes superb jelly and marmalade, particularly when in combination with the peel and juice of a lemon.

Helen Brown's West Coast
Cook Book, 1952, reissued 1991

FEIJOA

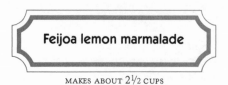

Feijoa lemon marmalade

MAKES ABOUT 2½ CUPS

Mrs. Brown gave no recipe for feijoa jelly or marmalade, but her advice is right on target. The lemon modifies the fruit's characteristic musky aroma without overwhelming it.

1 lemon (4 ounces)
Water
1 pound ripe feijoas (about 4 large)
Sugar

Slice lemon crosswise as thin as possible; discard stem and blossom ends, and seeds. Place sliced lemon in a 2-cup glass measure, and add water to 1½-cup mark. Let stand, uncovered, about 12 hours, or overnight, to leach out pectin.

Place solids in a blender, and add just enough soaking liquid to cover blade assembly (save the remaining liquid). Reduce to a not-quite-smooth purée. With a small sharp knife peel the feijoas, slice them crosswise a scant ¼ inch thick, then cut into matchstick-size pieces. Transfer lemon purée and reserved liquid to a 3-quart saucepan, cover, bring quickly to a boil, and boil rapidly 5 minutes. Add prepared feijoa, and boil about 5 minutes longer, or until feijoa is tender. At this point, you may pack the stock in freezer containers, seal, chill, label, and freeze for later use.

I prefer to complete the marmalade in a saucepan on the range top; the time differential between this method and microwaving is insignificant. Either way,

Sugar tends to harden fruit

Firm raw fruit, citrus peel, and vegetables will toughen if you cook them in a heavy syrup. They should be precooked until tender in a plain or lightly sweetened liquid — water, cider, unsweetened fruit juices, or juice concentrates. Soft berries, however, will retain their shape better in preserves if you let them form their own syrup by mixing them with sugar and letting them set for several hours, until the sugar dissolves.

you will get better results if you cook it in two batches, of 1 cup and 1½ cups each. Place 1 cup of prepared fruit in a 1½-quart saucepan, stir in ¾ cup of sugar, bring quickly to boil, and boil 10 to 12 minutes, stirring occasionally, until gel tests done. Pack at once into a hot, sterilized 8-ounce jar or two 4-ounce jars, seal, cool, label, and refrigerate. Repeat, using 1½ cups fruit stock and 1 cup of sugar.

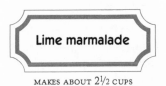

Lime marmalade

MAKES ABOUT 2½ CUPS

A spread for people who like bitter marmalade. The vegetable coloring is optional, but you will get a much more appetizing color if you use it.

> **¾ cup fresh lime juice (3 large or 4**
>   **small limes, about ¾ pound total)**
> **3 cups water, divided**
> **3 cups sugar**
> **Green vegetable coloring (optional)**
> **2 tablespoons light rum (optional)**

Place the juice in a 1-cup measure. Strip membrane and pulp residue from peel, and set aside all of it. Use a sharp knife or scissors to cut peel into matchstick-size slivers, adding them to the juice until it reaches the 1-cup level.

Place remaining peel and reserved membrane and pulp in a small bowl, and add 1 cup of the water.

Place prepared juice and slivered peel in another bowl and add remaining 2 cups of water.

Let both mixtures stand 12 to 24 hours. Then place juice and peel mixture in a wide 3-quart saucepan and strain the other mixture into it, squeezing to extract as much liquid as possible. Bring quickly to boil, and boil rapidly about 30 minutes, or until peel is tender and translucent. Remove from heat, and measure. If needed, add water to reach the 3-cup level. At this point you can freeze the stock for later use.

Or make 1 to 3 cups of marmalade. For 1 cup of stock, use a 1½-quart

Lime marmalade (continued)

saucepan; for 3 cups, a 3-quart saucepan. Add an equal measure of sugar to the juice, bring quickly to a boil, and boil rapidly (timing may vary from 10 to 25 or 30 minutes, depending on the amount being cooked at one time). Boil until gel tests done. Remove from heat, tint with a few drops of vegetable coloring, and stir in rum, if desired. (Avoid rum extract; its flavor makes the marmalade taste like an artificially flavored lollipop.) Cool and stir about 5 minutes, to prevent floating peel. Ladle into hot, sterilized jars, seal, and cool. Label and store at least 1 week before using.

> *"Don't forget the butter for*
> *The Royal slice of bread."*
> *The Alderney*
> *Said sleepily:*
> *"You'd better tell*
> *His Majesty*
> *That many people nowadays*
> *Like marmalade*
> *Instead."*
>
> A. A. Milne, *When We*
> *Were Very Young,* 1924

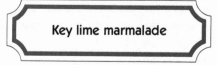

Key lime marmalade

MAKES ABOUT 3 CUPS

This pale, green-gold marmalade has the flavor of genuine Key lime pie, but without all the sugar and fat calories. My favorite uses for it in baking are as a substitute for sugar in cheesecake, or as a topping for store-bought cheesecake, or for sweetening the cheese layer in Cheesecake Squares (page 227). It is also delicious on toast or muffins, with or without cream cheese.

Key limes are available in limited quantities all year round in specialty shops and some upscale supermarkets. They are imported from Haiti by a Florida company.

1 pound Key limes (11 to 15 fruit)
Water
Sugar

The peel of Key limes, which is thin and leathery, is easiest to grind with an old-fashioned food grinder or an electric grinder, using a plate or cylinder with fine holes. The blender method that follows is my second choice. Whichever method you choose, first halve, juice, and seed the limes; reserve seeds, juice, and peel. Cut the peel halves in half again; either put through a grinder as described above or add enough water to an electric blender container to barely cover the blades. Chop the peel coarsely, in 2 batches if necessary. Place this mixture in a 4-cup measure, add the reserved juice and additional water to reach the 4-cup level. Tie the seeds in a double thickness of cheesecloth or place in a small stainless steel mesh tea ball, and add to the fruit mixture. Let stand 12 to 24 hours to leach out the pectin. Transfer the mixture to a 3-quart saucepan, bring to a boil quickly, and boil rapidly for 10 to 15 minutes, or until peel is tender and translucent. At this stage you may freeze the stock (you should have about 3 cups).

Complete the marmalade in 2 or 3 batches. Measure 1 or 1½ cups of the stock into a 1½-quart saucepan, add an equal volume of sugar, and stir to dissolve sugar, as you bring the mixture to a quick boil. Boil rapidly for about 3 minutes for the 1½ cups of stock, or until gel tests done. Start testing at 1½ minutes for 1 cup of stock. Pack into hot, sterilized jars, seal, and cool. Label and store a week or more to mellow before using.

NOTE

This makes a traditional bitter marmalade. For a milder version, strain the juice, and save it to make Key Lime Marmalade Sherbet (page 235) or for other uses. Grind the peel as directed above, place it in a 4-cup measure, add water to the 4-cup level, and proceed as described above.

Pineapple-apricot marmalade

MAKES ABOUT 1½ CUPS

This marmalade is so easy to prepare in a microwave oven that I never bother with conventional range top cooking.

> 1 (6-ounce) package dried apricots
> 1 (8-ounce) can crushed pineapple in heavy syrup
> ¼ cup frozen unsweetened pineapple juice concentrate, undiluted
> 6 tablespoons sugar, or more to taste

Cut apricots into ¼-inch strips. Set an open 8-ounce canning jar upside down in the center of a 2-quart microwavable glass measure or casserole. Distribute the prepared apricots around it. Strain the syrup from the crushed pineapple over the apricots, reserving the pineapple; add the juice concentrate, cover (vent

Pineapple-apricot marmalade (continued)

if using plastic wrap), and microwave (see pages 33–35 for details) on high for 5 minutes. Uncover, remove jar with jar lifter, stir, and let stand, covered, for 20 minutes to allow apricots to soften and plump. Stir in reserved pineapple and sugar, and microwave uncovered on high 5 to 7 minutes, or until marmalade holds its shape when stirred. It will thicken more as it cools. Ladle into hot, sterilized jars, seal, and cool. Label and refrigerate.

A stack cake by another name

Today we would probably call it a stack cake. The sixteenth edition of Directions for Cooking, *by Miss Leslie in 1842 called a rich buttery cake made with 10 eggs a Jelly Cake. It consisted of griddle cakes layered with "grape jelly, peach marmalade, or any other sweetmeat that is smooth and thick."*

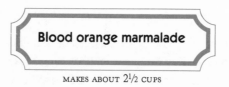

Blood orange marmalade

MAKES ABOUT 2½ CUPS

These specialty oranges are well worth searching out in fancy food markets and upscale supermarkets; some are imported from Italy, others are grown in California. Although the peel tends to be orange colored mottled with red, the flesh is a deep red, and the finished marmalade is a deep rose color.

> **3 small blood oranges (about 1 pound total)**
> **2½ cups water**
> **¼ cup fresh lemon juice**
> **Sugar**

Slice the oranges crosswise as thin as possible, and then cut into quarters or sixths. Discard ends and any seeds you find. Place prepared oranges and water in a 1-quart bowl or measure, cover, and let stand at least 12 hours to leach out pectin. Transfer mixture to a 4-quart saucepan, bring quickly to a boil, and boil 30 minutes. Stir lemon juice into marmalade stock. At this point, you may refrigerate or freeze the stock (you should have about 2½ cups) for later use.

To make about 12 ounces of marmalade, measure 1½ cups of stock into a 1½-quart saucepan, add 1 cup plus 2 tablespoons of sugar, stir to dissolve it as you bring mixture quickly to boil; boil rapidly about 4 or 5 minutes, or until gel tests done. To make 1 cup of marmalade, use the same size saucepan and ¾ cup of sugar. Cooking time will be slightly less. Ladle into hot, sterilized jars, seal, invert for 5 minutes, then set upright to cool. Label and store a week or so for flavor to mellow.

Microwave directions (See pages 33–35 for details.) To prepare the marmalade in a microwave oven, measure 1 cup of stock prepared according to first paragraph of recipe into a 2-quart microwavable glass measure, stir in juice and ¾ cup of sugar until sugar dissolves, and microwave about 5 minutes, or until gel tests done. Ladle into a hot, sterilized jar, seal, cool, label, and store a week or two for flavors to mellow. Repeat with remaining 1½ cups of stock and 1¼ cups of sugar; you may need to extend the cooking time by 30 seconds or more.

Variation Substitute navel oranges for the blood oranges.

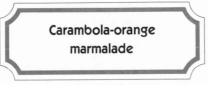

**Carambola-orange
marmalade**

MAKES ABOUT 2 CUPS

**1 navel orange (6 to 7 ounces)
1 cup water, divided
1 pound ripe carambolas
Sugar**

Cut the orange into chunks and pulse/chop medium fine in a food processor with ¼ cup of the water. Place the orange and its liquid in a 2-cup glass measure or small bowl, add the remaining ¾ cup of water, and let stand at least 12 hours for pectin to leach out. Trim brown edges from carambolas, and slice them into stars on a mandoline. Discard ends and any seeds  that you find. Transfer orange mixture to a 3-quart saucepan, bring quickly to a boil, and boil rapidly 5 minutes, stirring occasionally to prevent sticking. Add carambola slices, and boil 5 minutes longer. At this point, you may freeze the stock for later use.

To prepare 1 cup of marmalade, measure 1 cup of stock into a 1½-quart saucepan, stir in ¾ cup of sugar, bring quickly to boil, and boil rapidly 5 to 10 minutes, or until gel tests done. To cook 1½ cups of stock, you will need 1 cup plus 2 tablespoons of sugar. For the entire batch, use a 3-quart saucepan and 1⅞ cups of sugar, and extend the cooking time as necessary. Ladle into hot, sterilized jars, seal, invert for 5 minutes, then set upright to cool. Label and store.

Grapefruit's grandfather

Imagine a grapefruit that is almost as sweet as an orange and has juice cells so firm they don't squirt in your face when you spoon out the flesh. That is a pummelo, often called Chinese grapefruit because the Chinese and Chinese-Americans prize it as part of their New Year's celebration. Until recently one had to seek them out in Chinatowns in major cities. Now they are being grown in California and sold in specialty shops and some upscale supermarkets.

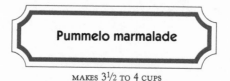

Pummelo marmalade

MAKES 3½ TO 4 CUPS

The first pummelo (or pomelo) I tasted—in Kweilin, China, in 1982—was so lacking in juice and flavor that I never wanted to try another. The second one changed my mind. Just before the Chinese New Year celebration in midwinter 1989, I bought an American-grown pummelo almost as big as a basketball in New York's Chinatown. The pulp was firmer than our familiar grapefruit, but sweeter. I also quickly discovered that this Southeast Asian grandparent of grapefruit is splendid for preserving—either as marmalade or candied peel (page 192).

> 1 large pummelo (1½ to 1¾ pounds)
> 4 cups water
> ¼ cup fresh lemon juice
> ¾ to 1 cup sugar for each cup of
>   cooked peel and pulp

Either score the peel into sixths or eighths with a small, sharp knife; or halve the fruit crosswise as you would a grapefruit. If you choose the first method, use your fingers to pry off the peel in large pieces, and remove excess white pith. Then, separate the segments and pull away the membrane, reserving it to extract its pectin.

If you halve the fruit, use a grapefruit knife and/or grapefruit spoon to release the segments from the membrane, then cut the halves of peel into smaller pieces, and strip away the remaining membrane, reserving it to extract its pectin. Discard any seeds you may find. Place the pummelo peel and pulpy segments in the water in a large bowl. Tie the membrane in a cheesecloth square, and add it to the bowl. Cover, and let stand about 24 hours.

Transfer entire mixture to a 6-quart saucepan, cover, bring quickly to a boil, and boil rapidly about 20 minutes, or until peel is tender when pierced with a wooden pick. With tongs, remove peel to a cutting board to cool; place the cheesecloth bag in a strainer set over a 1-quart measure, and let stand until dripping slows to a trickle. Discard the bag of membranes and add the cooked pulp to the measure. When the peel is cool enough to handle, cut it into thin strips, or chop in a food processor. Add the lemon juice and the pummelo peel to the pulp mixture. You should have about 3½ cups stock. At this stage, the stock may be refrigerated for up to a week, or frozen for longer storage.

To prepare the marmalade, cook 1 cup of stock and ¾ cup of sugar in a 1½-quart saucepan until gel tests done; or 1½ cups of stock with 1 cup plus 2 tablespoons of sugar in a 2-quart saucepan; or the entire batch with 2½ cups plus 2 tablespoons of sugar in a 4-quart saucepan. Ladle into hot, sterilized jars, seal, and cool. Label and store a couple of weeks before using.

Ginger marmalade

MAKES ABOUT 4 CUPS

Ginger marmalade is good on cream cheese sandwiches or toast or as a glaze for cheesecake. I also like to use it instead of sugar to sweeten hot tea. The apple pulp remaining after the juice has been extracted may be put through a food mill to remove seeds and skin, and sweetened and spiced to taste to serve as applesauce. The recipe appeared in slightly different form in *Gourmet* magazine. It is reprinted here with permission. Recipe is easily halved.

> ¾ pound fresh gingerroot
> Water
> 3 pounds tart apples, quartered, stems
>   and cores removed
> 6 cups water
> 3 cups sugar
> ¼ cup fresh lemon juice

Peel ginger and shred in a food processor using medium shredding disc. In a 1½-quart saucepan combine ginger with enough boiling water to cover by 1 inch. Boil mixture, uncovered, for 30 minutes. Drain in a colander, discarding water, and rinse under cold water to stop further cooking. Drain again, place ginger in a bowl, cover with water and a lid or plastic wrap, and set aside for at least 12 hours.

In a 4-quart saucepan place apple quarters and the 6 cups water. Bring to boil over high heat and boil, stirring and mashing the fruit with the back of a spoon, for about 40 minutes. Drip the juice through a clean jelly bag wrung out

Ginger marmalade (continued)

in hot water or 2 thicknesses of dampened cheesecloth into a 2-quart measure. You should have about 4½ cups juice. If there is more, return it to the saucepan and reduce it over high heat to 4½ cups. Drain the ginger well and add it with the sugar and the lemon juice to the saucepan. Stir to dissolve sugar, bring mixture to a boil over moderately high heat, and boil 25 minutes, or until gel tests done. Remove pan from heat, and stir and skim foam for 5 minutes to keep ginger from floating to the top in the jars. Ladle marmalade into hot, sterilized jars, seal, invert for 5 minutes, then set upright to cool. Label and store at least a week to mellow before serving.

Mock orange marmalades

In the days when oranges were a pricey luxury, women often combined them with carrots to make an affordable substitute for orange marmalade. One cookbook author, Helen Watkeys Moore, used ground carrots, lemons, vinegar, and sugar for her Mock Marmalade in Camouflage Cookery, 1918. *The Mock Orange Marmalade in* The Rural Cook Book, *a collection of recipes from New York State farm women published by* The Rural New Yorker *magazine in 1907, replaces some of the oranges with yellow tomatoes. "This is an original recipe and a delightful substitute for the genuine orange marmalade, though much cheaper," the compiler wrote.*

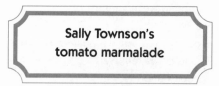

**Sally Townson's
tomato marmalade**

MAKES ABOUT 5 CUPS

Sally Townson's tomato marmalade, which was given to me by a friend in Buffalo, New York, is very similar to the Mock Orange Marmalade recipe that appeared in 1907 in *The Rural Cook Book,* with recipes selected from several thousand received from farm women statewide.

> **2¼ pounds firm, ripe tomatoes**
> **Pulp and slivered peel of 2 medium**
>   **oranges (5 or 6 ounces each)**
> **Pulp and slivered peel of 1 medium**
>   **lemon (about 3 ounces)**
> **4½ cups sugar**

Peel and core tomatoes, and cut into chunks.

Place tomatoes and prepared orange and lemon pulp and peel in a 4-quart saucepan. Bring quickly to a boil, stirring to prevent sticking. Boil 15 to 20 minutes, or until peel is tender; stir occasionally. Measure. You should have about 4½ cups. If not, add cold water to make up the difference.

Return fruit mixture to saucepan, bring to boil again, and stir in sugar all at once. Continue to heat and stir until sugar has dissolved and mixture again boils. Boil rapidly, and stir often, about 30 minutes, or until peel is translucent and syrup passes gel test. Skim if necessary. Ladle into hot, sterilized jars, seal, invert for 5 minutes, then set upright to cool. This marmalade may take as long as 48 hours to set in hot weather. Label and store at least a week before serving.

When you have fmall Pine-Apples in Fruit, which are not noble enough to be brought to the Table, twift off their Crowns, and pare them; then flice them, and put them into a Syrup of Water, Sugar, and Pippins; and boil them with half their quantity of Sugar added to them, with a little White Wine, breaking them with a Spoon, as they boil, till they come to a Mafh, or are a little tender. Then take them from the Fire, and put the Marmalade into Glaffes to keep, and cover every Glafs with white Paper, preferving them in a dry Place.

This is said to be the first pineapple recipe in
English, attributed to Richard Bradley in *The Country
Housewife and Lady's Director, Part II*, 1732.

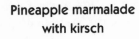

Pineapple marmalade with kirsch

MAKES 4 TO 5 CUPS

2¼ cups fresh ripe pineapple
  (about one 4-pound fruit or two
  smaller ones)
¼ cup fresh lemon juice
3¾ cups sugar
1 (3-ounce) pouch liquid pectin
2 tablespoons kirsch

Peel, core, and coarsely chop pineapple in a food processor. Place prepared pineapple in a wide 4-quart saucepan; stir in lemon juice and sugar. Bring

Pineapple marmalade with kirsch (continued)

quickly to a rolling boil that cannot be stirred down. Add pectin, and boil hard 1 minute, stirring constantly. Remove from heat, stir in kirsch, and skim and stir about 5 minutes. Ladle into hot, sterilized jars, seal, invert for 5 minutes, then set upright to cool. Label and store a few days for flavor to mellow. This marmalade sets very slowly and should be allowed to stand undisturbed until it is cold.

> *It was ten years later, in 1873, that the orange industry really got going [in California] . . . Then came lemons and grapefruit and the less common citrus fruits — limes, kumquats, tangerines, limequats, citrons, tangelos, and calamondins.*
>
> Helen Brown's West Coast Cook Book, 1952, reissued 1991

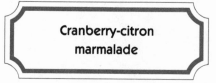

Cranberry-citron marmalade

MAKES ABOUT 2 CUPS

Citron recipes in old American cookbooks almost invariably call for citron melon, a wild fruit similar to watermelon, to be put up the same way — as pickled rind, in a spicy sweet-and-sour syrup. My recipe uses the true citron, or *Citrus medica*, a variety believed to be indigenous to either China or Southeast Asia. It was taken to Greece and China during the campaign of Alexander the Great in 300 B.C., and reached Rome in the first century A.D. At various times through history, it has been used as an antidote to poison, an air freshener, and to mothproof clothing and season meat. It is cultivated today principally in Italy, Greece, Israel, and Puerto Rico, although at this writing, John Kirkpatrick, a member of the Sunkist Growers cooperative, has some acreage planted in the variety known as Etrog at his ranch in Exeter, California. Etrog, sometimes spelled esrog, is the sacred Jewish lemon that must be harvested in a prescribed size, shape, and green-gold color to be used in the ritual of the Feast of Tabernacles each fall. Most true citron in America today is available almost exclusively as a candied peel used in winter holiday baking. It can be substituted for raw citron in this marmalade; see variation that follows recipe.

This recipe was inspired by a recipe from an Israeli friend, Dalia Carmel Goldstein. Dalia uses etrog with imperfections that have made it unacceptable for the Jewish holiday ritual. Yellow fruit may be used, but if you can get it while still green, it will have more flavor and aroma.

> 2 small (8-ounce) citrons or 1 medium
>   (12-ounce), preferably green
> 1½ cups water
> 6 ounces (1½ cups) cranberries, fresh
>   or frozen
> ½ teaspoon finely grated gingerroot
> ¼ teaspoon ground cardamom
> Pinch each of ground cinnamon,
>   ground cloves, and ground allspice
> ⅛ teaspoon dried crushed red pepper
> 1½ cups sugar

Halve the citron; discard the seedy flesh and surrounding membrane, and shred the rind in a food processor, using a fine disc. Measure out 1 cup, packed, and freeze any leftovers for later use. Set an open 8-ounce canning jar upside down in the center of a 2-quart microwavable flameproof lidded casserole. Distribute the shredded citron around it, add water, cover with vented lid, and microwave (see pages 33–35 for details) on high for 10 minutes. Sort, rinse, drain, and add the cranberries, cover, and microwave 5 minutes longer, or until berries have burst and mixture is juicy. Measure, and add water if necessary to reach the 2-cup level.

While the rind and the cranberries cook, stir the gingerroot and the other spices into the sugar, and set aside. Return cooked fruit to the microwave vessel, stir in sugar/spice mixture, and microwave uncovered on high for 5 minutes; stir, and microwave about 7 minutes longer, stirring every couple of minutes from the outside toward the center, until mixture thickens perceptibly. It will continue to cook for 2 or 3 minutes after you remove it from the microwave, and overcooking makes a very stiff spread. If that should happen, return the marmalade to the flameproof casserole, add 1 or 2 tablespoons of water, and melt, stirring, on a range top burner. Ladle into hot, sterilized jars, seal, cool, label, and refrigerate. Store it at least a week for flavors to meld.

Range top directions Place the shredded citron rind in a 3-quart saucepan with 1½ cups of water, bring quickly to a boil, and boil 10 minutes. Add cranberries, and boil 10 minutes longer. Crush with a potato masher during the last 10 minutes, and watch carefully to prevent sticking. Stir the ginger and other spices into the sugar, add to the pan, return it to a boil quickly, and cook about 3 minutes from the time the mixture reaches a boil. Quickly ladle into hot, sterilized jars; seal, cool, label, and store a week or so before serving.

Variation To make the marmalade with candied citron, substitute either an 8-ounce piece of candied citron or the same weight of diced candied citron. Soak

Cranberry-citron marmalade (continued)

the unchopped citron at least 12 hours in 1½ cups of water so that it can be chopped or shredded in a food processor without making a sticky mess. Drain, reserving soaking water while you chop the diced citron medium fine in a food processor or shred the whole piece in a food processor using the finest disc. Place the citron, the reserved soaking water, and the cranberries in a 4-quart saucepan, bring quickly to a boil, and boil about 10 minutes, until berries have popped and are pulpy. Add only 1 cup of sugar, and the ginger and other spices, then boil about 3 minutes, or until gel tests done. Ladle marmalade into hot, sterilized jars, seal, cool, label, and store as described in previous paragraph.

How to peel a pineapple

Pineapple shells are so hard that a heavy carving knife with serrated or scalloped edge is the safest instrument to use for removing the thorny crown and quartering the fruit lengthwise. Wear a rubber glove or protect your hand with a dishcloth, laying the fruit on its side, and grasping the crown to cut it off. A grapefruit knife with curved blade is best for removing the core and the fruit from the shell.

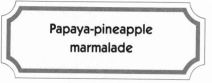

Papaya-pineapple
marmalade

MAKES ABOUT 3 CUPS

Here is a Hawaiian recipe, based on a much sweeter version I found in the third edition of *Fruits of Hawaii* by Carey D. Miller, Katherine Bazore, and Mary Bartow (1957). I have reduced the sugar content, and sometimes substitute lime peel and lime juice for the lemon.

> 1 small ripe, fragrant pineapple
> 1 ripe papaya (about 1¼ pounds)
> 1½ teaspoons grated lemon or lime
>   peel, colored part only

¹/₄ cup fresh lemon or lime juice
1¹/₂ cups sugar

Peel and core the pineapple, cut into chunks, and pulse/chop in a food processor. Measure 1¹/₃ cups; drain for 5 minutes to remove excess juice; save the juice for other uses, or drink it. Peel and halve the papaya lengthwise, and cut pulp into small cubes. Place the drained pineapple, the papaya cubes, the lemon or lime peel and lemon or lime juice in a 3-quart saucepan, bring to boil over high heat, and boil rapidly until papaya cubes are translucent, about 10 to 15 minutes. Stir in sugar, and boil about 30 minutes, or until marmalade thickens, and a spoonful of the syrup holds its shape on a cold saucer. It will thicken more as it cools. Ladle into hot, sterilized jars, seal, invert for 5 minutes, then set upright to cool. Label and refrigerate.

A handful of orange seeds

The first fruit trees introduced to America from Europe were sour, or Seville, oranges grown from a handful of seeds brought by Christopher Columbus in 1493 on his second voyage in search of the East Indies. Other explorers also brought seeds to America, and in little more than a century the sweet orange supplanted the sour in Spanish settlements. Pioneers from the South planted orange seeds along the Gulf Coast and in what is now Mexico. Franciscan monks who established missions in southern California in 1769 carried orange seeds with them, and hundreds of groves of sweet oranges were growing there by 1848, when California achieved statehood.

Seville orange marmalade

MAKES ABOUT 3 CUPS

In *The Scots Kitchen* (1929), F. Marian McNeill ranks Seville orange marmalade as one of Scotland's two chief culinary gifts to the world. "The great Dundee manufacturers spread the popularity of marmalade in the south. Its first stronghold was Oxford, where it figured at undergraduate breakfasts as *squish.*"

Seville orange marmalade (continued)

About 1¼ pounds Seville oranges
(2 large or 4 small)
4 cups water
1 tablespoon fresh lemon juice for
each cup of cooked peel mixture
1 cup sugar for each cup of cooked
peel mixture

Halve the oranges crosswise, and juice, reserving seeds as well as juice and peel. Cut the peel halves in half again. Place the peel, pulp, juice, seeds, and water in a 2-quart bowl, and let stand about 24 hours.

Transfer mixture to a 4-quart saucepan, bring quickly to a boil, and boil rapidly about 20 to 30 minutes, or until peel is tender and translucent. Drain through a colander set in a deep bowl; discard seeds. When peel is cool enough to handle, cut it into very narrow strips or pulse/chop in a food processor. If you don't mind a slightly cloudy jelly, add the peel to the juice after you have drained it through a colander. For a clear jelly, drip the juice through a jelly bag before adding peel. Stir in lemon juice. At this stage, you may refrigerate or freeze the stock for later use.

To prepare the marmalade, measure the stock in whatever amount you want into a saucepan of appropriate size (a 1½- or 2-quart pan for 1 or 1½ cups of stock, or a 4-quart pan for 3 cups of stock). Stir in an equal volume of sugar, and boil rapidly until gel tests done. Because of its high pectin content, it may reach the gel point after 10 minutes of boiling. If after it sets it is too stiff, remelt it with a tablespoon or two of either water or sweet orange juice, and reheat. Ladle into hot, sterilized jar(s), seal, cool, label, and store a couple of weeks for flavor to mellow.

FRUIT BUTTERS AND REDUCED-CALORIE SPREADS

Fruit butters are among the most wholesome of fruit sweets, as they contain a large amount of fruit to a small amount of sugar.

Ruth Berolzheimer, editor of revised World
War II edition, *Victory Binding of the American
Woman's Cook Book,* first published in 1938

ive of the 11 fruit butters in this chapter were prepared in slow cookers of 2-quart or 1-quart capacity. While a larger size may be used, the results are less satisfactory because the surface of the butter may not reach all the heating elements. If you convert the recipes to use a larger appliance, you may need to increase the size of the recipe to meet the manufacturer's recommendation for fill level.

If you do not have a slow cooker or a counter top oven with a slow-cook setting, do the preliminary cooking of the raw fruit in a saucepan on a range top (you may have to increase the liquid content in some recipes), and the final cooking in a conventional oven or a convection oven.

After puréeing the cooked fruit, add the sugar and spices, if desired; then, transfer the mixture to shallow, ovenproof glass baking dishes to a depth of 1 inch; and bake about 2 hours in a conventional oven preheated to 325 degrees Fahrenheit. Stir every ½ hour, until butter is thick. If you use a convection oven, set the temperature for 275 degrees. Even at the lower temperature, the cooking time should be shorter. Nine of the recipes in this chapter appeared in slightly different form in *Woman's Day* magazine in September 1980.

NOTE

The fruit butters and reduced-calorie spreads that follow may be packed in either hot, sterilized jars or plastic freezer containers. I prefer the sterilized jars largely because sterilization seems to prolong the refrigerator shelf life of fruit butters and spreads with low-sugar content.

A simple Thanksgiving

On September 22, 1724, the Schwenkfelders, a small band of Protestant religious refugees from Germany, reached Philadelphia. Two days later the forty or so families who had survived persecution and death en route to a new life in the American colonies held a Thanksgiving feast of bread, apple butter, and water. "Today the descendants of the Schwenkfelders are well able to hold a costlier celebration," Katherine Burton and Helmut Ripperger wrote in 1951 in the Feast Day Cookbook, *adding that they nevertheless continued their ritual of a meal of bread, apple butter, and water following a Thanksgiving service.*

Apple butter

MAKES ABOUT 2 CUPS

If you use a single sweet apple variety such as Cortland, you may need no additional sugar. If you mix sweet and tart varieties (McIntosh, Northern Spies, Winesaps, Cortlands), you may want to add a little sugar or one of the Native Americans' typical sweeteners—honey or maple syrup.

> **2 pounds apples**
> **1 (6-ounce) can frozen apple juice**
>   **concentrate, thawed, or ¾ cup**
>   **boiled apple cider (see Note)**
> **Sugar or maple syrup (optional)**
> **Ground cinnamon, ginger, mace, or**
>   **coriander (optional)**

Peel and core apples and purée them in a food processor with the thawed apple juice concentrate or boiled cider. Empty the purée into a 2-quart slow cooker, and cook, covered, on high for about 8 hours, or until very thick. Taste for sweetness, and add sugar or maple syrup, if desired. This will thin down the butter somewhat. Cover, and continue to cook on high until thick. Stir in spices of your choice, starting with ¼ to ½ teaspoon of one or more, and tasting after each addition. Divide among hot, sterilized jars or freezer containers, cool, cover tightly, label, and refrigerate or freeze. Keeps at least 1 month in refrigerator, or 6 months or more in freezer.

NOTE

Boiled apple cider is regular-strength fresh (unpasteurized) cider that has been boiled rapidly to measure half its original volume. This concentrates the flavor and sweetness.

> *Hour after hour, the huge [apple butter] kettle swinging on its iron crane in many a farmyard steamed and bubbled and stewed, its sweet and spicy aroma scenting all the air, while someone stood guard over it, swaying the long-handled stirrer back and forth to keep the rich, thickening mass from sticking to the sides.*
>
> Della T. Lutes, *Home Grown,* 1937

Apple-cranberry butter

MAKES ABOUT 2 CUPS

6 ounces (about 1½ cups) fresh or
  frozen raw cranberries
1 pound sweet apples, preferably
  Cortlands
½ cup boiled cider (see note, above)
¼ cup maple syrup
¼ cup sugar

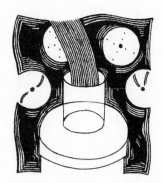

Wash, drain, and sort the cranberries. Peel and core the apples, cut them into chunks, and purée them in a food processor with the cranberries. Empty purée into a 2-quart slow cooker, cover, and cook on low for 2 hours. Stir in maple syrup and sugar, cover, and cook on high about 4 hours longer, or until butter is thick and dark. Pack in hot, sterilized jars or freezer containers, cool, cover tightly, label, and refrigerate or freeze.

One cook's marmalade is another's fruit butter

There is no such thing as an original recipe. What I call Guava Butter was Guava Marmalade to a Florida woman who contributed her recipe to a cookbook published in 1898 to commemorate the turn of the century Columbian Exposition in Chicago. Recipes in The Home Queen Cookbook *were collected from more than 200 World's Fair Lady Managers, governors' wives "and other Ladies of Position and Influence." The donor of the marmalade recipe was Florida's alternate lady manager, Chloe (middle name illegible) Reed.*

Guava butter

MAKES ABOUT 2 CUPS

Unless you are a Floridian with guava trees in your yard, the hardest part of this recipe is finding enough half-ripe guavas to prepare it. If I cannot get fruit that shows signs of ripening, I usually buy ¼ to ½ pound extra, anticipating a certain amount of spoilage. Bruised or blemished fruit may be used if you carefully cut away the damaged parts. If you are lucky enough to find fruit with a wonderfully spicy aroma and color that has begun to lighten, hold them a few days until the aroma permeates the room, then make the butter. Or buy feijoas instead. (Recipe follows.) This egg-shaped fruit resembles guava in appearance and aroma, so much so that it is nicknamed pineapple guava—although it is a different botanical species altogether. Either fruit makes a spread so aromatic even freezing does not destroy the fragrance.

1 pound half-ripe, fragrant guavas
3 to 4 tablespoons water
2 tablespoons fresh lime juice
1 to 1½ cups sugar
½ teaspoon finely grated gingerroot
(optional)

Peel the guavas thin, and pulse/chop them to a coarse texture in a food processor. Place the chopped guava in a 3-quart microwavable glass casserole, add the water, and microwave (see pages 33–35 for details), uncovered, on high for 5 minutes; stir, and microwave 2 minutes longer, or until fruit is soft. Let stand 2 minutes. Using a wooden spoon, push pulp through a strainer to remove seeds; use a rubber scraper to save as much pulp as possible. Stir in lime juice, sugar, and gingerroot, if desired. Return mixture to the casserole, and microwave, uncovered, on high, 3 to 5 minutes, or until thickened but not stiff. Pack into hot, sterilized jars or freezer containers; cool, seal, label, and refrigerate or freeze.

If you have used the larger amount of sugar, final cooking time could be less than 3 minutes. If after cooling, the butter is too stiff, thin it with additional lime juice, return it to the microwave, reheat to a simmer, and repack.

Feijoa butter

MAKES ABOUT 2$\frac{1}{2}$ CUPS

The yield is higher from feijoas because, unlike guavas in the previous recipe, feijoas are completely edible, except for their skin. The addition of lemon gentles the musky aroma.

>   **1 lemon (4 ounces)**
>   **Water**
>   **1 pound ripe feijoas (4 large)**
>   **1$\frac{1}{2}$ cups sugar**

Halve the lemon; discard seeds and end pieces. Place just enough water in a blender container to cover the blades; add lemon, cut into chunks, and pulse/blend to a coarse texture. Empty mixture into a 2-cup liquid measure, and add water to reach the 1$\frac{1}{2}$-cup level. Let stand, uncovered, about 12 hours, or overnight to leach out the pectin.

Boil the mixture, covered, in a 1- or 1$\frac{1}{2}$-quart saucepan for 10 minutes. Put through a strainer, pushing with a wooden spoon to obtain as much liquid as possible. You should have about $\frac{3}{4}$ cup.

Peel the feijoas, and purée in a food processor. Place the lemon mixture, the feijoa purée, and the sugar in a 3-quart saucepan, bring quickly to a boil, stirring constantly to prevent spattering and sticking, and boil steadily, stirring, until butter is thick but not stiff. Pack into hot, sterilized jars or freezer containers, seal, and cool. Label and refrigerate or freeze.

FEIJOA

The multi-purpose quince

A century before the Pilgrims landed in New England, quinces were growing in apple and pear orchards in Brazil, planted there by Portuguese settlers. Eventually they were grown throughout New England and carried west by pioneers. Most of today's quinces are grown in California's San Joaquin Valley, but trees also survive to produce dooryard fruit in many states. Quinces were widely used in desserts and even meat dishes in the early days of this country. In rural areas people soaked the seeds to make glue. Until this century the glue was used as, among other things, a hair-setting liquid.

Quince butter

MAKES ABOUT 3 CUPS

Because raw quinces are so hard to core, I have tried several different methods of preparing them for cooking. They can be microwaved whole, but are apt to cook unevenly and to burst if you fail to prick the skin beforehand. I really prefer the old-fashioned, long boiling method because only that method, I have found, develops the characteristic deep amber color and full flavor of the fruit.

> 1¾ to 2 pounds fully ripe quinces
> 1½ cups water or defrosted apple
>   juice concentrate or boiled cider
>   (see note, page 105)
> 1 cup sugar
> 2 tablespoons fresh lemon juice

Peel and core the quinces, and cut them into chunks. Quince oxidizes (darkens) quickly when peeled. But it doesn't matter because the fruit darkens even more as it cooks. Place prepared quinces and water or apple juice concentrate or boiled cider in a 2-quart slow cooker, cover, and cook on high for 2 hours. Stir in sugar and lemon juice, and continue cooking, covered, for about 4 hours more, or until thick and a deep amber color. This produces a textured purée. If you want a smoother spread, let cool slightly, then purée in a food processor. Pack into hot, sterilized jars or freezer containers, cool, cover tightly, label, and refrigerate or freeze for future use.

This butter keeps a month or more in the refrigerator, and retains its flavor for at least 6 months in a freezer at zero degrees Fahrenheit. Recipe may be doubled, using a 3½- or 4-quart cooker; increased cooking time may be necessary.

Tangerine butter

MAKES ABOUT 2 CUPS

Is it a butter? Or a marmalade? You be the judge. Since the purée is so fine, I have arbitrarily put this recipe among the fruit butters. It is not worth making unless you can get the old-fashioned Dancy variety tangerines, with their loose peel and characteristic flavor. Clementines and Mandarines, which are also tangerines, are good to eat raw, but in a marmalade or butter, I find their flavor indistinguishable from that of other sweet orange spreads.

¾ pound tangerines (3 medium)
1¼ cups plus 2 tablespoons sugar

Peel and seed tangerines, and discard strings that cling to the peel and pulp segments. Place peel, pulp, and sugar in a food processor and chop until a gritty purée is achieved. Transfer purée to a 2-quart microwavable measure or casserole with vented cover; cover and microwave on high for 5 minutes. Stir, and microwave (see pages 33~35 for details), uncovered, on high for 5 to 7 minutes longer. Let stand 2 minutes. Ladle into hot, sterilized jars or freezer containers, cool, cover tightly, label, and refrigerate or freeze.

"Something smells awful good in here," remarked Dick, coming in with the evening paper open in his hand. I looked quickly at the headlines ... An astronaut was expressing his readiness to start to the moon in less than two years ... The apple butter spurted up again, splashing the newspaper. As I turned to pull the kettle back from the gas flame, I realized how much the glazed, spurting surface of the apple butter resembles the cratered far-off face of the moon as shown in the photographs displayed in the observatory at Mt. Palomar ...

Rachel Peden, *Rural Free, A Farmwife's Almanac of Country Living,* 1969

Crabapple butter

MAKES ABOUT 2 CUPS

A beautiful pale pink spread to eat immediately or freeze for later use.

1½ pounds crabapples
1 (12-ounce) can unsweetened apple
   juice concentrate, defrosted
Pinch of ground ginger
⅜ to ½ teaspoon each of ground
   cinnamon, ground mace, and ground
   coriander
Sugar (optional)

Remove stem and blossom ends from the crabapples, and pulse/chop them coarsely in a food processor. Place prepared crabapples and juice concentrate in a 4- to 5-quart saucepan, bring to a boil, and boil rapidly about 30 minutes, or until crabapples are mushy and liquid has almost totally evaporated. Stir occasionally to prevent sticking. Let cool before puréeing in a food mill. Stir in spices. Taste, and add sugar, if desired, 1 tablespoon at a time until you reach the sweetness level you want. Pack into hot, sterilized jars or freezer containers, cool, cover tightly, label, and refrigerate or freeze.

Butter and jam on a slice of white bread was a middle-class Anglo-American symbol of status in the 18th century. Apple butter and cottage cheese on a slice of rye bread was the Pennsylvania-German equivalent.

William Woys Weaver, *Sauerkraut Yankees*, 1983

Pineapple-apricot butter

MAKES ABOUT 2½ CUPS

This is a lightly sweetened version of the Pineapple-Apricot Marmalade (page 89) popular in the sixties and seventies. If you use canned pineapple, buy the most flavorsome brand you can find.

> **2 cups ripe, fragrant fresh pineapple**
> **chunks or 1 (20-ounce) can crushed**
> **pineapple in its own juice**
> **1 (6-ounce) package dried apricots**
> **1 (6-ounce) can unsweetened pine-**
> **apple juice concentrate, defrosted**
> **Sugar**

Drain the pineapple, saving the juice for other uses. Place an open 8-ounce canning jar upside down in the center of a 2-quart microwavable nonplastic measure or casserole, distribute the apricots evenly around the jar, add the juice concentrate, cover (vent if using plastic wrap), and microwave (see page 33 for details) on high until juice boils. Remove measure from oven, remove jar with jar lifter, re-cover, and let stand until the apricots are soft and plump. Transfer apricots and syrup to a food processor, add the drained pineapple chunks or crushed pineapple, and process to a relatively smooth purée. Return mixture to the cooking vessel, add ¼ to ½ cup of sugar or more to taste, and microwave, uncovered, on high about 5 minutes, or until butter is glossy and holds its shape. Pack into hot, sterilized jars or freezer containers, cool, cover tightly, label, and refrigerate or freeze.

Applebutter boiling

And now the butter-boiling came —
    That set the rural hearts ablaze —
That came as sure as autumn came;
Would that it yet came all the same
    As in those dreamy autumn days —
With fiddle, frolic, dance and play,
With rustic song and rural lay.

Across a rugged bench astride,
    A busy, artless, rustic sits
And pares the apples for the rest,
Who, 'mid the music, song and jest,
    Now cut the apples into snits;
While, two by two, well paired, by turns,
Stir, lest the boiling butter burns.

Good butter must be slowly boiled —
    According to the old-time way;
And so they boiled and stirred it slow,
Until the cocks began to crow,
    And then began the sport and play,
And dance went on and seldom ceased
'Til rosy morn adorned the East.

Before they took the kettle off
    They stirred the fragrant spices in;
And then, with ladle, tin, or gourd,
The boiling mass was dipped and poured;
    Amid the noisy clang and din,
From copper-kettle, burning hot,
Into the well-cooled, earthen pot.

From a longer poem "Cider-Making and Butter-Boiling" in H. L. Fisher's Olden Times: York, Pennsylvania, or, Pennsylvania Rural Life, some fifty years ago, and other poems, 1888 as quoted in Ann Hark and Preston A. Barba's Pennsylvania German Cookery: A Regional Cookbook, 1950

Paradise butter

MAKES ABOUT 4 CUPS

In the economical tradition of our grandmothers, I make fruit butter from the pulp left over from making Paradise Jelly.

> **3½ to 4 cups of pulp from Paradise
> Jelly (page 82)**
> **½ cup honey**

Purée pulp in a food processor. Stir in honey, place in a 1-quart slow cooker, cover, and cook about 2 hours if the purée is at room temperature, or 1 to 1½ hours if it is still warm. To cut cooking time to 1 hour, reheat the pulp and honey in the crockery liner with a vented cover in a microwave oven (700-watt oven with turntable) about 5 minutes on high. Transfer the crock to the cooker base for finishing. Pack the butter in hot, sterilized jars or freezer containers. Cool, cover tightly, label, and refrigerate or freeze. Keeps for months in the refrigerator, and up to a year in a zero-degree freezer.

Gingery pear butter

MAKES ABOUT 1¼ CUPS

The pears you use should be fully ripe—golden yellow and dripping with sweet juices. Pears, incidentally, ripen best after picking.

> **1 teaspoon ascorbic acid mixture
> (page 245)**
> **¾ teaspoon water**
> **1½ pounds ripe, juicy pears**
> **2 tablespoons sugar**
> **½ to ¾ teaspoon finely chopped crys-
> tallized ginger or drained preserved
> stem ginger**

Place ascorbic acid mixture and water in the workbowl of a food processor with steel chopping blade. Add peeled, cored pears, cut into chunks, and process to a

Gingery pear butter (continued)

smooth purée. Transfer to a 2-quart saucepan, and boil, stirring, over high heat for 5 minutes. Transfer to a jelly bag, and let drip 15 minutes, reserving the juice for other uses.

Return pulp to saucepan. Add sugar and ginger, and reheat just to a boil, stirring constantly to prevent sticking and spattering. Pack immediately in a hot sterilized jar or freezer container, cool, cover tightly, label, and refrigerate or freeze.

Microwave directions   (See pages 33–35 for details.) Place the uncooked puréed pear mixture in a 2-quart microwavable glass measure or casserole, and microwave on high until mixture boils, about 5 minutes, stirring after first 3 minutes. Pour into jelly bag and let drip 15 minutes, reserving juice for other uses. Return pulp to measure or casserole. Stir in sugar and ginger, and reheat in microwave until butter boils. Immediately fill a hot, sterilized jar or freezer container, cool, cover tightly, label, and refrigerate or freeze.

A taste for fruit in natural juice, circa 1812

The manner of making use of fruits, preserved by the process I have pointed out, consists, 1st. in putting such fruit into a fruit jar, in the same state in which it is in the bottle, without adding any sugar, because many persons, more especially ladies, prefer fruits with their natural juice.

Nicolas Appert, the Frenchman who invented vacuum canning, *The Art of Preserving All Kinds of Animal and Vegetable Substances for Several Years,* 1812

Reduced-calorie fruit spreads

If you love the flavor of jam, but not the extra calories, try these freezer spreads—you can make them any time of year, using frozen fruit and berries when fresh are out of season. Most of the spreads contain a little sugar, which has one major advantage over the juice concentrates used in commercial products. The concentrates tend to dilute the flavor of the primary fruit, while sugar—even in small amounts—enhances the fruit's flavor.

My personal favorites among the recipes in this chapter are the simplest recipes—just fruit, water or juice, a flavoring extract or spirits, and only enough sugar to complement the fruit flavor without overwhelming it. A few recipes use packaged powdered pectin, not for its jelling properties, but as a thickener.

Of course, you can also use the new reduced-calorie pectins that work with or without sugar, but the yields in most recipes are far greater than my small batches. For a discussion of these pectins, and suggestions for use, see page 15.

You will find many uses for the juices drained from the fruits and berries before making the spreads: in molded desserts, syrups, ices, and other frozen desserts, yogurt drinks, or with mixers such as seltzer or club soda.

The University of California leaflet that inspired my recipes recommends water bath processing (pages 10–11) if you want to store the spreads at room temperature: 15 minutes for half-pints; 20 minutes for pints. I do not recommend water bath processing in this case because freezing them is easier and just as safe. Most of the spreads are decidedly tangy. If you prefer something sweeter but do not want to add more sugar, stir in artificial sweetener to taste after the spreads have cooled.

Like traditional preserves, these spreads all taste better if they are allowed to mellow at least a week before serving. They keep up to six months at zero degrees Fahrenheit, or up to six weeks in the refrigerator. Spreads made with artificial sweeteners tend to spoil faster than sugar-sweetened products because even a small amount of sugar has some preservative effect.

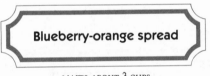

Blueberry-orange spread

MAKES ABOUT 3 CUPS

Thinned with a little orange-flavored liqueur, this also makes an unusual and flavorful sauce for vanilla ice cream or orange sherbet.

> **3 pint baskets ripe blueberries, or**
> **3 (12-ounce) packages frozen**
> **unsweetened blueberries**
> **½ cup fresh orange juice**
> **1 teaspoon grated orange peel**
> **¾ cup sugar**

Wash, drain, and stem the blueberries if fresh. Place the orange juice, peel, and berries in a 4-quart saucepan, cover, bring quickly to a boil, uncover, and reduce heat slightly. Stir almost constantly to prevent spattering and sticking, and cook rapidly for 10 minutes. Pour into jelly bag, and let drip into a bowl 15 minutes. Return pulp to the saucepan, and refrigerate juice for other uses.

Stir sugar into pulp; stirring almost constantly, cook rapidly 10 minutes, or until thickened. Ladle into hot, sterilized jars or freezer containers, cool, cover tightly, label, and refrigerate or freeze.

Microwaved blueberry-orange spread

MAKES ABOUT 3 CUPS

Reduce all ingredients by half, and prepare blueberries as described in first paragraph of the preceding recipe. Set an open 8-ounce canning jar upside down in the center of a 2-quart microwavable glass measure or casserole, arrange berries around it, add orange juice and grated peel, and microwave (see pages 33~35 for details), uncovered, on high, for 5 minutes, or until all berries have burst. You may need to add a minute or two cooking time if berries are frozen. Drip mixture through a jelly bag into a bowl for 15 minutes. Return pulp to the cooking vessel, stir in sugar until it dissolves, then microwave, uncovered, on high 3 minutes or more, until mixture thickens. It will thicken still more as it cools. Pack as directed in last paragraph of preceding recipe.

Piña colada spread

MAKES ABOUT 1½ CUPS

You may use fresh pineapple and grated, unsweetened coconut in this spread, but the difference in flavor is so insignificant and the added work so much greater that I never bother. For a fancy cheese spread to serve with toast and tea, stir a few spoonfuls of this into softened cream cheese.

> 1 (20-ounce) can crushed pineapple
>   in pineapple juice
> ¼ cup flaked coconut
> Half of a 1¾- or 2-ounce package of
>   regular powdered fruit pectin
> 1½ tablespoons dark rum, or 1
>   teaspoon rum extract

Place pineapple in jelly bag; let drip into bowl for 15 minutes. Place pulp in a 3-quart saucepan, and refrigerate juice for other uses.

In a saucepan over medium heat stir pineapple until hot; stir in coconut, pectin, and rum (not extract) until pectin is dissolved. Remove from heat. If using rum extract, stir in at this time. Pack in a hot, sterilized 12-ounce jar or freezer container, cool, cover tightly, and refrigerate or freeze.

Microwaved piña colada spread

MAKES ABOUT 1½ CUPS

Using ingredients from preceding recipe, drain pineapple as described in first paragraph of the recipe. Set an open 8-ounce canning jar upside down in a 3-quart microwavable casserole with vented cover, arrange drained pineapple around it, and microwave (see pages 33–35 for details), covered, on high about 5 minutes, or until fruit is hot. Remove from oven, add coconut, pectin, and rum or rum extract, stirring continuously until pectin has dissolved and spread is thick. Fill a hot, sterilized 12-ounce jar or freezer container, cool, cover tightly, label, and refrigerate or freeze.

Reduced-calorie orange marmalade

MAKES ABOUT 3 CUPS

Because its sugar content is so low, this marmalade remains opaque instead of clearing up like the traditional variety—but the taste is great, on toast, in sandwich cookies, or as a cheesecake topping.

> 2 large thick-skinned navel oranges
>   (about 10 ounces each)
> 1½ cups water
> ⅔ cup sugar
> 1 (1¾-ounce) package powdered
>   pectin

If using a food processor, first cut the oranges into 1-inch wedges, and chop, 1 cupful at a time. Use the steel blade and an on-off motion, and empty the container after each load. If using a knife, first peel the oranges; cut the pulp into small pieces, and coarsely chop the peel. You should have about 2 cupfuls.

Reduced-calorie orange marmalade (continued)

Place chopped pulp and peel in a 2-quart saucepan with the water. Bring to boil quickly over high heat, and adjust heat so mixture boils steadily for 30 minutes. Stir often to prevent sticking. Mix sugar and pectin together, and stir into cooked fruit; boil 5 minutes more, stirring almost constantly to prevent sticking. Remove from heat; quick-chill a spoonful in the freezer; taste, and add more sugar if desired. Fill hot, sterilized jars or freezer containers, cool, cover tightly, label, and refrigerate or freeze.

> *"Quinces, Cherries, andd Damsins set the Dames a-work,"* wrote the seventeenth-century writer John Josselyn of Massachusetts, noting that in every house he found marmalades and preserved Damson plums. Fruits were not only dried, but candied, preserved in syrup, made into jams, or pressed to make sweet wines.
>
> Richard J. Hooker, A *History of Food and Drink in America*, 1981

Plum-rum spread

MAKES ABOUT 1½ CUPS

Damsons make a particularly delicious spread, but they are often hard to find in markets today, and I've found that Italian prune plums work as well in this spread. The rum may be omitted from this recipe, but the jam will not taste as good. Do not substitute rum extract—the flavor tastes artificial—and even though the rum flavor diminishes as the spread ages, the extract is still not as good as the real thing.

> 1½ **pounds ripe prune plums**
> 2 **tablespoons water**
> ¼ **cup sugar**
> 1½ **tablespoons dark rum**

Pit and quarter the plums. Set an 8-inch open canning jar upside down in the center of a 2-quart microwavable glass measure or casserole. Distribute the plum quarters around it, add the water, cover (vent if using plastic wrap), and microwave (see pages 33–35 for details) on high 5 to 7 minutes, or until fruit is soft and pulpy. Let stand 2 minutes. With a jar lifter, remove the jar, mash the fruit, stir in the sugar and rum, and microwave, uncovered, on high for 10 minutes, stirring every 3 minutes. Let stand 2 minutes. Fill a hot, sterilized jar or freezer container, cool, cover tightly, label, and refrigerate or freeze.

NOTE

This spread can be made on the range top, and the difference in cooking time is insignificant; but I prefer the microwave because the spread erupts and splatters when cooked the old-fashioned way.

> *Take oranges of medium size,*
>   *The peel remove, I pray,*
> *From each a round cut from one end,*
>   *And scoop the seeds away.*
> *Fill up the little cups thus formed*
>   *With strawberry preserve.*
> *The flavor mixed with orange juice*
>   *Is more than most deserve.*
>
> Imogen Clark, *Rhymed Receipts,* 1912

Strawberry-rhubarb spread

MAKES ABOUT 2½ CUPS

After many experiments I finally gave up the idea of developing a low-sugar strawberry jam—like most berries, the strawberry's juice content is so high that even as little as 15 minutes' draining left too little pulp. But in the classic combination with rhubarb, the jam yield—and the flavor—are great.

1 (20-ounce) bag frozen unsweetened
   strawberries, or 2 pint baskets fully
   ripe fresh strawberries (1¼ pounds)
8 ounces fresh or frozen rhubarb
¾ cup sugar
1 (1¾- or 2-ounce) package
   powdered fruit pectin

Hull and halve or quarter extra-large strawberries, and cut trimmed rhubarb stalks into ½-inch pieces if you are using fresh fruit. Discard rhubarb leaves, which contain toxic amounts of oxalic acid.

In 3-quart saucepan over low heat cook strawberries and rhubarb, stirring often, until juices begin to flow freely. Raise heat slightly, bring to boil, stirring often. Stirring almost constantly to prevent sticking and spattering, boil 5 minutes.

Remove from heat; crush fruit with potato masher. Pour into jelly bag; let drip 5 minutes into bowl. Return pulp to saucepan; refrigerate juice for other use.

Strawberry-rhubarb spread (continued)

Stir sugar and pectin into pulp; stirring, quickly bring to boil; boil 1 minute. Remove from heat. Ladle into a hot, sterilized jar or freezer container, cool, cover tightly, and refrigerate or freeze.

Microwave directions (see pages 33–35 for details) Set an open 8-ounce canning jar upside down in the center of a 3-quart microwavable and flameproof glass ceramic casserole with vented lid. Distribute the prepared fruit evenly around the jar, starting with the strawberries. If the berries and/or rhubarb are frozen, cover the casserole and microwave on defrost setting until juice starts to flow; follow the oven manufacturer's guidelines for timing. Microwave, covered, on high about 9 minutes for frozen berries and fruit, or about 5 minutes for fresh. Let stand 3 minutes. Fruit should be soft when pierced with a fork.

Remove from heat, remove the jar with jar lifter, and crush the fruit with a potato masher. Pour into a jelly bag and let drip into a bowl for 5 minutes only. Return pulp to microwave casserole, and refrigerate juice for other uses. Stir sugar and pectin together in a small bowl; add all at once to the fruit mixture, and cook on a range top, stirring constantly over medium heat until mixture boils. Boil 1 minute, remove from heat, and ladle into hot, sterilized jars or freezer containers. Cool, cover tightly, and refrigerate or freeze.

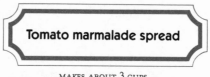

Tomato marmalade spread

MAKES ABOUT 3 CUPS

I like to serve this one as a spread on cream cheese or as a relish with ham, cold roast pork, or turkey.

> **2 pounds ripe tomatoes (about
>   5 medium)**
> **2 medium lemons (3- to 4-ounce size)**
> **1 medium orange (6 to 7 ounces)**
> **⅔ cup sugar**
> **2 tablespoons orange-flavored liqueur
>   (optional)**

Cut tomatoes into 1-inch chunks; you should have about 6 cups. Slice lemons and orange very thin, discarding end pieces and seeds.

Place tomatoes, lemons, and orange in a 4-quart saucepan over high heat. Stirring often, bring to a boil. Reduce heat, and continue to stir often as the spread boils for 25 to 30 minutes, or until peels are tender and translucent. Stir in sugar, and cook rapidly, stirring often, for 15 minutes (does not need to drip through jelly bag). Remove from heat, stir in liqueur, if desired. Ladle into hot, sterilized jars or several freezer containers, cool, cover tightly, label, and refrigerate or freeze.

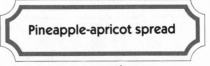

Pineapple-apricot spread

MAKES ABOUT 2½ CUPS

1 (6-ounce) package dried apricots
1 (20-ounce) can crushed pineapple
**   in its own juice**
¼ cup sugar

Cut apricots into ¼-inch strips, and place in a 1½-quart saucepan. Drain pineapple juice into the pan, and bring to a boil, stirring often. Reduce heat slightly, and cook rapidly, stirring often, for 10 minutes, or until juice has thickened and apricots are soft. Remove from heat, crush fruit with a potato masher, and stir in pineapple and sugar until sugar has completely dissolved. Fill hot, sterilized jars or freezer containers, cool, cover tightly, label, and refrigerate or freeze.

Microwaved pineapple-apricot spread

MAKES ABOUT 2½ CUPS

Using ingredients from preceding recipe, cut the apricots into ¼-inch strips. Set an open 8-ounce canning jar upside down in the center of a 2-quart microwavable glass measure or casserole. Arrange apricot strips around the jar, and drain the pineapple juice over them. Microwave (see pages 33–35 for details), uncovered, on high for about 5 minutes. Remove jar with a jar lifter, and let fruit stand 5 minutes to soften and plump up. Crush with a potato masher, and stir in pineapple and sugar until sugar dissolves. If jam is not quite thick enough, return it to the microwave for a few minutes more cooking. Pack as directed in preceding recipe.

Amaretto-flavored peach spread

MAKES ABOUT 3 CUPS

Be sure to use real amaretto liqueur, not noyeau or any of the other almond-flavored drinks. Any moderately priced brand will do. A dollop of this jam thinned with a little more amaretto makes a luscious sauce for peach ice cream or sliced peaches—fresh, frozen and partially defrosted, or canned in their own juice.

> 2 to 3 pounds ripe peaches, or
>   2 (20-ounce) bags frozen
>   unsweetened peach slices
> 1 tablespoon fresh lemon juice
> 1 (1¾- or 2-ounce) package powdered
>   fruit pectin
> ⅓ to ½ cup sugar; use larger amount
>   if using almond extract
> 3 tablespoons amaretto liqueur, or 1
>   teaspoon almond extract

Peel and pit fresh peaches or slightly defrost frozen ones. In a food processor pulse/chop the peaches to a coarse texture with the lemon juice, to measure about 4 cups. Empty mixture into a 2-quart saucepan, and bring to a boil over high heat, stirring often to prevent sticking. Reduce heat slightly; stirring almost constantly, cook rapidly 15 minutes. Ladle into a jelly bag, and let drip into a bowl for 15 minutes.

Return pulp to saucepan, and refrigerate juice for other uses. Mix the pectin with the sugar, and add to the fruit mixture while stirring to prevent lumping. Cook rapidly, stirring almost constantly, about 15 minutes, or until mixture thickens. Stir in liqueur, and cook 5 minutes more. If you use almond extract, stir it in off the heat and do not cook further. Ladle into hot, sterilized jars or several freezer containers, cool, cover tightly, label, and refrigerate or freeze.

When Captain Haden developed the Haden mango near Miami, he did a greater kindness to the state than the Plant or Flagler Railroad systems. The texture is like cream melting on the tongue. The flavor is as though nightingales were singing to the palate. What the gods gorged on, on Olympus, is called nectar and ambrosia, but mangos are plainly meant.

Marjorie Kinnan Rawlings, *Cross Creek Cookery*, 1942

MAKES ABOUT 2½ CUPS

Mangoes have a long season—February through September—but the best time to make this spread is in June or July, when they are most plentiful, and so sweet you may not even need the quarter cup of sugar.

**3 large ripe mangoes (about
1 pound each)**
1 tablespoon fresh lemon or lime juice
¼ cup sugar (optional)

Holding each mango over the workbowl of a food processor to catch the juice, cut slices from the flat pits. With a grapefruit spoon or other sharp-edged spoon, scrape the flesh into the workbowl. Cut remaining flesh from the pits, scrape flesh from the strips of peel, and purée.

Place purée in a 2-quart saucepan, and add lemon or lime juice and sugar, if desired. Bring quickly to a boil, reduce heat, and cook rapidly about 20 minutes, stirring often to prevent sticking. Ladle into hot, sterilized jars or freezer containers, cool, cover tightly, label, and refrigerate or freeze. Recipe may be halved.

Microwave variation　Using ingredients from preceding recipe, make the purée as described in the first paragraph of that recipe. Place the purée in a 2-quart microwavable glass measure or casserole, add lemon or lime juice and sugar, if desired, and microwave (see pages 33–35 for details), uncovered, on high, about 10 minutes. Stir every 3 or 4 minutes, until spread is thick. Pack containers as described in last paragraph of preceding recipe.

PICKLES AND RELISHES

On the table spread the cloth,
*   Let the knives be sharp and clean,*
Pickles get and salad both,
*   Let them each be fresh and green;*
*   With small beer, good ale, and wine,*
*   O ye gods! how I shall dine!*

English folk song, quoted by
Evan Jones in *A Food
Lover's Companion*, 1979

o some people a full cookie jar is a security blanket. To others it may be a quart of ice cream in the freezer. Mine is a jar of my aunt's Bread-and-Butter Pickles (page 135), plus a jar of Piccalilli (page 164), although in a pinch I can chop some of the pickles to make a quick relish.

Pickles don't seem to be as popular today as they were when I was growing up. And that's a shame. Their tart, tangy, spicy flavors do as much for bland, low-fat foods as for fried chicken, hamburgers, and hot dogs. In the first instance, they make up for the flavor lost when you reduce fat content. Conversely, the sharpness of pickles and relishes cuts oiliness in other foods.

Some pickles and relishes make good ingredients for other recipes. The classic example is probably tartar sauce, in which cucumber relish is stirred into mayonnaise to be served with fish or seafood. A similar spread is good on sandwiches. I also add cucumber or pepper relish to my meat loaf or chicken or turkey loaf mixtures. Tuna salad also benefits from chopped pickles or a not-very-sweet pickle relish. Fruit chutneys and other sweet-and-sour relishes are particularly good in or with chicken or turkey salads or sandwiches.

It is true that man cannot live by pickled cucumbers alone,
or even make a complete meal of them without accompani-
ment. But it is equally true that there are some noble
gustatory experiences that would not merely be incomplete,
but almost unthinkable, without their pickled cucumber
garnish.

Paul Levy, *Out to Lunch*, 1986

Frozen sliced sweet dill pickles

MAKES ABOUT 1 QUART

One might reasonably expect frozen pickles to be limp, soggy, and unappetizing. These are not. But don't ask me to explain why they have a crispness that rivals even pickles made with pickling lime. I don't know the answer. I do know that everyone I have ever served these to asked for the recipe. The carambola pickle following is a variation on the theme.

1 pound 3-inch unwaxed cucumbers
¾ pound small yellow onions
4 teaspoons table salt
2 tablespoons water
¾ to 1 cup sugar
½ cup cider vinegar
1 teaspoon dried dill weed (or more
    to taste)

With a food processor thinly slice the cucumbers and onions.

Mix the prepared cucumbers, onions, salt, and water in a 2-quart bowl (not aluminum), and let stand about 2 hours. Drain, but do not rinse.

Return the vegetables to the bowl, and add the sugar, the vinegar, and the dill. Let stand, stirring from time to time, until sugar has dissolved completely and liquid covers the vegetables. Pack in glass or plastic freezer containers, leaving 1 inch of headspace, seal tightly, label, and freeze.

Defrost either in the refrigerator or at room temperature. Defrosting time will vary greatly, depending on the size of the freezer containers and the temperature.

Carambola: a fruit with an identity crisis

The carambola has more aliases than a gangster on the run. "Carambola" was the original Portuguese name for the ribbed fruit that looks like golden stars when it is sliced crosswise. The Portuguese name came from samara, *the Sanskrit word for "food-appetizer," Jane Grigson and Charlotte Knox write in* Cooking with Exotic Fruits & Vegetables *(1986). Elsewhere it is called the Coromandel gooseberry (by English residents of Southeast Asia); the Chinese gooseberry in southern China, but the yang t'ao, or goat peach, in northern China, where kiwifruit is called Chinese gooseberry. Even today, say Grigson and Knox, "a request for [a Chinese gooseberry] may well get you a kiwifruit in London, but a carambola from an English-speaking merchant in Hong Kong."*

Frozen sweet carambola pickles

MAKES ABOUT 2 CUPS

Appearance isn't everything, but it helps. These star-shaped pickles are fine on burgers and other sandwiches, and they really dress up a salad in terms of flavor and looks.

> **1 pound small carambolas, green or**
> **   semiripe**
> **½ pound small yellow onions**
> **1 teaspoon salt**
> **2 tablespoons water**
> **¾ cup sugar**
> **½ cup white vinegar**

Trim the brown edges from the carambolas, and slice crosswise on a mandoline or with a knife; discard seeds. Thinly slice the onions. Mix the prepared carambola with the onions, salt, and water in a 2-quart nonaluminum bowl, and let stand 2 hours. Drain, but do not rinse.

Return the solids to the bowl, add sugar and vinegar, and let stand, stirring occasionally, until sugar has dissolved completely, and liquid covers the solids. Pack in freezer containers, leaving ¾- to 1-inch headspace; seal tightly, label, and freeze at least 24 hours before defrosting for serving.

Pickled snap peas

MAKES ABOUT 2 PINTS

Use the plumpest snap peas you can find. They are sweetest when the pods are full and round. Serve as a snack as is, or with a dip made of Ajvar (page 206) and yogurt.

1 pound snap peas
2 to 4 peeled garlic cloves
1/4 to 1/2 teaspoon dried crushed red
    pepper, or to taste
1 cup white rice vinegar or rice wine
    vinegar
1 cup water
1 tablespoon sugar
1 tablespoon salt

String the peas, and pack them upright in hot, sterilized wide-mouth pint jars in two vertical layers, adding a garlic clove or 2 on each layer. Sprinkle crushed red pepper over the top layer.

Combine vinegar, water, sugar, and salt and bring to a boil. Fill jars almost to overflowing. Peas should be covered by at least 1/4 inch with the brine. Seal, cool, label, and refrigerate at least 2 weeks before serving.

Oriental pickles are winning new fans in America

"Rice and pickles are to the Japanese what bread and cheese are to the English, and French bread and wine to the French," Shizuo Tsuji *wrote in* Japanese Cooking: A Simple Art *(1980). "Pickling began in ancient times as a means of preserving food, and over the years pickles became an important part of the Japanese meal—in many cases the only food served besides rice." As growing numbers of Japanese restaurants in American cities serve growing numbers of American patrons, we, too, are developing an appetite for their lightly vinegared or brined vegetables and even the peppery pickled ginger slices that are served with sushi.*

Pickled cabbage
Japanese style

MAKES A SCANT 1 QUART

1 pound green cabbage
1 1/4 cups white rice vinegar
1 1/2 teaspoons salt
1 to 1 1/4 tablespoons sugar
1/4 cup water
1-inch square of lemon peel, yellow
    part only

Core the cabbage, remove any damaged outer leaves, and tear or cut it into bite-size pieces. Place the prepared cabbage in a glass bowl. Measure the vinegar, salt, sugar, and water into a 1 1/2-quart saucepan, bring to a boil over high heat, stirring to dissolve the sugar. Pour boiling liquid over the cabbage and tuck the lemon peel into the center. Cover with a plate or saucer that will fit inside the bowl, and weight it with about 8 pounds of canned foods securely sealed in new plastic food bags. Let stand at room temperature about 12 hours, or until liquid covers the cabbage. With tongs, transfer the cabbage to a 1-quart jar, pour the pickling brine over it, and press down to pack the cabbage below the surface of the liquid. Cover, label, and refrigerate at least 2 days before serving.

To serve, use tongs to remove cabbage from the jar. Serve with a few drops of soy sauce, if desired. It keeps 1 to 2 months in the refrigerator.

Kimchi comes in many varieties

Korean War veterans in the fifties—like World War II veterans in the forties— brought home a taste for foods they had first sampled in the war zone. During the war Korean kimchi (or kimchee) was off limits to our fighting men because the cabbage version of the peppery relish was often pickled too long and under less than ideal conditions, Jeanne Voltz writes in The California Cookbook *(1970). "Made at home," she added, "it is completely safe and not so pungently soured as the real article."*

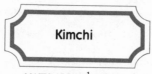

Kimchi

MAKES ABOUT 1 QUART

My first taste of *kimchi* was at a Korean restaurant in Honolulu in the 1950s. The name had been anglicized to *kimchee,* and the cabbage was incendiary, primarily from the bits of red chiles visible in the brine. Its primary ingredient was green cabbage and only later did I learn that Chinese cabbage (napa) is more traditional for the cabbage variety. Other *kimchi* vegetables include turnips, carrots, and cucumbers. And still other *kimchis* are made with fish and seafood. Judy Hyun, author of *The Korean Cookbook* (1970), writes that "Kimchi, for better or worse, finds its way to the table daily, like bread in the West." Certainly that is true in a fast-growing number of Korean restaurants in cities like New York, where half a dozen or more dishes of *kimchis* are brought to the table at the start of a meal. In Western meals, it makes a good substitute for cole slaw with sandwiches, cold meats, and poultry.

> 1½ pounds Chinese cabbage (napa)
> ½ cup salt dissolved in
>   1½ quarts water
> ¼ cup sliced scallions, including green
>   tops
> 1½ teaspoons each of finely chopped
>   gingerroot, finely chopped garlic,
>   and dried crushed red pepper, or to
>   taste
> ¼ cup plus 2 teaspoons sugar

Cut cabbage into 1½-inch squares, and place in a large mixing bowl with the saltwater solution. Weight the cabbage with a plate or a water-filled jar to keep it submerged; if necessary, add water so the cabbage is covered. Let stand about 3 hours, or until cabbage has wilted. Drain it well, and rinse 2 or 3 times to remove excess salt; drain well again. Stir in the remaining ingredients, and pack firmly into a scalded 1-quart or 1-liter jar, cover tightly, and refrigerate 2 to 3 days before serving. The *kimchi* keeps for months in the refrigerator, its spiciness and aroma becoming stronger with age.

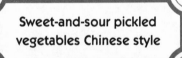

Sweet-and-sour pickled vegetables Chinese style

MAKES ABOUT 1 QUART

In some Chinese-American restaurants a dish of pickles—either cabbage, hot with chiles, or sweet-and-sour mixed vegetable pickles like these—will be brought to the table soon after guests are seated, just as bread is brought to table in Western restaurants. My recipe has evolved from those in several Chinese cookbooks, including *Chinese Recipes for the Home Kitchen* by Li Nianpei (1985).

¼ to ½ cup sugar or its equivalent in
    artificial sweetener
1 cup white rice vinegar or
    white vinegar
½ cup water
½ teaspoon salt
1 or more small dried hot chiles or
    1 teaspoon crushed red pepper
About 1½ pounds green cabbage
2 medium carrots
2 broccoli stalks

First, make the syrup. Place sugar, vinegar, water, salt, and chiles in a 1½-quart saucepan, and stir over high heat until the sugar has dissolved and the mixture boils. Remove from heat and let cool to room temperature. If you use an artificial sweetener, add it to the syrup after it has reached room temperature.

While the syrup cools, core the cabbage, separate it into leaves, and tear them into bite-size pieces. Peel the carrots and broccoli stems (save florets for other uses) and slice them thin on the diagonal. Bring 2 quarts of water to a boil in a 4-quart saucepan. Add the prepared vegetables all at once, stir, turn off the heat, and let them blanch for 2 minutes; drain, and spread the vegetables in a shallow layer on a platter to cool.

Sterilize a 1-quart or 1-liter jar, pack the vegetables into the jar, fill to overflowing with the syrup, cover, and refrigerate at least a week before using. They keep for months in the refrigerator.

Variation   Add 1 teaspoon of crushed Szechuan peppercorns to the syrup, and use any firm vegetables you fancy—sliced bell peppers, green beans, snow peas, turnips, and/or radishes.

The old stone jar of mustard pickles

After the kraut is cured, it can be put into the freezer, if you have room. Old-timers remember how good the cold top layer was in deep winter when you went out to the summer kitchen to fill a bowl from one of the five-gallon stone jars. Beside it was the stone jar of mustard pickles, grape-leaf-covered, with an old white-china plate on top, and a clean stone weighing it all down.

Rachel Peden, *Rural Free, A Farmwife's Almanac of Country Living,* 1969

MAKES ABOUT 5 PINTS

Crispness, tartness, and a pronounced mustard flavor are what I look for in this type of pickle. The vegetables remain crunchy because they are simply heated—not cooked—first in the soaking water, and then in the sauce. I like mustard pickles with just about any kind of cold meat or poultry and even with oily fish such as salmon, Spanish mackerel, and shad. The tangy sauce seems to make the fish taste less rich. The recipe may be halved, if five pints seems excessive.

1 pound small unwaxed cucumbers
1 pound hard green cherry tomatoes
    or larger tomatoes
1 pound bell peppers
¾ pound small white onions, fresh or
    frozen
½ pound cauliflower florets
½ cup uniodized table salt, or pickling
    salt, or ½ cup plus 3 tablespoons
    coarse (kosher) salt
5 cups water
½ cup flour
3 tablespoons dry mustard
1 teaspoon each of ground turmeric,
    celery seed, and mustard seed
½ teaspoon each of whole cloves and
    whole allspice
1 cup packed light brown sugar
4 cups cider vinegar

Cut cucumbers crosswise into ½-inch-thick slices. Core and halve the cherry tomatoes, or core larger ones and cut into 1-inch chunks. Stem and seed the bell peppers, and cut into ¼-inch chunks. Scald and peel the onions if using fresh ones. Frozen onions need not be defrosted. Place the cucumbers, tomatoes, cauliflower, peppers, onions, salt, and water in a large bowl. Stir well to dissolve the salt, and weight with a plate and a jar filled with water or food cans protected by new plastic food storage bags. Let stand 18 to 24 hours.

The next day, heat the vegetables in the brine in a wide 4-quart saucepan, stirring often, until they are hot to the touch. Drain well in colander.

While the vegetables heat, mix the flour, spices, and sugar in a wide 4-quart saucepan. Gradually stir in the vinegar. Place over medium heat, and stir constantly until mixture is as thick as heavy cream sauce.

Add the hot, well-drained vegetables and continue stirring until they are very hot and sauce is boiling. Adjust heat to keep mixture hot while you quickly pack into hot, sterilized jars. Vegetables should come within ¾ inch of top, and sauce should cover them within ¼ inch of top. Seal, label, and store at least a month before using.

A mystery: how bread-and-butter pickles got their name

Where bread-and-butter pickles got their name is a mystery. None of the dozens of books I have consulted offered a clue. William Woys Weaver, a culinary historian and author, theorizes that the name may have referred originally to a variety the Pennsylvania Dutch called sandwich pickles — pickles to be eaten with or in sandwiches. The trade association representing pickle manufacturers thinks bread-and-butter pickles may have been developed as a substitute filling for cucumber tea sandwiches when fresh vegetables were out of season.

Onie's bread-and-butter pickles

MAKES ABOUT 4 PINTS

Onie is the family nickname for Aunt Lena Wolf, who was my father's oldest sister and a fine cook. Like most cooks of her time (she was born in 1865), she rarely wrote out precise directions for her recipes. I have her bread-and-butter

Onie's bread-and-butter pickles (continued)

pickle recipe in her own angular script on a blank page in a dog-eared book, *Good Things to Eat,* published in Topeka, Kansas, in 1921. It calls for one gallon of cucumbers and four large onions, and it makes about eight pints, although she neglected to note this in writing. I halved her recipe for this book. If you want to make the whole thing, either cook it in two batches or use a larger, wider pan. My recipe also is easily halved.

> 4 pounds unwaxed cucumbers
> 　　(3 to 4 inches long)
> 1/2 pound onions (2 large)
> 1/2 cup coarse (kosher) salt, or
> 　　6 tablespoons uniodized table salt
> 　　or pickling salt
> Water
> 2 1/2 cups sugar
> 1 1/2 teaspoons each of celery seed,
> 　　mustard seed, and ground turmeric
> 2 1/2 cups cider vinegar

Slice cucumbers and onions as thin as possible with a mandoline or a food processor.

Layer prepared cucumbers and onions with salt in a 4-quart bowl (not aluminum). Cover with cold water, and refrigerate, covered, 4 to 5 hours, or overnight.

Drain, rinse, and drain again, then refrigerate in a colander set in the bowl while you prepare the syrup.

Place sugar, spices, and vinegar in a 6- to 8-quart saucepan, stirring to dissolve sugar. When mixture boils, add well-drained vegetables all at once. Stir to encourage even heating, and heat just to the boiling point.

Adjust heat to keep mixture hot but *not* boiling while you use a slotted spoon to fill hot, sterilized jars within 3/4 to 1 inch of top. Cover with boiling syrup almost to overflowing. With a tea strainer, remove spices remaining in pan, divide them among the jars, and seal. (Discard leftover syrup. You may have as much as 2 cups, but it's too watered down by the cucumbers to be reused.) Seal, cool, label, and store at least a month before using.

> *In 1728 the* Boston News Letter *estimated the food needs of a middle-class "genteel" family. Breakfast was bread and milk. Dinner consisted of pudding, followed by bread, meat, roots, pickles, vinegar, salt, and cheese. Supper was the same as breakfast.*
>
> Richard J. Hooker, A *History of*
> *Food and Drink in America,* 1981

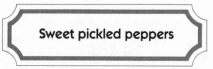

Sweet pickled peppers

MAKES ABOUT 5 CUPS

I was tempted to rename this Rainbow Relish, now that red and green peppers have been joined by yellow, orange, and even a dark chocolate color. The flavor is the same, no matter what colors you select, and a mixture makes just as appetizing a pickle as all red ones. The bitterness that some people object to in raw bell peppers is missing altogether. These are good with meat, poultry, and fish, in salads or sandwiches. You may want to avoid using green bell peppers, only because their color fades to an unappetizing olive drab in cooking. The recipe is easily halved.

> 3 pounds ripe bell peppers in
>   various colors
> 1 cup coarse (kosher) salt, or ¾ cup
>   pickling or uniodized table salt
> 2 tablespoons mixed pickling spice
> 1¾ cups cider vinegar
> 1¾ cups sugar

Stem and seed the peppers, and cut into ¼-inch rings. In a large bowl or nonreactive saucepan put peppers, add salt, and water to cover, and soak 6 to 8 hours.

Tie pickling spices loosely in a double thickness of dampened cheesecloth or place them in a metal tea ball. Combine vinegar, sugar, spice bag, and ¾ cup plus 2 tablespoons of water in a 4-quart saucepan. Bring to boil and boil 10 minutes.

Drain pepper rings, rinse in cold water, and drain again. Add to the syrup, bring to a boil again, and boil steadily 10 to 12 minutes, or until peppers are tender.

With a slotted spoon, fill hot, sterilized jars with peppers within ½ inch of the top. Boil liquid rapidly until syrupy, and pour over peppers, filling jars to within ¼ inch of the rim. Discard spice bag. Seal, cool, label, and store at least a month before serving.

James Beard's olive oil pickles

MAKES ABOUT 5 PINTS

I first saw Jim's recipe in his syndicated newspaper column, and it sounded so good I wanted to try it at once. As he wrote, the pickles are crisp and good and different served with cold meats and fish and even on cream cheese sandwiches. They're also great in cold meat salads. Jim's recipe called for cucumbers and onions by size, but I have measured them by weight, as that is how I buy them at markets and vegetable stands. The recipe is easy to halve.

> 3½ pounds unwaxed cucumbers (3 to
>   4 inches long)
> 1½ pounds onions, peeled
> ¾ cup coarse (kosher) salt, or about
>   ½ cup uniodized table salt or
>   pickling salt
> 1 teaspoon powdered alum (optional)
> 1 quart wine vinegar
> ½ to ¾ cup olive oil
> 1⅓ cups packed light brown sugar
> 2 tablespoons celery seed
> 3 tablespoons mustard seed

Slice the cucumbers and peeled onions a scant ¼ inch thick on a mandoline or in a food processor with medium slicing disc.

Mix prepared cucumbers and onions, salt, and alum, if desired, in a 4-quart bowl (not aluminum) and let stand about 8 to 12 hours, or overnight, in a cool place.

The next day, drain and rinse the vegetables and the bowl. Return the vegetables to the bowl, and add the vinegar. It should cover them. Add more if necessary to do so. Let stand 1 to 4 hours, preferably the latter.

Drain vinegar into a 4-quart saucepan. Add remaining ingredients, and bring to a boil, stirring. Pour boiling hot syrup over the cucumber-onion mixture, pack at once in hot, sterilized pint jars, and seal. Label and store at least a week before using.

Don't be alarmed if you have as much as 2 cups of liquid remaining after packing the pickles. The hot syrup draws a lot of water out of the vegetables. The resulting liquid is not flavorful enough to save.

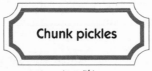

MAKES 4 TO 5½ PINTS

This is a very old recipe. It came from a ninety-one-year-old resident of Connecticut, who got it from her mother. The daughter made the pickles with cucumbers and grapes grown in her own yard. Hers are the best sweet pickles I've ever tasted—lightly sweetened, lightly spiced, and crisp. Unlike most pickles, they taste best at room temperature. Chilling overwhelms their delicate flavor.

> **About 4 pounds unwaxed cucumbers**
> **¼ cup coarse (kosher) salt, or**
>   **3 tablespoons uniodized table salt**
>   **or pickling salt**
> **¼ teaspoon powdered alum (optional)**
> **1½ cups sugar**
> **1½ cups cider vinegar**
> **1½ cups water**
> **1 teaspoon mixed pickling spice**
> **2 grape leaves for each jar (optional)**
> **3 or 4 green grapes (Thompson**
>   **seedless or unripe grapes of other**
>   **varieties) for each jar**
> **1 small sprig fresh dill per jar**

Scrub cucumbers in cold water with a vegetable brush before cutting them into ¾- to 1-inch chunks. Cut out any bruised spots that could spoil the whole lot. Place cucumber chunks in a 4-quart mixing bowl (not aluminum), add salt, and

Treating hard water

If the area in which you live has hard water, it will have to be specially treated to prevent its natural mineral content from darkening pickles and interfering with the pickling process. To do this, simply boil the water that you are going to use for brine. Let it cool, then strain through 4 thicknesses of clean, dry cheesecloth and add white or cider vinegar in the ratio of 1 tablespoon per quart of water.

Chunk pickles (continued)

cover with water. Weight them with a plate or plates to keep the chunks from floating. Let stand, covered or uncovered, 16 to 24 hours.

Drain brine into a wide 4-quart saucepan, add alum, if desired, heat to boiling, and pour back over cucumbers. Let them stand 12 hours more, again weighted to prevent floating.

When you're ready to pack cucumbers, make a syrup by combining sugar, vinegar, 1½ cups water, and spices in a 2-quart saucepan. Bring to a boil, and keep hot until ready to fill jars. Drain the chunks, and discard the brine. Starting with a grape leaf in the bottom of each jar, adding 3 or 4 grapes at random, and ending with a sprig of dill on top, pack the chunks snugly in hot, sterilized wide-mouth jars. As each is packed, set it back in the sterilizer containing several inches of hot water. When all the jars are filled, add hot water to sterilizer if necessary to bring level almost to tops of jars. Cover and heat until cucumber chunks are hot to the touch, but don't allow the water to boil. It might splash over into the open jars.

When chunks are hot, remove one jar at a time from sterilizer, pour off any water that has accumulated (this shouldn't be necessary if you've kept an eye on the kettle to avoid overheating), and fill almost to overflowing with boiling syrup. Top with a grape leaf, clean rim and threads of jar, and seal. Repeat until all are filled. Label and store at least 2 months before using. (The yield varies, depending on the diameter of the cucumbers.)

Poke melia — a Russian pickle

This Receipt was given to
Benjamin Franklin on his Departure
from Paris in 1785 by a Russian.

Put a layer of white oak leaves and black currant leaves, mixed, at the bottom of an oak cask, and then put in a layer of cucumbers; strew over them horse-radish, garlic, race ginger, whole pepper, allspice and cloves, then layers of leaves, cucumbers and spices successively till the cask is full. Fill the cask with salt and water strong enough to bear an egg, and half a gallon of good cider vinegar. They will be fit for use in about two weeks.

Recipe from the 24-page facsimile bicentennial edition (1976) of *The National Cookery Book,* compiled from original receipts for the Women's Centennial Committees of the International Exhibition of 1876 in Philadelphia. The original book contained over 300 pages.

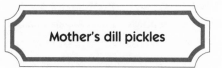

Mother's dill pickles

MAKES ABOUT 3 QUARTS

As a child, I liked these pickles better than lollipops. Truly. The sharp, salty, spicy tang of the pickles was particularly appealing with salami or liverwurst sandwiches on a typically hot, humid summer day in Arkansas. Now that I have given up salami and liverwurst sandwiches for lower-fat meats such as turkey-ham, dill pickles help fill the flavor gap that results when fat content is sharply reduced.

> 2 fresh grape leaves per quart
>   jar (optional)
> 2 large or 4 small sprigs fresh dill per
>   quart jar
> About 3½ pounds small unwaxed
>   cucumbers (1 inch or less in
>   diameter and about 3 inches long)
> 2 to 4 peeled cloves of garlic per
>   quart jar
> 1 teaspoon mixed pickling spice per
>   quart jar
> Pinch of alum per quart jar
> 7 cups water
> ⅓ cup coarse (kosher) salt, or ¼ cup
>   pickling salt or uniodized table salt
> ½ cup cider vinegar
> 1 (1-inch) dried chile pepper per quart
>   jar (optional)

Wash and dry grape leaves and dill. Scrub cucumbers under cool, running water and trim away any bad spots. Place garlic, spices, and alum nearby, and place the

Keeping pickles crisp

Many old recipes call for grape leaves in the top and bottom of jars containing pickles. The leaves were thought to help keep the pickles crisp. I still use grape leaves from habit, but for really crisp pickles, alum helps more—and pickling lime does the best of all.

Mother's dill pickles (continued)

water, salt, and vinegar in a 2½-quart saucepan to heat while you pack the pickles. Stir the brine occasionally until salt has dissolved.

In each hot, sterilized wide-mouth quart jar, pack 1 grape leaf, 1 or 2 sprigs of dill, a vertical layer of cucumbers, 1 or 2 garlic cloves, a second layer of cucumbers, another garlic clove or two, 1 or 2 dill sprigs, 1 teaspoon of pickling spice (and the hot chile pepper, if desired), a pinch of alum, and another grape leaf.

When all the jars are full, bring the brine to a boil, and pour it, boiling hot, over the cucumbers to fill jars almost to overflowing. Clean rims and threads and seal. This recipe makes about 3 quarts, but the brine is enough for about 4 quarts. Purposely. When the pickles have stopped fermenting, you'll need extra brine to make up for loss during fermenting. If the solids are exposed to air, the pickles will mold and spoil.

Important not to seal the lids

Sometimes the lids will seal, forming a vacuum as they should for most pickle products. They should not remain sealed for this type of pickle, which needs air during fermentation. So check the jars after they are cool, and release any lids that have sealed. Store the jars in a shallow pan or dish to catch overflowing brine. When the cucumbers are a uniform olive green color and the bubbling has stopped, remove lids and clean them and the jar threads and rims. Add more brine to cover solids completely, reseal, and label. Chill before serving.

Cracker barrel pickles

An unidentified contributor to Food 'N Folklore, *published in Bismarck, North Dakota, in 1973, recalled that her large family, 16 in all, "put up one cracker-barrel of cucumbers and when they had melons, they were also pickled with dill. My grandmother put ripe tomatoes in with the cucumbers. She used these, carrots and beets to make vegetable soup . . . Instead of fresh cabbage they used sauerkraut in vegetable soup. They also used to put whole cabbage leaves in with the sauerkraut and used them to make pigs-in-blankets."*

Food 'N Folklore was compiled by Beata Mertz and
published by the North Dakota Historical Society
of Germans from Russia in Bismarck, N.D.

Dora Thea Hettwer's schleiss gurken

MAKES ABOUT 5 PINTS

This German recipe for sliced pickles is the best of its kind I've ever tasted. They are milder and a little sweeter than my mustard pickles, and I like them particularly with cold cuts, potato salad, and beer.

2½ pounds small unwaxed cucumbers
1 pound small white onions, peeled
6 tablespoons coarse (kosher) salt, or
    4½ tablespoons uniodized table salt
    or pickling salt
2½ cups small cauliflower florets
    (about ½ pound)
¼ cup flour
1¾ cups sugar
2½ tablespoons ground mustard
4½ teaspoons each of celery seed and
    mustard seed
½ teaspoon curry powder
3 cups cider vinegar
½ pound red bell peppers

Slice the cucumbers and the peeled onions about ¼ inch thick in a food processor or on a mandoline. Dissolve the salt in 6 cups of boiling water, and let cool. Place the cucumbers and onions in separate bowls, and divide the cooled brine between the two. Weight with plates and jars of water to keep the vegetables from floating. Let stand 8 to 12 hours.

When you are ready to finish the pickles, cover the cauliflower with boiling water, and boil rapidly about 3 minutes. Drain at once, and cover with cold water to stop the cooking. Drain again.

Rinse and drain the cucumbers and onions, and place them with the cauliflower in a 4- or 5-quart saucepan.

Mix the flour, sugar, and spices in a 2-quart saucepan, breaking up lumps before stirring in the vinegar slowly. Stem, seed, and dice bell peppers, add to saucepan, and bring quickly to boil, stirring constantly. Continue to stir and boil mixture 5 minutes, until the sauce thickens slightly. Remove from heat and keep warm while heating the pickle mixture.

Dora Thea Hettwer's schleiss gurken (continued)

Cover the pickle mixture with boiling water and return to boiling point, stirring often. Drain the vegetables well in a colander, return them to the pan, and add sauce. Stir often as you bring the mixture to a boil over high heat. When it boils, adjust heat to keep pickles hot without cooking them, and quickly pack them in hot, sterilized jars, covering with sauce to within ¼ inch of top. Seal, cool, label, and store at least a month before using.

What's for lunch?
A peanut butter and dill pickle sandwich

Private investigator Kinsey Milhone packs her lunch before going out on a job:

"I unplugged the coffeepot, poured the balance of the coffee into a thermos, and then made myself a peanut butter and dill pickle sandwich, which I put in a brown paper bag like a school kid."

Sue Grafton, *"D" Is for Deadbeat,* 1987

Salt-free pickles

Traditional recipes for the next two pickles require a lot of salt, both for safe preservation and flavor. The Salt-Free Sour Pickle recipe from *Craig Claiborne's Gourmet Diet* (1980) increases the amount of vinegar substantially and requires refrigerator storage to make up for the omission of salt. The results are sharper than traditional sour pickles, but very good indeed. The Salt-Free Dill Pickle recipe (opposite) is based on the same principles. If your refrigerator space cannot accommodate three quarts of pickles at a time, it is easy enough to make one. Some of the spice measurements are not exactly divisible by three, and a little more or less of them won't make a noticeable difference in the end results.

Salt-free sour pickles

MAKES ABOUT 3 QUARTS

3 pounds small Kirby cucumbers
6 large sprigs fresh tarragon
6 large sprigs fresh thyme
12 small onions, peeled
8 peeled garlic cloves

1 teaspoon coriander seeds
2 teaspoons black peppercorns
1 quart white vinegar
3 cups water
1 tablespoon sugar
12 whole cloves
1 teaspoon whole allspice

Sterilize three 1-quart glass pickle jars. Make layers of cucumbers, tarragon, thyme sprigs, and onions. Add occasional cloves of garlic, the coriander seeds, and black peppercorns. Combine the vinegar, water, sugar, cloves, and allspice in a saucepan and bring to a boil. Pour the boiling liquid over the cucumbers. Seal tightly and let stand until cool. Label and refrigerate for at least 1 week before using.

Salt-free dill pickles

MAKES ABOUT 3 QUARTS

3 to 3½ pounds small unwaxed
    cucumbers
6 to 9 stalks fresh dill, preferably with
    seed heads
1 quart cider vinegar
3 cups water
1 tablespoon sugar
9 peeled garlic cloves
½ pound white onions, 1 inch or less
    in diameter (optional)*
3 teaspoons mixed pickling spice

Scrub cucumbers with vegetable brush. Remove blossoms, if any, and trim stems even with ends of cucumbers. Rinse dill under running water and shake off excess water. Place vinegar, water, and sugar in a saucepan of at least 2½ quarts' capacity, and bring to boil. While brine is heating, pack jars with layers of dill, garlic, cucumbers, and onions, beginning and ending with dill and garlic. Add 1 teaspoon of mixed pickling spice to each jar. Pour boiling hot brine into jars, filling within ½ inch of top, and seal. When jars are completely cool, wash and dry, label, and refrigerate at least a week before serving. They keep for a month or more.

*If fresh pearl onions are not available, use frozen small boiling onions.

The old tin dinner pail broadcast its contents

In the days when farm children carried lunch to school in a tin dinner pail, you could guess the contents by the smells that were released when the lid was pried off. In Home Grown, *Della T. Lutes (1937) recalls that "the odor of sour pickles predominated, injudiciously mixed with the aroma of chocolate cake or fried cakes."*

Chinese pickled garlic

MAKES ABOUT 1 PINT

I first tasted pickled garlic in a restaurant in Beijing, China, that specialized in food of the north. A bowlful accompanied Mongolian hot pot, a lamb dish cooked in a firepot on the table. Our American tour leader ate them as if they were peanuts. Later, in Shanghai's Number 1 department store I was able to buy a jar of them, and the recipe following is my adaptation. You may find them a bit sharp for eating out of hand, but they add a piquant flavor to salads (slice thin or chop fine in a food processor) and to stir-fry dishes.

Pickled garlic from both China and Thailand can sometimes be found in markets in American Chinatowns. The heads are much smaller than American garlic and are pickled whole.

> ¾ to 1 pound fresh garlic (small heads preferred)
> 1 cup white rice vinegar or rice wine vinegar of at least 4.2 percent acidity
> 1 teaspoon salt
> 2 tablespoons sugar

Separate garlic into cloves; scald, and peel them. Place vinegar, salt, and sugar in a 2-quart saucepan, stir to dissolve salt and sugar, and bring quickly to a boil. Add peeled garlic cloves, and let mixture return to a boil, stirring so it heats evenly. Pack at once into a hot, sterilized 1-pint or half-liter jar, and cover almost to overflowing with the brine. Cover, cool, label, and refrigerate at least a month before using. They keep for months in the refrigerator.

Garlicks, *tho' used by the French, are better adapted to the uses of medicine than cookery.*

Amelia Simmons, *American Cookery*, 1796

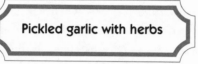

Pickled garlic with herbs

MAKES ABOUT 1 QUART

True garlic lovers may snack on these, but I prefer to chop them for use in salad dressings, or use them to enliven sauces for meat, poultry, fish, or seafood. The recipe is based on one obtained by the California-based Fresh Garlic Association from a resident of Gilroy, California, who does not recall where she got it. Gilroy, just south of San Francisco, holds an annual garlic festival, which has spawned such recipes as garlic chip cookies, garlic pudding, chocolate-dipped garlic cloves, and garlic jelly. Although these pickles can be made any time of year, there is less waste if you make them in summer, soon after the annual harvest.

1 pound fresh garlic
1 cup white vinegar
1 cup white table wine or dry vermouth
2 fresh chopped chiles, or 1 teaspoon
    dried crushed red pepper
1 sprig fresh thyme, or ½ teaspoon
    dried thyme leaves
1 sprig fresh rosemary, or ½ teaspoon
    dried rosemary
1 bay leaf
½ teaspoon peppercorns
2 tablespoons sugar
1 teaspoon salt

Break garlic heads apart, place the garlic cloves in a 2-quart saucepan, cover with boiling water, stir once, drain immediately, and cover with cold tap water to stop them from cooking. Drain again, and slip off skins; cut away any bruises or spoilage (more apt to occur in storage garlic than in the fresh crop).

Return peeled garlic to the saucepan, add the remaining

Pickled garlic with herbs (continued)

ingredients, bring to a boil, and boil 5 minutes; cover, and let stand 24 hours. Bring to a boil, and again boil for 5 minutes. Transfer to hot, sterilized jar(s), cover, and cool to room temperature before refrigerating for up to 3 months. Allow a couple of weeks for flavors to meld before using.

Handle pickling lime with care

Protect your hands with rubber gloves when you use slaked lime solutions. Prolonged contact with the mixture may irritate or burn wet skin. If it should come in contact with your eyes, immediately flush thoroughly with water, and call a physician.

Bernice Bixler's lime pickles

MAKES ABOUT $5^1/2$ PINTS

The lime that makes these pickles incredibly crisp is not fruit, but calcium hydroxide, usually labeled pickling lime, slaked lime, or hydrated lime. Generations of Southerners and Midwesterners have used a solution of this fine white powder and water to make pickles so crisp they crackle when you bite into them.

At this writing, two brands of pickling lime are sold in supermarkets and other shops that carry canning supplies. One of the two is also sold by direct mail from the manufacturer (see Source List, page 250). Because the formula differs from the pharmaceutical product (labeled calcium hydroxide U.S.P.), the amount to be used in solution differs. Follow the manufacturer's directions for making lime water, using 1 cup of the powdered lime per gallon of water.

My brother Mark, who is a chemical engineer, tells me not to worry about the use of pickling lime as a food additive. Because it cannot dissolve completely in water, you will never get more than a few hundred parts per million in the cold water solution. A second soaking of the cucumbers in fresh water removes any powder deposited on their surface.

You can make Mrs. Bixler's pickles and my Green Tomato Pickles (page 150) without lime water. The flavor will be the same — sweet and sour, slightly spicy. But the texture will be far less crisp and, I think, not as delicious.

3½ pounds small unwaxed cucumbers
1 cup pickling lime, dissolved as
    manufacturer directs in 1 gallon
    cool water
5 cups cider vinegar
2¾ cups sugar
2 teaspoons coarse (kosher) salt, or
    1½ teaspoons uniodized table salt
    or pickling salt
½ teaspoon each of whole cloves and
    celery seed
1 teaspoon mixed pickling spice

Using a mandoline or a food processor, slice the cucumbers as thinly as possible.

Place prepared cucumbers in the lime water solution in a pan or bowl of at least 8-quart capacity (not aluminum), and let stand about 24 hours. The next day, use a skimmer or a slotted spoon to remove the cucumber slices to a 4-quart bowl (not aluminum). Rinse them well in cool water, and drain well, repeating the process a second time. Cover with cool tap water and let stand about 3 hours.

While cucumbers are soaking, place vinegar, sugar, salt, and spices in a 2-quart saucepan, bring to boil, and stir until sugar dissolves. Remove from heat and let cool.

Drain the cucumber slices well, return them to bowl, cover with syrup, and let stand 12 hours or overnight.

The next day, place cucumbers and syrup in a wide 6- or 8-quart saucepan, bring to boil, stirring occasionally, and boil 35 minutes, or until slices look clear.

Use a slotted spoon to divide cucumber slices among hot, sterilized jars within ½ inch of top. Bring syrup to boil, fill jars almost to overflowing, seal, and label. Let stand at least a week before using, but a month is even better.

Throw it out

Don't bother saving pickling brine or syrup that was left over after heating solids in them. These liquids will be too diluted by the juice that seeped out of the cucumbers or other solids to make a good product.

Green tomato pickles

MAKES ABOUT 4 PINTS

Like Bernice Bixler's Lime Pickles, these are kept especially crisp by presoaking in a solution of water and pickling lime. Pickles made without the lime water soak are just as flavorful but less crisp. The recipe is easily halved.

If as much as ½ cup of the syrup is left over, cook a few carrot sticks in it in a covered saucepan until they are tender but still crisp. Chill and serve as a snack.

> ½ cup pickling lime
> 2 quarts water
> 3 pounds hard green plum tomatoes,
>   sliced
> ½ pound small white onions, peeled
>   and sliced
> 1½ cups sugar
> 3 cups cider vinegar
> 1 teaspoon each of peppercorns and
>   whole allspice
> ¼ teaspoon whole cloves
> 2½ inches broken stick cinnamon
> ¼ teaspoon each of mustard seed,
>   celery seed, and grated crystallized
>   ginger per pint of pickles

Stir pickling lime into water in a large bowl, taking care not to splash it on yourself. Add sliced tomatoes and onions, and let stand about 24 hours. Stir occasionally.

The next day, drain and rinse the vegetables, drain again, and soak them in cold water to cover for 2 to 3 hours.

Drain the vegetables in a colander while you prepare the syrup. Mix the sugar and vinegar in a wide 4-quart saucepan. Tie the peppercorns, allspice, cloves, and cinnamon in a dampened cheesecloth square 3 or 4 layers thick or place them in a metal tea ball. Add the spice bag to the pan, bring quickly to a boil, and boil rapidly 5 minutes. Add the vegetables all at once, and cook about 15 minutes, stirring occasionally, and timing from the point at which the syrup returns to a boil. Spoon, boiling hot, into hot, sterilized jars. Add mustard and celery seeds and crystallized ginger, and make sure the solids are covered by about ½ inch of syrup. They'll expand as they cool. Seal, cool, label, and store 4 to 6 weeks before using.

Quick dill slices

MAKES ABOUT 4 CUPS

I make these whenever I have a windfall from gardening friends and no time or not enough cucumbers to put up winter pickles or relish. They keep almost indefinitely in the refrigerator, and while they can be eaten at once, they're milder when they're a few weeks old. They go beautifully with fish or cold meat loaf.

The measurements are only approximations. And you can add some thinly sliced mild onions if you like. If you pack the pickles in an attractive, tightly stoppered apothecary jar, you can serve straight from it at the table.

> **About 1½ pounds unwaxed**
> **cucumbers**
> **1 tablespoon salt**
> **Several sprigs fresh dill, or about**
> **2 teaspoons dried dill weed**
> **White wine vinegar or rice wine vine-**
> **gar or cider vinegar (about 2 cups)**

Slice cucumbers thin in a food processor. Layer cucumber slices with salt in a colander, and cover with a plate weighted with a heavy can or jar. Let stand about 1 hour. Then rinse to remove excess salt, drain well, and layer with the fresh or dried dill in a jar or dish you can cover tightly. Cover with vinegar and refrigerate.

Pickling salts

Plain and iodized table salt are safe for use in pickling, but the noncaking ingredients added to both types may cloud pickle brine. Canning or pickling salt will not. Reduced-sodium salt may be used in recipes in which it is present for seasoning only. Fermented pickles—such as dill or sour pickles—require full-sodium salt for its preservative effect.

Free lunch in a gold rush boom town

Barrooms did a lively business during the Gold Rush of the 1860s and 1870s in Nevada and northern California. They sold the drinks but served a "free lunch" to go with the booze. "These generous repasts, for such they were, were designed to appease an appetite, not make one," authors Helen Evans Brown, Philip S. Brown, Katherine Best, and Katherine Hillyer wrote in The Virginia City Cook Book *(1953). "That they also raised a thirst was nicely calculated. Hungry men go home to eat, well-fed ones remain to drink away a dryness. A favorite at the free lunch, besides ham, sundry sausages, cheeses, and salads, were pickled eggs and pickled pigs feet. Good they were, too, and still available [in the 1950s] in local bistros — though not for free."*

Mother's pickled beets

MAKES ABOUT 1½ PINTS

This sharp pickle is good with either fish or cold meats and poultry. It will keep for weeks in the refrigerator if you can hide it from raiders. When all the beets and onions have been eaten, recycle the brine by filling the jar with hard-cooked eggs. Return the jar to the refrigerator until the egg whites have turned a uniformly deep pink. They can be eaten after two days but are better after a week. Sliced or quartered, the eggs make a beautiful garnish for salads and platters of cold food.

If this pickle is too sharp for your taste, dissolve ¼ cup of sugar in a little of the vinegar over medium heat and add it to the jar when you pour the cold vinegar on. Or substitute ¼ cup water for the same amount of vinegar.

About 1 pound beets
2 small onions, peeled
1 teaspoon salt
About 1 cup cider vinegar or red
    wine vinegar

Leave roots and at least 1 inch of stem on the beets to help keep their color. Scrub them well before cooking. I like to pressure cook them to retain maximum flavor, but it's almost impossible to suggest cooking time because beets vary so widely in size. Follow the manufacturer's directions for pressure cooking, or test beets with a fork if you steam or boil them in a saucepan.

Rinse the cooked beets in cool, running water only until they're cool enough to handle. Break off the roots and stems, and rub off the skin.

In a food processor slice the beets and the onions about ¼ inch thick, and pack while warm into a hot, scalded 1½-pint wide-mouth jar, alternating beet slices with raw onion rings.

Add the salt, and cover with vinegar. Seal. Refrigerate as soon as the jar has cooled, and keep refrigerated at least a week—but two weeks are better. The beets are ready when the onion rings have turned a uniform deep pink.

A lighter hand with the spices

"Cloves are the strongest of the spices put in pickles and should be used less freely than mace or cinnamon," Janet McKenzie Hill wrote in the 1927 edition of Canning, Preserving and Jelly Making. *She suggested a tablespoonful of cinnamon, eight or ten cloves, and one inch of gingerroot as a good proportion for a quart of pickles. Mace, which is the lacy reddish-brown covering of nutmeg kernels, was widely used in nineteenth-century preserving, but seems to have fallen out of favor today. Too bad, for it adds a very pleasant flavor to pickles and relishes as well as to fruit.*

Nika Hazelton's sweet-sour plum relish *(saure pflumli)*

MAKES ABOUT 4 PINTS

Most pickled plums are too sharp for my taste, so I was delighted to find this recipe in Nika's *The Swiss Cookbook*. It is, as she wrote, an old-fashioned relish for any kind of roast or boiled meat and fowl, and for cold cuts. I have expanded her directions slightly but otherwise made no changes.

For a spicier relish, I sometimes substitute ginger-flavored currant wine for the dry red wine. Recipe is easily halved. If you do halve the recipe, use 1 cup plus 3 tablespoons of sugar, and 7 cloves, and divide remaining ingredients evenly.

Nika Hazelton's sweet-sour plum relish (continued)

2¹/₃ cups sugar
1¹/₂ cups dry red wine
1¹/₂ cups red wine vinegar
15 whole cloves
4 inches stick cinnamon, broken
3 pounds firm, ripe, purple Italian
    (prune) plums

Place sugar, wine, and vinegar in a 2-quart saucepan. Tie spices loosely in two thicknesses of dampened cheesecloth or place in a metal tea ball. Add spice bag to syrup, bring to boil, and simmer, covered, 5 minutes. Cool.

While syrup cools, wash and dry plums, prick them three times each with a small skewer, and place them in a 3-quart bowl. Cover with cooled syrup, and let stand about 8 hours, or overnight. The syrup will not cover the fruit completely at first, but do not add more.

The next day, drain syrup, bring to boil, and let cool again before pouring it back over fruit. Let stand another 8 hours. Then place plums and syrup in a wide 4-quart saucepan and cook over lowest possible heat until the skins begin to tear in one or two places and plums are hot. If the syrup boils or the plums cook too long, the skins will shrivel and the fruit will shrink.

Use a slotted spoon to divide plums among hot, sterilized wide-mouth jars, and drape a clean towel over them to protect the fruit while you quickly boil down the syrup to the consistency of heavy cream. Set syrup aside until it is warm, then cover the plums with it, seal, label, and refrigerate. Allow 2 to 3 weeks for the relish to mellow.

Mock mangoes

Mangoes were a popular nineteenth-century pickle in the United States — not the aromatic tropical fruit we savor today, but stuffed fruits and vegetables in a sweet-and-sour sauce somewhat similar in flavor to authentic Indian mango pickles, William Woys Weaver writes in A Quaker Woman's Cookbook *(1982). "They became popular in England during the eighteenth century, mostly as a less expensive substitute for the real imported article ... The pickle was popularized in this country through English cookbooks ... Green bell peppers were generally used for 'mangoes' in Pennsylvania and western Maryland, and muskmelons in Tidewater Maryland. Other cooks used tomatoes, peaches, or cucumbers."*

Pickled peaches

MAKES ABOUT 1 QUART

Ah, yes. I remember them well. Clingstone peaches, studded with cloves and packed into quart jars, with sticks of cinnamon tucked in among them. We ate them with meat or poultry. I liked them best with roast duck. Nowadays I follow the example of a well-known New York City cooking teacher, who provided a recipe in her book, *Cooking with Lydie Marshall* (1982), for pickled peach vinegar made with canned peaches. Another version of quick pickled peaches appears in the 1963 edition of *Vineyard Fare,* compiled by The Vineyard Haven Branch of the Martha's Vineyard (Massachusetts) Hospital Auxiliary. The recipe donor, Edna J. Andrews, used the same ingredients, plus the syrup from the can. Yes, you can substitute frozen unsweetened sliced peaches for those canned in heavy syrup, but the flavor and texture will suffer. The heavy syrup helps keep the peaches firm.

> 1 teaspoon each of whole cloves and
>   whole allspice
> 1 (20-ounce) can cling peach halves in
>   heavy syrup
> 1/2 cup sugar
> 1/2 cup cider vinegar
> 1 (4-inch) stick cinnamon

Tie the cloves and allspice berries in a cheesecloth bag, and drain the peaches, reserving syrup for other uses. Mix the sugar, vinegar, and spices in a 2-quart saucepan, bring to a boil, and boil 5 minutes, until sugar has dissolved. Add drained peach halves and return mixture to a boil. Pack in a hot, sterilized quart jar or refrigerator container with a tight-fitting lid. Cool to room temperature, cover, and refrigerate. Let stand a week or two, tasting a piece of peach from time to time until the pickle is as spicy as you wish. With tongs, remove and discard the bag of spices and the cinnamon stick.

As a young girl growing up in Brooklyn, my idea of heaven was dinner at Manhasset's Patricia Murphy's. I pictured myself seated in that sumptuous dining room, nibbling at the proffered relish tray while I perused the menu and sipped my Pink Lady. It was not the meal that I coveted, but only that lazy susan, brought unbidden, with its exotic pickled watermelon rind and chow chow.

Willa Gelber in the Good Living
section of the New York *Daily News*,
Valentine's Day, 1990

Pickled watermelon rind

This old-fashioned pickle is increasingly hard to get in stores, so you may find it worthwhile to make it at home. Although the process can take three days or more to complete, the actual labor involved is minimal. When I was a child, pickled watermelon rind turned up regularly on our supper table as a relish to add flavor to simply cooked meats and poultry. There was a time when this and a small assortment of other sweet-and-sour relishes were as routinely served as bread at dinner or suppertime in many Southern and Midwestern homes and restaurants.

If you halve the recipe, measure the spice oils with a medicine dropper. They are very strong, and it is easy to overseason if you use a partially filled 1/8 teaspoon measure instead.

This is a flexible recipe, easy to adjust at any point in terms of flavoring and proportion of syrup to solids.

Watermelons today have thinner rinds than those of a generation or more ago, so the old recipes that call for 1-inch cubes just don't work. You're lucky to get 1/2-inch cubes. And they're easier to pack than large cubes because you can get more into a jar.

Buy 2 1/2 to 3 times the weight in melon that you want in unpeeled rind. Cut or scoop out the red meat and save it for other purposes. Use a large, very sharp knife to cut the rind into strips about 3 inches wide and then into 1/2-inch strips. I find a knife with a serrated edge is best for this step, and a grapefruit knife is best for removing any vestiges of pink meat and the hard, dark green outer skin. Cube the prepared strips, and measure them.

Cover every 4 cups of cubes with a brine of 3 tablespoons uniodized table salt or pickling salt dissolved in 1 1/2 quarts of water. If necessary, prepare more brine made in the proportion of 1 tablespoon salt to each 2 cups of water. Weight with a plate and a jar of water to keep rind from floating. Let it stand about 24 hours at room temperature in cool weather, or in the refrigerator if it's hot.

The next day, drain the rind, rinse it in cold water, and drain again. Tip the rind into a large saucepan, cover with boiling water, and cook 8 to 10 minutes, timing from the point at which water reboils. When the rind is easy to pierce with a toothpick, drain it well, measure, and cover with this boiling syrup for each 8 cups of uncooked rind:

> **4 cups sugar**
> **2 cups white vinegar or white**
>   **wine vinegar**
> **⅛ teaspoon oil of cloves, or**
>   **1 teaspoon whole cloves**
> **⅛ teaspoon oil of cinnamon, or**
>   **4 inches stick cinnamon, broken**

I find spice oils give a better flavor without discoloring the pickles. They are more expensive than whole spices and often hard to find, but they can be ordered by mail (for sources, see page 250). If you prefer whole spices tie them loosely in four layers of cheesecloth or place them in a metal tea ball.

Boil the sugar, vinegar, and spice oils or whole spices in a 1- or 1½-quart saucepan for 5 minutes, then pour syrup on cooked rind. If the syrup does not cover fully, boil a bit more, using 2 parts sugar to 1 part vinegar, but do not use more spices at this point.

Weight the rind to keep it submerged, and let stand, uncovered, about 24 hours.

The next day, taste a cube of rind. If it's too mild, drain the syrup into a 1- or 1½-quart saucepan and add more solid spices to the bag or tea ball or a few more drops of spice oils. Bring to boil again, and pour back over rind. Weight it as before, and let stand another 24 hours.

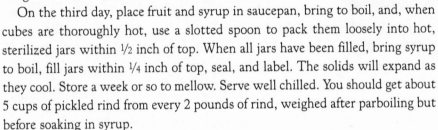

On the third day, place fruit and syrup in saucepan, bring to boil, and, when cubes are thoroughly hot, use a slotted spoon to pack them loosely into hot, sterilized jars within ½ inch of top. When all jars have been filled, bring syrup to boil, fill jars within ¼ inch of top, seal, and label. The solids will expand as they cool. Store a week or so to mellow. Serve well chilled. You should get about 5 cups of pickled rind from every 2 pounds of rind, weighed after parboiling but before soaking in syrup.

For a fancier pack, I like to cut the rind in circles, but there's a lot of waste to this method and the quantity per jar is less.

Even with the tremendous variety of ready-made jams, jellies, pickles and bottled condiments at their fingertips, American homemakers find preserving a rewarding experience . . . Every American cook has at least one canned specialty that her family enjoys.

Ann Seranne, editor, *America Cooks, The General Federation of Women's Clubs Cookbook,* 1967

Cantaloupe pickle

MAKES ABOUT 2 PINTS

Syrup left over after the pickles have been eaten can be recycled to make quick refrigerator pickles. Just heat it to boiling, and pour it over sliced peaches (fresh, frozen, or canned, drained). Let cool, cover, and refrigerate for a few days.

Both the original recipe and the quick version make a good accompaniment to pork and lamb roasts and ham, and a spicy salad dressing for fruit or poultry salads.

> ½ cup pickling lime dissolved as label
>   directs but in only 2 quarts water
> About 3 pounds firm, unripe
>   cantaloupe
> 3 cups sugar
> 2 to 4 tablespoons packed finely
>   grated crystallized ginger
> 1½ cups cider vinegar

Mix the pickling lime solution in a 4-quart bowl (not aluminum).

Halve the melon or melons from stem end to blossom end and discard seeds. Cut halves crosswise into 1-inch slices and pare them thin, removing just the netted skin and leaving a thin layer of green flesh, if possible. I find the curved, serrated blade of a grapefruit knife does the best job both for peeling and for trimming away soft flesh surrounding the seed cavity. Cut the strips into cubes and measure. You should have about 6 cups. Add cubes all at once to the pickling lime solution, and let stand about 4 hours.

Drain, rinse in a colander, and drain again. Rinse the bowl, return cantaloupe to it, cover with fresh water, and let stand 2 hours.

Drain cantaloupe thoroughly. Place in a wide 4-quart saucepan, add remaining ingredients, and stir to dissolve sugar. Weight with a plate to keep fruit submerged, and let stand 18 to 24 hours. Refrigerate only if room is very hot.

The next day, bring to a boil quickly and adjust heat to boil steadily about 1¼ hours, or until cubes look opaque and syrup has reduced. If too much liquid has boiled away after 45 minutes, add ¼ cup water.

Spoon cubes into hot, sterilized jars within ½ to ¾ inch of top. Bring syrup to full boil and fill jars almost to overflowing. Clean rims and threads and seal. Label and store at least a month.

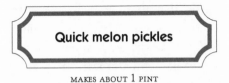

Quick melon pickles

MAKES ABOUT 1 PINT

These are not quite as crisp as pickles made from fresh melons.

> ¼ cup pickling lime dissolved in
>   1 quart cold water
> 1 (16-ounce) package frozen mixed
>   melon balls
> 1 cup sugar
> 1 to 2 tablespoons packed finely
>   grated crystallized ginger
> ½ cup cider vinegar

Make the pickling lime solution in a glass mixing bowl. Add the frozen melon balls, stir, and weight with a plate to keep them submerged. Let stand about 12 hours, or overnight.

Drain, rinse, cover with cold water, and let stand 4 hours; repeat this step two more times. Drain the melon balls and return to the washed, dried bowl. Mix the sugar, ginger, and vinegar in a small saucepan, bring to a boil, and boil about 5 minutes, until sugar has dissolved. Pour the syrup over the melon balls. The syrup will increase in volume as time passes. Let stand overnight, drain, boil the syrup again, and again pour it over the melon balls and weight as before. Let stand overnight. Drain, bring syrup to a boil, and boil until it is reduced to about 1 cup.

Place melon balls in a hot, sterilized pint jar, cover with the syrup, cool, seal, and refrigerate for a few days before serving.

Sweet quince pickle

MAKES ABOUT 2 PINTS

The success of this recipe depends largely on the quality and ripeness of the quinces. When they are a light golden yellow and aromatic at the time of purchase, the pickle is a joy to behold and to eat—rich, amber colored, spicy, and full of flavor. Green quinces will ripen at home, but they make a less flavorful pickle.

I've deliberately omitted the volume of prepared fruit from the recipe because much depends on the size of the quinces you can obtain and also how you slice them. If you have no kitchen or diet scale you can measure the prepared fruit accurately enough by standing on bathroom scales, first with a plastic bag of sliced quinces in hand and then without—just subtract the difference to estimate the weight of the fruit.

2½ to 2¾ pounds ripe quinces
3¼ cups sugar
¾ cup cider vinegar
¾ cup water
½ teaspoon each of whole allspice and
**   whole cloves**
About 8 inches stick cinnamon

Peel, core, and slice quinces ¼ inch thick. Steam the prepared quinces in a shallow layer in a covered steamer 15 to 20 minutes, or until a toothpick or small skewer pierces the slices easily. If your steamer is small, cook the fruit in two or more batches; accumulate cooked fruit in a bowl of at least 2½-quart capacity.

While the fruit cooks, assemble the syrup ingredients in a 1½-quart saucepan. Place the sugar, vinegar, and water in it. Place allspice and cloves in a metal tea ball, and add it and the cinnamon to the pan. When all the fruit is cooked, bring the syrup to a boil, stirring, and then boil rapidly without stirring for 5 minutes. Pour, boiling hot, over quince slices, and weight them with a saucer or small dish and a jar of water. As the mixture cools, the syrup will gradually cover the fruit. Let stand, uncovered, 12 hours or overnight.

The next day, turn the mixture into a wide 4-quart saucepan, bring quickly to boil, stirring occasionally, and boil rapidly 20 to 25 minutes, or until quinces look almost transparent, syrup is rosy, and gel tests done. Remove from heat, stir and skim, if necessary, about 5 minutes to cool slightly and prevent floating fruit. Discard spices and pack at once in hot, sterilized jars or glasses, seal, and label. It is just as good after one year as after one day.

Microwave directions   (see pages 33–35 for details) A high-powered microwave does a superior job of precooking this sweet pickle. It is best done in two batches. Place half the prepared quince slices in a 2-quart nonplastic micro-wavable measure or baking dish; add ½ cup water, and a vented cover, and microwave on high for 7 minutes, stir-

ring after the first 4 minutes. Let stand 2 minutes. Empty the cooked quince into a bowl, and repeat with remaining quince. While quince is cooking, prepare the syrup as previously described, add all the quince, and continue to follow previous directions for finishing the pickle.

Helene Robinson's pepper hash

MAKES ABOUT 3 PINTS

For hamburgers, this old-fashioned relish is hard to beat. I also like it mixed with cottage cheese. The recipe came to me from my Kansas cousin, Patricia Sears, who got it from a friend in Wichita in 1927. If you halve the recipe, pack it in 12-ounce jars. Or divide everything by three, and make just a pint.

> 1½ pounds green bell peppers (about
>   6 medium)
> 1½ pounds red bell peppers (about
>   6 medium)
> 1½ pounds yellow onions
> 1½ cups sugar
> 1 cup cider vinegar
> 2¼ teaspoons coarse (kosher) salt, or
>   1½ teaspoons pickling salt or
>   uniodized table salt

Stem and seed the bell peppers, and peel the onions. Pulse/chop the vegetables coarsely in a food processor, in batches if necessary. You should have about 9 cups total. Line a large colander with a double thickness of woven cheesecloth,

Helene Robinson's pepper hash (continued)

and drain the chopped peppers and onions. Transfer the drained vegetables to a heatproof nonreactive bowl, cover with boiling water, and let stand 5 minutes.

Drain again, and place vegetables in a wide 2½- or 3-quart saucepan. Stir in sugar, vinegar, and salt. Bring to boil quickly, reduce heat, and boil steadily 20 to 30 minutes, or until vegetables are cooked but not mushy. Ladle into hot, sterilized jars, seal, cool, label, and store at least a month before using.

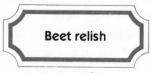

Beet relish

MAKES ABOUT 3½ PINTS

Mixed with mayonnaise, sour cream, or yogurt, this makes a beautiful pink and tangy salad dressing, or a sauce to serve with fish. I also like to substitute it for beet horseradish to accompany gefilte fish (poached fish balls). It is also good with or in meat loaf or similar loaves made with ground chicken or turkey. The recipe is easily halved.

> ½ pound green bell peppers
> ½ pound onions
> 1¼ pounds cabbage
> 1 pound cooked beets (for cooking
>   suggestions, page 153)
> 1 cup sugar
> 1 teaspoon uniodized table salt
> 1 cup cider vinegar
> 1 tablespoon dehydrated horseradish,
>   or 2 tablespoons prepared
>   horseradish, drained, or 1 to 2
>   tablespoons of fresh-grated
>   horseradish

Stem and seed the bell peppers; peel the onions, and core the cabbage, discarding any damaged outer leaves. Pulse/chop the bell peppers, onions, cabbage, and beets in a food processor to a coarse texture.

In a 4-quart saucepan, boil the vegetables, sugar, salt, and cider vinegar for about 30 minutes, stirring occasionally, until mixture is thick. Add horseradish during the last 5 minutes. Ladle into hot, sterilized jars within ¼ inch of rims. Release air bubbles with a plastic knife or bubble releaser; seal, cool, label, and store at least a month before serving.

"Turmeric" is Indian saffron, and is used very much in pickling as a coloring.

Emma Frances Voris, *The New Columbian White House Cookery,* 1893

India relish

MAKES ABOUT 4 PINTS

Chances are this relish got its name from English families who had spent some time in colonial India, and who had developed a taste for the spice blends now called curry powders.

The relish differs from most nineteenth-century recipes in that it contains olive oil and curry powder as well as other traditional curry spices. Because it is heated rather than cooked, it remains crisper than other relishes, and is especially good with cold meats of all sorts and in tuna salad.

1 pound green bell peppers
1/2 pound red bell peppers
1 pound cabbage
1 pound onions
About 1/2 pound unwaxed cucumbers
3 tablespoons uniodized table salt or
    pickling salt, or 1/4 cup coarse
    (kosher) salt
1 1/3 cups packed light brown sugar
4 teaspoons mustard seed
1 tablespoon celery seed
1/8 teaspoon ground turmeric
1/4 teaspoon ground black pepper
3 cups cider vinegar, divided
5 tablespoons ground mustard
1/2 teaspoon curry powder
1/4 cup olive oil

Stem and seed the bell peppers, core the cabbage, and peel the onions. Coarsely pulse/chop the bell peppers, cabbage, onions, and cucumbers in a food processor, in batches if necessary.

Mix prepared vegetables and salt in a bowl (not aluminum) of at least 2 1/2-quart capacity.

India relish (continued)

Mix sugar with mustard and celery seeds, turmeric, and black pepper in a wide 4-quart saucepan. Stir in 2½ cups of the vinegar, and bring to boil quickly. Boil steadily for 5 minutes, then pour mixture over the vegetables and let stand, uncovered, until cool.

Mix ground mustard and curry powder in a 1-cup measure, and stir in the

remaining ½ cup vinegar slowly until no lumps remain. Stir in olive oil, and set aside.

Drain syrup back into the saucepan, bring to boil quickly, and add the vegetables all at once. Heat and stir just until vegetables are thoroughly hot. Do not let the mixture boil. Stir in the spiced vinegar and oil mixture and pack at once in hot, sterilized jars and seal. Cool, label, and store at least 6 weeks before using.

Besides all the fruits, there were a host of vegetables that Grandmother pickled. One interesting old "receipt" book has a recipe for "Pickled Lily." This no doubt refers to piccalilli, having been spelled as granny thought the name sounded. Green tomato pickle in all its various forms was a favorite of the olden times.

Mary Emma Showalter, *Mennonite Country Cookbook*, 1950

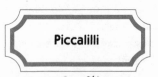

Piccalilli

MAKES ABOUT 3½ PINTS

When I was growing up in Arkansas, piccalilli was a relish we ate with cold cuts and hamburgers. Years later, a friend from New England told me it is traditional with baked beans in her part of the country. It is obviously a close relative of the preceding recipe for India Relish, and some old American recipes call it just that. Piccalilli probably reached our shores via English sea captains and army officers who would have developed a taste for this highly seasoned chopped vegetable pickle during service in colonial India. Some old American recipes even call it Indian pickle. The recipe may be halved.

1¼ pounds green tomatoes
¾ pound cabbage

¼ pound bell peppers, preferably half
   red and half green
1 hot chile (5 to 6 inches long)
½ pound onions
1 tablespoon each of mustard seed
   and celery seed
1 tablespoon coarse (kosher) salt, or
   2 teaspoons uniodized table salt or
   pickling salt
2 cups cider vinegar
1¼ cups sugar

Core the tomatoes and the cabbage; stem and seed the bell peppers and the chile, and peel the onions. Pulse/chop all the vegetables to a coarse texture in a food processor, in batches if necessary.

Combine chopped vegetables and all remaining ingredients in a wide 4-quart saucepan. Bring to boil quickly, stirring occasionally. Boil slowly about 30 minutes, or until mixture thickens slightly. Ladle, boiling hot, into hot, sterilized jars, seal, cool, label, and store at least a month before serving.

Chow-chow—Oriental in origin, an American tradition

Chow-chow. The name sounds Chinese, but the spices used suggest Indian origins. In The Mystic Seaport Cookbook, Lillian Langseth-Christensen (1970) says this spicy vegetable relish was brought from India and China by New England whaling ships. Eleanor Early, in her New England Cookbook (1954), gives the credit to New England sailors aboard clipper ships in the China trade. They "became fond of an Oriental preserve made of mixed fruits, and christened it 'chow-chow'—and that, I suppose, is how 'chow' became slang for food. After the sailors came home they called all mixed foods chow-chow," she writes, adding that after a time the name came to mean a particular mixed relish.

Peppery pear relish

MAKES ABOUT 3½ PINTS

The Chinese, who invented chow-chow as a mustard-flavored mixed vegetable pickle, might be surprised at this Texas version. The main ingredient is fruit, and it is particularly good with ham, pork, hamburgers, and cold cuts. I came across it in Alma Lee Holman's Cookbook column in the Taylor (Texas) *Press*. The version she printed called for 25 pears and 12 hot peppers. I've reduced both the size of the recipe and the potency, leaving some leeway in the number of peppers to use. Recipe is easily halved.

> 2¼ to 2½ pounds pears
> 1 pound onions (3 medium)
> 3 to 6 bottled or pickled hot red
>   peppers
> 1½ teaspoons coarse (kosher) salt, or
>   1 teaspoon table salt or pickling salt
> ½ cup prepared yellow mustard
> ¾ cup cider vinegar
> ¾ cup sugar
> 1 teaspoon celery seed
> 1 teaspoon ground coriander

Peel and core the pears, and peel the onions. Coarsely pulse/chop the prepared pears, onions, and hot peppers in a food processor.

Mix all the ingredients in a wide 2½-quart saucepan, bring to boil over medium heat, stirring occasionally, and adjust heat to boil steadily about 45 minutes, or until thick. Stir occasionally. Ladle, boiling hot, into hot, sterilized jars, seal, cool, label, and store at least a month before serving.

> *Great-grandfather never allowed any of his brood to leave food on their plates at the table. Even the fat meat or "speck" had to be eaten. Great-grandma once more rallied to the need of filling her place as a "helpmeet," this time for her children. She made all kinds of sauces and relishes to pour over that fat meat, and thus helped it to slide down easily!*
>
> Mary Emma Showalter, *Mennonite Community Cookbook,* 1950

Chili corn relish

MAKES ABOUT 2¼ CUPS

In the 1980s Mexican food—or more specifically, Tex-Mex food—became the third most popular ethnic cuisine in America—after Italian and Chinese. About the same time raw chiles began to show up in supermarket produce departments

well beyond the borders of California, Arizona, and the Southwest, and cross-cultural cookery caught on. Corn relish, a staple in the Midwest and the South for generations, tastes even better, I think, with chopped fresh chiles. When fresh local corn and bell peppers are out of season, simply substitute frozen corn and bottled roasted red peppers or pimientos for for the fresh produce. Serve with burgers (beef, turkey, or chicken).

½ cup finely minced cilantro
  (coriander)
1 teaspoon ground cumin
1 or 2 small hot chiles, such as
  jalapeños
1 small red bell pepper
1 small yellow bell pepper
¼ cup finely minced onion
½ cup cider vinegar
¼ cup sugar
¾ teaspoon salt
2 cups (about 4 ears) corn kernels,
  fresh or frozen

Pulse/chop the cilantro in a food processor, and set it aside. In a small skillet, toast the cumin a few minutes, until slightly darkened and aromatic. Stem and seed the chiles and bell peppers, and peel the onion and cut it into chunks; pulse/chop them together in a food processor to a coarse texture, stopping to scrape down the sides of the bowl as

CORIANDER

necessary. Transfer the cumin and the contents of the workbowl to a small saucepan of at least 1½-quart capacity, add vinegar, sugar, salt, and corn, and simmer over moderate heat, stirring occasionally, just long enough to set the milk in the corn kernels, 4 minutes or so. Cool before stirring in the chopped coriander.

Chili corn relish (continued)

Microwave directions   Stir all the prepared ingredients except the cilantro together in a 2-quart microwavable casserole, cover, and microwave on high (see pages 33–35 for details), 4 to 5 minutes if the corn is fresh, 6 to 7 minutes if it is frozen; stir after the first 3 minutes when using frozen corn. Transfer to a refrigerator container and cool. Cover and refrigerate at least 24 hours before serving. Stir in coriander before serving.

NOTE

For a hotter relish, stem the chiles and chop them with seeds and veins intact.

> *Ah, we sigh, her apple dumplings! Her fried chicken! Her popovers and gingerbread and rice fritters! Oh, the cool, mysterious cellars from which she fetched up the pickles, the jellies, the mincemeat, the preserved fruit — all done by her own hands, and all ambrosia!*
>
> *. . . Like most myths, the tale possesses just a faint core of validity. That Grandmother often had talent, I admit. That she set as good a table as we do now, I stoutly deny. My contention is that any housewife today, provided she is not impoverished, illiterate, or unconquerably indifferent to the pleasures of the palate, can contrive better dishes than Grandmother ever imagined.*
>
> Phyllis McGinley, *Sixpence in Her Shoe,* 1964

Bess Dewing's sweet/hot pickle relish

MAKES ABOUT 7½ TO 8½ CUPS

The real difference between this and other piccalilli-type relishes is the spiciness that comes from fresh hot chile peppers. If they are not available, substitute crushed dried pepper, starting with about 1½ teaspoons. After cooking, stir in more if the relish is too mild for your taste. You might mix it with cottage cheese on a salad plate, or stir it into mayonnaise to serve with cold fish steaks or fillets. The recipe is easily halved.

¾ pound bell peppers, preferably half red and half green

2 hot chile peppers (each 5 to 6 inches
   long)
3/4 pound onions
2 1/2 pounds unwaxed cucumbers
3 tablespoons coarse (kosher) salt, or
   2 tablespoons uniodized table salt
   or pickling salt
3 cups cider vinegar
1 1/4 cups sugar
1 1/2 teaspoons mustard seed
3/4 teaspoon ground turmeric
1 tablespoon each of whole cloves and
   broken stick cinnamon
1 1/2 teaspoons whole allspice
3/4 teaspoon cracked nutmeg*

Stem and seed the bell peppers and the chiles, and peel the onions. Pulse/chop the bell peppers, chiles, onions, and cucumbers to a coarse texture in a food processor. You should have about 8 cups.

Transfer the vegetables to a 3-quart or larger bowl, stir in the salt, and weight with a plate to keep vegetables from floating as the brine forms. Let stand 12 hours, or overnight.

Then drain and rinse the vegetables, and drain well again. Transfer them to a 4-quart saucepan; add the vinegar, sugar, mustard seed, and turmeric. Place the cloves, cinnamon, allspice, and nutmeg in a metal tea ball or tie loosely in three or four thicknesses of dampened cheesecloth. Add the spice bag to the pan, and simmer, uncovered, 1 hour, stirring occasionally.

Discard the spice bag, and ladle relish, boiling hot, into hot, sterilized jars. Seal, cool, label, and store at least 1 month before serving.

---

*This is a good way of using end pieces of nutmeg from a grinder. Wrap one or two loosely in a corner of a clean dishtowel and whack them sharply with a hammer. Measure the amount you need; reserve any leftover chunks to flavor milk for custard or rice pudding.

CHUTNEYS, CONSERVES, COMPOTES, CONDIMENTS, CONFECTIONS, AND A CONCENTRATE

Chutneys may be preserved or made fresh daily

Chutneys may be preserves—that is, they may be bottled and kept indefinitely, or they may be made fresh daily, Madhur Jaffrey writes in An Invitation to Indian Cooking *(1973). Whichever route you choose, the flavor will be better if you buy whole spices and grind them yourself with a mortar and pestle or an electric spice mill. It is also cheaper. Whole spices retain their full flavor much longer than powdered or crushed ones. These Indian-style relishes have been popular in America since colonial times.*

 hy, you may wonder, is a recipe for tomato concentrate (page 195) in a chapter on chutneys, conserves, compotes, condiments, and confections? Because, like tomato concentrate, those chutneys, conserves, compotes, condiments, and confections may be used in a similar manner—as ingredients in other dishes such as sauces and desserts. Specific suggestions accompany some recipes, and I hope they will inspire you to develop others. Even candied fruit peel can be chopped and folded into dessert sauces, and the fruit pastes can be melted down with fruit juice or wine or spirits to make quick dessert sauces.

As relishes or side dishes, the recipes in this chapter have a long tradition, particularly in the South, the Southwest, the Midwest, and on farms throughout the country. True, compotes are more often served as desserts, but I share the view put forth in the 1947 edition of *The Original Picayune Creole Cook Book* which states unequivocally that "All Compotes may be served as desserts or *entremets* [side dishes]."

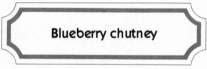

Blueberry chutney

MAKES ABOUT 2 PINTS

Try this chutney with roast turkey, duck, or goose. It is also good with meats and curries. Mixed with mayonnaise or plain yogurt, it makes a piquant dress-

Blueberry chutney (continued)

ing for salads made with meat, poultry, and/or fruits. This recipe is easily halved.

> 2 pint baskets ripe blueberries, or
> 2 (12-ounce) packages frozen
> unsweetened blueberries
> 1/4 pound onion (1 medium)
> 1 1/2 cups red wine vinegar
> 1/2 cup golden raisins
> 1/2 cup packed light brown sugar
> 2 teaspoons yellow mustard seed
> 1 tablespoon grated crystallized ginger
> 1/2 teaspoon ground cinnamon
> Pinch each of salt and ground nutmeg
> 1/2 teaspoon dried crushed red pepper

Wash, drain, stem, and sort fresh blueberries, and place in a 4-quart saucepan, or empty the frozen berries, unthawed, into the saucepan. Chop onion finely in a food processor, and add remaining ingredients. Combine onion mixture with blueberries.

Boil over medium heat, stirring occasionally, about 45 minutes, or until chutney is thick. Ladle into hot, sterilized jars, seal, cool, label, and store about a month before serving.

The difference between chutney and pickle (both of which may contain salt, vinegar, sugar, seasonings, spices, and vegetables or fruits) is the texture. Chutney . . . can be in the form of a sauce, dip, thick pulpy spread, or finely minced preserve, while a pickle contains clearly distinguishable pieces of vegetables or fruit. Pickle can be sweet or hot. Major Gray's Sweet Mango Chutney in India would be referred to as Sweet Mango Pickle because it contains large chunks of mango.

Julie Sahni, *Classic Indian Vegetarian and Grain Cooking,* 1985

Green tomato chutney

MAKES ABOUT 3 PINTS

Yet another flavorsome use for the glut of green tomatoes from home gardens in the fall. Vincent and Georgiana Banks, from whose English recipe mine is adapted, called for shallots in this peppery chutney, and I do think shallots make a superior relish. But if they are hard to find or too expensive, by all means substitute small pickling onions. Recipe may be halved.

> 2 pounds green tomatoes
> ½ pound tart green apples
> 6 dried chile peppers (each
>   1 inch long)
> ½ pound peeled shallots or
>   small onions*
> ½ cup packed golden raisins
> 1 cup packed dark brown sugar
> 1 tablespoon grated crystallized ginger
> 1½ teaspoons minced garlic (about 3
>   cloves)
> 1¼ cups cider vinegar

Cut the tomatoes into ½-inch cubes, to measure about 6 cups. Peel, core, and dice the apples, to measure about 2 cups. If you are using dried whole chiles, break them up and remove some seeds, if you want a milder chutney. For easy peeling of the shallots or onions, first cover them with boiling water, stir, drain, and immerse in cold water to prevent their cooking. Drain again, and peel.

Place all the ingredients in a wide 4-quart saucepan, bring to a boil quickly, and boil about 30 minutes, or until the chutney is as thick as jam. Stir occasionally to prevent sticking. Ladle into hot, sterilized jars, seal, cool, label, and store.

*If shallots are not available, substitute either raw pearl onions or frozen small boiling onions.

Naturally sweet nectarine chutney

MAKES ABOUT 3½ PINTS

The only refined sugar in this relish is the little used in manufacturing crystallized ginger, and even the excess there should be rinsed off before you grate the confection. The nectarines and orange juice provide all the sweetening you need. I serve the chutney with curry, of course, but I also like it with roast turkey instead of cranberry sauce, and with cold roast pork and ham. Recipe may be halved.

1½ pounds firm, ripe,
    unpeeled nectarines
½ pound red onions
3 tablespoons (about 2 ounces) grated
    crystallized ginger, or ½ teaspoon
    ground ginger
2 cups fresh orange juice
½ cup white wine vinegar or white
    vinegar
2½ cups packed (a 15-ounce box)
    golden raisins
2 to 2½ inches stick cinnamon
¼ teaspoon dried crushed red pepper
1 teaspoon salt
½ teaspoon ground mace
½ cup blanched almonds, halved

Wash, dry, and pit the nectarines and slice them thin on a mandoline or with a sharp knife. Peel and dice the onions, to measure about 2 cups. If you use crystallized ginger, rinse it before grating to remove excess sugar.

Place all the ingredients except almonds in a wide 4-quart saucepan. Bring to boil over medium heat; adjust heat to boil slowly about 40 minutes. Stir occasionally at first, more often during the last 15 minutes, to prevent sticking. Stir in almonds, and boil, stirring, 5 minutes more. Spoon at once into hot, sterilized jars, seal, cool, and label. Store at least a month before using.

This is totally different from traditional sweet, hot mango chutney. It is more sharp than sweet, steeped in thin syrup instead of thick, and spiced with green peppercorns instead of chiles. I first tasted a jar of it put out by a famous Paris food store; it was good but expensive. So I worked out my own version, which not only is much cheaper but, frankly, has a fresher, livelier flavor. Rather than serve the chutney only with curry dishes, I offer it with roast duck and goose, pork and ham, or use it to make sauce for ham steak.

Bottle any leftover syrup to use for thinning mayonnaise for fruit salads. Or, if the quantity remaining is large, pour it over dried fruit, bring to a boil, cover, and let stand until the fruit is plump, to make a quick refrigerator compote to go with meat or poultry.

> 1 ripe pineapple (4½ pounds)
> 2 tablespoons coarse (kosher) salt, or
>   4 teaspoons table salt or pickling salt
> 1 cup sugar
> 1 cup white vinegar or white
>   wine vinegar
> ½ cup dried currants
> 2 tablespoons whole mustard seed
> 2 tablespoons canned or bottled green
>   peppercorns, drained, rinsed,
>   drained again, and mashed slightly

Peel and core pineapple and cut into ¼-inch-thick wedges. Mix pineapple with salt, and place in a colander or large strainer set over a deep bowl or pot (not aluminum). Let stand 1 hour. Discard brine, rinse pineapple in cool water to remove excess salt, and drain well.

Place sugar and vinegar in a wide 2½-quart saucepan and bring to boil quickly, stirring to dissolve sugar. Add currants, mustard seed, and peppercorns to syrup. Then add pineapple with a slotted spoon, shaking it first so any salty liquid remaining will not go into the pan. Stir to mix, and continue cooking only until fruit is thoroughly hot. Taste a piece to be sure.

Adjust heat to keep mixture hot but not boiling, and quickly spoon it into hot, sterilized jars, making sure syrup covers the solids by about ¼ inch and

Pineapple chutney (continued)

leaving as much headspace in each jar. Strain out the spices (some tend to float, and others sink), and divide them among the jars. Cool, seal, label, and store at least 1 month.

Yogurt-based fresh chutneys

With the proliferation of Indian restaurants in New York and other cities with growing numbers of Indian immigrants, we Americans are coming to appreciate a far wider range of chutneys, including the soothing, yogurt-based raitas. "Indians use yogurt as Europeans use sour cream," Madhur Jaffrey *writes in* An Invitation to Indian Cooking. *(1973) "Apart from cooking with it and using it as a marinade, we use it for hundreds of relishes. Raitas are one of them. Here cooked or raw vegetables are added to well-mixed yogurt, seasonings are sprinkled in, and the dish is cooled before being served."*

Fresh green chutney with Chinese parsley and yogurt

SERVES 6

If you share my enthusiasm for the flavor of fresh coriander, do use this chutney in everyday meals. Madhur Jaffrey says it should be made the day it is eaten, and can be served in a small bowl as a relish, or over meat, cooked fish, or vegetables. I often serve it as an oil-free salad dressing.

1 packed cup chopped Chinese parsley (coriander greens or cilantro)
1 fresh hot green chile, sliced, or ¼ teaspoon ground cayenne pepper (optional)
1 (8 ounce) container plain yogurt
½ teaspoon salt (add more if you need it; the sourness of yogurt can vary with its age)
⅛ teaspoon freshly ground pepper

> ½ teaspoon roasted, ground
>   cumin seeds*
> 1 tablespoon lemon juice

*To roast cumin, place desired amount of whole seeds in a heavy skillet (iron is best) over medium heat. Stir 2 to 3 minutes, or until seeds turn a darker brown. Remove from heat, then grind.

Put the parsley and chile in the container of an electric blender with 3 tablespoons of water and blend until you have a smooth paste (you may need to push the parsley down a couple of times).

In a nonmetallic bowl, combine the yogurt, salt, pepper, cumin, lemon juice, and paste from the blender. Cover and refrigerate until ready to use.

To serve: Bring the cooled bowl to the table. You could serve it with almost any Indian meal. People should take just a tablespoon at a time.

NOTE

That is the Indian tradition of service. At my table it is used as liberally as a sauce, especially with plain broiled chicken, turkey cutlets, or fish.

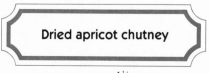

Dried apricot chutney

MAKES ABOUT 1½ CUPS

This is so easy to make in a microwave, and the results are so good, that I no longer use the range top cooking method.

> 1 small onion (about ¼ pound)
> 1 garlic clove
> 1 (6-ounce) package dried apricot
>   halves
> ½ cup water
> ½ cup red wine vinegar
> ½ cup packed light brown sugar
> 1 tablespoon finely grated preserved
>   stem ginger, drained, or
>   crystallized ginger
> 1 teaspoon coarsely crushed dried
>   coriander seeds

Peel the onion and slice it thin on a mandoline. Peel the garlic clove and slice it thin with a knife. Set an open 8-ounce canning jar upside down in the center of a 2-quart microwavable glass measure or casserole. Distribute apricots and onion around the jar, add the water and vinegar, cover (vent if using plastic wrap), and microwave (see pages 33~35 for details) on high for 5 minutes.

Dried apricot chutney (continued)

Remove from oven, remove jar with jar lifter, cover, and let stand until fruit is soft and plump, and much of the liquid has been absorbed. Stir in remaining ingredients, and microwave, uncovered, on high for 10 minutes. Ladle into a hot, sterilized 12-ounce jar, and use a bubble releaser around the sides. Seal, cool, label, and store a couple of weeks for flavors to mellow.

NOTE

If you double the recipe, make it in two batches.

Chiles — American natives

Chiles today range from Hungarian paprika (both mild and hot) to the fiery varieties of India and Southeast Asia, China, Thailand, and countless other nations whose hot climates are conducive to both the cultivation and consumption of peppery food. In fact, these pungent vegetables were unknown in Europe prior to the discovery of America. The Spanish carried seeds home with them in 1514, after finding the Aztecs and the Incas cultivating them in Mexico and Peru. Only after European explorers and traders carried them to the far corners of the earth did they become synonymous with the cooking of many nations around the world.

Mango or green pawpaw chutney

MAKES ABOUT TWO 1-PINT JARS

My favorite hot chutney recipe is this one, from Elisabeth Lambert Ortiz's *The Complete Book of Caribbean Cooking* (1973). As the name indicates, it can be made with either mangoes or papayas.

> 2 pounds hard, green (unripe) mangoes, or 2 pounds unripe pawpaw
> 8 ounces (about 1 cup) golden raisins, coarsely chopped
> 4 ounces cashew nuts, coarsely chopped
> 2 ounces fresh gingerroot, finely chopped

3 garlic cloves, minced
2 fresh hot red peppers, chopped
2 cups light brown sugar
2 cups malt vinegar
Salt to taste

Peel the mangoes or pawpaw and cut into 1-inch cubes. Put into a heavy saucepan with all the other ingredients, mix thoroughly, and simmer, stirring from time to time, until the mixture has thickened, about 30 minutes. Pour into hot, sterilized jars. Use with curries and cold meats.

NOTE

I use a food processor for the chopping, starting with the raisins and nuts; after emptying them into the saucepan, I chop the gingerroot, garlic, and hot peppers by dropping them down the feed tube while the motor is running. The cashews I use are roasted but unsalted.

Variation   I sometimes substitute mature but unripe fresh peaches, cut into chunks, or frozen unsweetened sliced peaches for the mangoes or papayas.

Conserves, like marmalades, may be made of large or small fruits. They differ from marmalades in that several fruits are often combined and nuts are usually added . . . when nuts are used, they are added after the cooking is finished because heat toughens the nut meats.

Ruth Berolzheimer, editor, *Victory Binding of the American Woman's Cook Book,* the World War II edition of a 1938 book

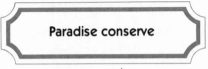

Paradise conserve

MAKES ABOUT 4 CUPS

Like Paradise Jelly (page 82), this beautiful red conserve is made with apples, quinces, and cranberries. It makes a fine partner for any kind of roast poultry and both feathered and furred game. My favorite apple varieties for this recipe are, in no particular order, Northern Spies, Winesaps, Cortlands, Baldwins, Jonathans, or McIntoshes. The quantities I have suggested in the ingredients list are not written in stone. Feel free to change them about if you wish—as long as the

Paradise conserve (continued)

total poundage remains unchanged, you should get the same yield. The larger the quinces, the greater the edible portion in relation to peel and core.

> ¾ to 1 pound ripe, aromatic quinces
> ¾ to 1 pound apples
> 6 ounces (1½ cups) fresh or frozen
>   cranberries
> 1½ cups ginger-flavored currant wine
> 1 cup sugar, or to taste

Peel and core the quinces and apples, and cut them into ½-inch pieces. Wash, sort, and drain the cranberries. Place prepared quinces and apples in a 3-quart saucepan. Add wine and sugar, stir to dissolve sugar, and boil rapidly 10 to 15 minutes, or until fruit is easily pierced with a food pick. Stir in cranberries, and continue to boil rapidly, stirring occasionally, until berries have burst and mixture begins to thicken. Ladle into hot, sterilized jars or freezer container(s); cool, cover, label, and refrigerate or freeze. This keeps for weeks in the refrigerator and up to a year in a zero-degree freezer.

Variations   Substitute either red table wine or cider or boiled cider (page 105, Note) or bottled apple juice for the ginger-flavored currant wine, and add 1 to 2 tablespoons of finely chopped crystallized ginger or drained preserved stem ginger or fresh gingerroot when you add the cranberries.

NOTE

One cup (¼ pound) of dried cranberries may be substituted for the fresh or frozen berries. If you do so, increase the liquid by ⅓ cup. Presoaking the dried cranberries is not necessary.

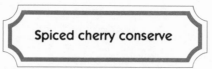

Spiced cherry conserve

MAKES ABOUT 2 TO 2½ CUPS

This relish is good with turkey, veal, and fresh pork. When fresh fruit is out of season, frozen unsweetened cherries make a fine substitute, although you may have to cook the relish longer; frozen fruit tends to release more juice than fresh fruit.

> 1⅓ pounds ripe dark sweet cherries,
>   or 1 (20-ounce) bag frozen
> pitted dark sweet cherries

1½ cups sugar

¼ teaspoon each of ground mace and
 ground cinnamon

Pinch of ground cloves

6 tablespoons red wine vinegar

2 tablespoons to ¼ cup blanched
 sliced or slivered almonds

Stem and pit the cherries if using fresh ones. In a 3-quart saucepan combine the sugar, spices, and vinegar. Bring quickly to a boil, stirring to dissolve the sugar. Add the cherries, and boil, stirring occasionally, about 40 minutes, or until a teaspoon of syrup thickens in 2 or 3 minutes on a prechilled saucer in the coolest part of the refrigerator or in the freezer. When the syrup is thick (it will thicken more as it cools), stir in nuts, if desired. Ladle the mixture into hot, sterilized jars, seal, cool, label, and store about a month for flavors to mellow.

Nectarine-honeydew conserve

MAKES 4 TO 5 CUPS

An unusual dessert sauce, this fruit and nut conserve is also delicious with popovers and other hot breads. You might also make it with peaches and cantaloupe instead of nectarines and honeydew.

1½ pounds semiripe nectarines

About half a 3¼-pound firm
 honeydew melon

Finely grated peel of 2 medium oranges

½ cup fresh orange juice or thawed
 frozen-orange-juice concentrate

3 cups sugar

½ cup blanched shredded almonds

Peel and pit the nectarines and cut into ½-inch cubes; you should have about 3½ cups. Peel and seed the honeydew melon, and cut into ½-inch cubes, to measure about 5 cups.

  Place nectarines, orange peel, and juice in a wide 2½-quart saucepan, and bring to boil quickly, stirring. Cover tightly, and reduce heat so mixture boils

Nectarine-honeydew conserve (continued)

slowly 10 to 15 minutes, or until fruit is tender when pierced with a toothpick. Stir often to prevent sticking.

Remove from heat and add honeydew, sugar, and nuts all at once. Return to heat, and bring to boil, stirring to dissolve sugar. Boil steadily about 10 minutes, until honeydew changes from bright to pale green.

Remove from heat and pour into a colander over a heatproof bowl. Let drain thoroughly, then return syrup to pan and boil rapidly about 10 minutes, or until thick and reduced by about half. Return fruit to the pan along with any syrup remaining in the bowl. Heat to boiling, spoon into hot, sterilized jars, and seal. Label and store at least a week before using.

Peach conserve

MAKES 3 TO 4 CUPS

The relatively low sugar content of this conserve seems to intensify the peach flavor, and the tartness makes it a delicious foil for salt meat—ham or corned beef—or rich dishes such as pork, duck, and goose.

> About 3½ to 4 pounds ripe peaches
> 3 tablespoons ascorbic acid mixture
>   (page 245), or 1 tablespoon each
>   of vinegar and salt dissolved in
>   2 quarts cold water
> 1 cup golden raisins
> 1¼ cups sugar
> ¾ cup fresh lemon juice
> 2 teaspoons whole mustard seed
> 4 inches stick cinnamon, broken
> ½ teaspoon whole cloves
> ½ cup coarsely broken walnuts
> 1 tablespoon brandy per half-pint jar

Peel and pit enough peaches to yield 2 quarts after slicing. Slice them directly into a 4-quart bowl containing the ascorbic acid mixture or acidulated water to prevent darkening. Do not use an aluminum bowl if the water contains salt. When all the fruit is prepared, drain it thoroughly (and rinse and drain again if you have used the vinegar-salt mixture). Place peaches in a wide 4-quart saucepan with the raisins, sugar, and lemon juice. Tie spices loosely in a double thickness of dampened cheesecloth or place in a metal tea ball, and add to the saucepan. Place over low heat until juices start to flow. Raise heat slightly, and cook, stirring occasionally, about 45 minutes, or until conserve thickens slightly.

Remove from heat, discard spices, stir in nuts, and ladle immediately into hot, sterilized jars within 1/2 inch of top. Add 1 tablespoon brandy to each jar, seal, and label. The just-cooked relish has a sharp, tart flavor that may tempt you to add more sugar. Don't. The conserve mellows as it ages, and additional sugar would make it more like a sweet preserve. Store at least 3 weeks, and chill before serving.

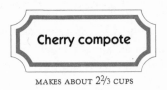

Cherry compote

MAKES ABOUT 2⅔ CUPS

The natural spiciness of fresh sour pie cherries is as irresistible for me as the fragrance of a fully ripe pineapple, and that spiciness is quite apparent in this lightly sweetened compote. I've given two sugar measurements, the smaller one to be used if you plan to serve the compote with the main course instead of dessert. As a dessert, I like the cherries and a spoonful or two of their sauce over vanilla ice cream or toasted pound cake. They are marvelous on cheesecake, too, if you drain the cherries well and thicken their sauce with cornstarch or arrowroot.

2 pounds ripe red sour cherries
⅔ to 1 cup sugar
2 teaspoons Vanilla Brandy (page 67)

Stem and pit the cherries. Mix cherries and sugar in a 1½-quart saucepan. Let stand at least 30 minutes, until syrup starts to form. Simmer 8 to 9 minutes. Stir occasionally. Remove from heat, and stir in vanilla brandy. Cool, cover, and refrigerate.

Dried fruit compote

MAKES ABOUT 3 CUPS

A preserve to make any time of year, this compote is tart enough to serve with roast meat and poultry. I like the apricot variety best, but the mixed dried fruit version is good, too, and less expensive to make.

Dried fruit compote (continued)

1 small navel orange
1 small lime
½ cup sugar
2 cups water
2 (2-inch) pieces of vanilla bean
2 (6-ounce) packages mixed dried fruit,
   or dried apricots
3 tablespoons cognac-orange liqueur
   (Grand Marnier) for the mixed fruit,
   or dark rum for the apricot version

Halve the orange and lime lengthwise. Place cut side down and slice the lime as thinly as possible, and the orange about ¼ inch thick. Discard end pieces. Stir sugar and water together in a 2-quart saucepan until sugar has dissolved. Tie vanilla bean in 2 thicknesses of dampened cheesecloth, or place in a small mesh tea ball. Add the vanilla bean to the syrup, bring quickly to a boil, lower heat, and simmer 5 minutes. Add the lime and orange slices, and the dried fruit, and boil steadily over medium heat about 30 minutes. Stir occasionally to prevent sticking. When the fruit is plump and tender, remove pan from heat, remove and reserve vanilla bean, and stir in the liqueur or rum.

Stir to mix the fruits well, and pack in hot, sterilized jars or several freezer containers. The syrup should cover the fruit, which will expand still more as it cools. Place a piece of vanilla bean on the surface of each filled jar. Seal, cool, label, and refrigerate or freeze. Wait at least a week before serving to allow flavor to mellow and peel to soften. Discard vanilla bean before serving.

Microwave directions   (see pages 33–35 for details) Prepare orange and lime as directed in the first paragraph, then stir all the ingredients except the liqueur or rum together in a 3-quart microwavable glass casserole with vented lid. Microwave, covered, on high for 5 minutes. Stir, cover, and microwave 5 minutes longer. Remove from oven, add liqueur or rum, and let stand, covered, until fruit is plump and soft, and has absorbed much of the syrup. If too much syrup remains, return the casserole, uncovered, to the microwave, and microwave, uncovered, on high at 3-minute intervals, until syrup has reduced and thickened. Pack as directed above.

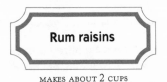

MAKES ABOUT 2 CUPS

This scarcely merits the name of recipe, as it requires only two ingredients and a few moments of preparation time. It has many uses: drained, the raisins may be added to fruit cakes, muffins or cupcakes, puddings (especially bread puddings), ice cream, and other frozen desserts. The raisins with their liquid can be used as is as an ice cream topping, or may be thickened with cornstarch or arrowroot, and cooked over medium heat until the sauce is clear to serve as a compote.

1 cup muscat raisins
Dark rum to cover well (about 1 cup)

Place both ingredients in a jar with a glass or plastic lid, cover tightly, and let stand at room temperature until the raisins are plump and soft. Add more rum if needed to cover the raisins fully. Keeps for months at room temperature.

Prunes (and apricots) in port

A jar of this fruit keeps almost indefinitely at room temperature. The prunes are delicious plain, with a little of their port syrup, but they're even better served with sweet or sour cream or plain yogurt and a dusting of sugar. Puréed, they add a whole new dimension to old-fashioned prune whip.

Quantities are hard to estimate. Some fruits absorb more liquid than others. I usually empty a 12-ounce package of bite-size pitted prunes into a clean, scalded apothecary jar with a plastic or ground glass stopper and cover the fruit by at

Prunes (and apricots) in port (continued)

least 1 inch with tawny port. After a couple of days, if the prunes expand above the surface of the port, I add more wine and reseal the jar. That's all. This usually takes 2 cups or more of port.

A mixture of prunes and apricots is also good, and for this I use:

> **1 box (11 ounces) pitted prunes**
> **1 package (6 or 8 ounces) dried apricots**
> **¼ cup sugar**
> **3 cups tawny port**

Put the ingredients in the order listed in a 1½-quart bowl, and cover tightly. When the fruit has plumped fully, and sugar has dissolved, pack into apothecary or canning jars and seal. The apricots will retain their chewiness and will darken after a few weeks almost as much as the prunes.

Brandied plums

MAKES ABOUT 3 PINTS

In our American tradition, compotes are fruits stewed or cooked in syrup and usually served as dessert. I also like them, and this plum compote in particular, as an accompaniment to game and other roast meats. For dessert, the plums are good alone or with ice cream or unfrosted cakes, especially angel food. You might also use any leftover syrup on canned or frozen fruit or fresh fruit such as ripe peaches or pears.

> **2 pounds ripe Italian (prune) plums**
> **2 cups sugar**
> **1 cup water**
> **Cognac or Vanilla Brandy (page 67)**

Prick each plum 3 or 4 times with a small skewer. Place prepared fruit in a deep 2-quart bowl. Bring sugar and water to boil in 1½-quart saucepan, stirring. Boil rapidly 5 minutes without stirring. Pour boiling syrup over plums, and stir to coat them. Weight with a saucer or plate and a jar of water. Let stand about 24 hours. The syrup will gradually cover the fruit.

The next day, sterilize 3 wide-mouth pint jars and lids. Place plums and syrup in a wide 2½-quart saucepan over very low heat, and stir occasionally to heat the fruit evenly. When skins begin to tear in one or two places and plums are heated through, use a slotted spoon to place drained plums in the jars — about a dozen per jar — to fill ¾ full. Boil the syrup rapidly about 10 minutes, to thicken slightly. Divide it among the jars, leaving approximately the top fourth of each one empty. Cover with a clean dishtowel and let cool. Top off with the brandy of your choice, filling jars within about ¼ inch of the top, and seal. Invert for 24 hours, then turn right side up and store at least 3 months before using. I always set the jars in shallow trays to catch overflowing syrup during fermentation. When fermentation stops, remove the lids. Clean lids, jar threads, and rims and outside of the jars, then reseal.

MAKES 3 TO 4 PINTS

Anjou pears are best for this recipe, largely because of their compactness and uniform shape. The long, slim necks on Boscs and Bartletts tend to overcook before the thicker base is done. Comice pears usually are too large to pack easily, and they are so good fresh it seems a shame to cook them. Seckel and forelle pears could be used, but I find their firm texture more suitable for pickling than preserving. Pear brandy—*eau de vie de poire*—lends a truly splendid flavor to this dessert but makes it so expensive you may prefer to reserve pear brandy for drinking and use regular grape brandy instead.

> **About 4¼ pounds, or a dozen 5- to**
> **6-ounce firm, ripe Anjou pears**
> **2 teaspoons ascorbic acid mixture**
> **(page 245) dissolved in 6 cups water**
> **2 cups sugar**
> **1½ cups water**
> **About 6 tablespoons *eau de vie de***
> ***poire* or other brandy per pint jar**

Peel, halve, and core the pears. Drop the pear halves, as you prepare them, into the ascorbic acid mixture and water in a bowl of at least 3-quart capacity. This helps prevent darkening. The easiest way to achieve uniform halves is to peel the whole fruit with a swivel-blade peeler, the kind you use for potatoes. Halve pears lengthwise, cut out stem and blossom ends with a small, sharp knife, and core with a small melon ball cutter.

Mix 1 cup of the sugar with the remaining 1½ cups of water in a wide 2½-quart saucepan. Bring quickly to boil, and boil rapidly 5 minutes. Add 6 pear halves, cut side up, and poach for about 5 minutes. Turn cut side down when they're half done. Continue poaching 5 to 10 minutes—until tender but still firm. Use a toothpick or small bamboo skewer for testing to avoid breaking

Brandied pears (continued)

the fruit. As each half is done, drain it well with a slotted spoon, and pack, cut side down, in hot, sterilized wide-mouth jars, filling them within about ½ inch of the tops. You'll probably get 6 to 8 halves into each jar—the pears shrink and settle.

When all the pears are poached, drain excess syrup from jars back into the saucepan, add the remaining cup of sugar, and boil rapidly about 10 minutes, until syrup thickens slightly. Divide it among the jars, leaving room for the brandy, and let cool. When the jars are cool, add brandy and a small piece of wadded waxed paper to keep the fruit submerged in the syrup. Seal, and stand the jars in a shallow container to catch syrup that overflows during fermentation. When fermentation, or bubbling, stops, remove the lids, clean the threads, rims, and lids, and reseal. Store 2 or 3 months to mellow before using.

Fermentation time varies, depending on temperature, but it usually lasts several weeks.

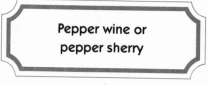

Pepper wine or pepper sherry

MAKES 1 PINT

These are piquant liquid seasonings from Barbados and Bermuda. Islanders use them as Americans do bottled red pepper sauces, shaking a few drops into soups, stews, and seafood. The method of preparation is the same on both islands, but Barbadians use white rum instead of wine, and the Bermudians use dry sherry. In the islands, fresh hot chile peppers would be called for, but the dried variety found in spice racks at supermarkets and specialty shops works equally well.

8 to 10 dried chiles (each about 1 inch long)
1 pint white or light rum or dry sherry

If you want to stabilize the peppers' strength, place the peppers in a clean, scalded 1½-pint mason jar, add the rum or sherry, cover, and set in a dark cupboard for a week to 10 days. Shake the bottle occasionally. Then put the mixture through a strainer lined with a double layer of dampened cheesecloth, and funnel the clear liquid into a clean, narrow-necked bottle with a screw lid. A vinegar bottle, the type that comes with both a removable plastic shaker cap and a regular cap, is ideal, or, for a gift, a pretty cruet with a shaker top.

Of course, you can simply put the chiles and the liquid in a jar and leave them, adding more rum or sherry as the liquid level drops, and discarding the chiles only when their strength diminishes.

WARNING

Never taste pepper wine or pepper sherry alone—it is fiercely hot. Shake a drop or two onto a forkful of fish or meat or into a tablespoon of soup instead. If it's too strong, just add more rum or sherry to reduce the potency.

Lemon- or orange-flavored mustard

MAKES ONE 8-OUNCE JAR

Both of these mustards are delicious with hot or cold fish or seafood, pork, ham, cold roast duck, even cold roast beef. Like all prepared mustards, the peppery flavor grows milder once the jars have been opened, so if you plan to use these condiments as gifts, make them as late as possible and be sure to tell the recipients to refrigerate them to conserve the mustards' strength as long as possible.

> 1 jar (8 ounces) Dijon-style
> prepared mustard
> 1/2 teaspoon lemon or orange extract
> 2 teaspoons freshly grated lemon or
> orange peel, the colored part only
> (from 1 lemon or 1/2 orange)

Use a rubber scraper to remove as much mustard as possible from its jar into a bowl of at least 1½-cup capacity. Stir in the extract and peel, blend well, and return mixture to original jar, or, for gift giving, a small apothecary jar with a tight stopper. Refrigerate.

The Scots had their own way of warming the stomach at the beginning of the day, by drinking a dram of whisky, and following it up with ale with a toast swimming in it. This pattern of breakfasting was undisturbed when tea-drinking began to grow popular in Scotland, early in the eighteenth

century. Some people continued with the customary dram, but replaced the ale with tea. Others replaced the dram as well, and ate warming sugar-preserved orange-peel or orange marmalade in its stead.

C. Anne Wilson, *The Book of Marmalade*, 1985

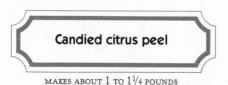

Candied citrus peel

MAKES ABOUT 1 TO 1¼ POUNDS

At some stage in history candied peels moved from breakfast to snack time and the dessert course. In 1742, Mrs. E. Smith called the confection orange chips in her *Compleat Housewife,* published in what is now Williamsburg, Virginia. Many people like the peel with coffee or tea. Others nibble them like candy.

3 cups citrus peel, cut into ¼-inch-wide
    strips*
2¼ cups sugar
¾ cup light corn syrup or mild honey
1½ cups water

*You will need 4 or 5 medium navel oranges, or 6 medium thick-skinned lemons, or 2 medium-to-large grapefruit or 2 medium or 1 large pummelo

Choose fruit with unblemished peel. While russet spots will not spoil the confection, they are unsightly. Score the peel from stem to blossom end into quarters for small fruit, sixths or eighths for large ones, and peel it with your fingers. Remove some of the white pith from pummelo peel, which is much thicker than grapefruit peel. Precook each variety separately in a large saucepan, using 6 cups of water for oranges, lemons, or grapefruit, or 8 cups of water for pummelos.

Place peel in a large pot, add water, bring to a boil quickly, and boil, uncovered, for 10 minutes. The peel will float at first, then sink as it absorbs more water. Drain in a colander, and repeat boiling one more time for orange, lemon, or grapefruit peel, or two or three times for pummelo, which is quite bitter. Each variety of peel should be tender and translucent before you begin the final cooking.

Drain well. Let cool until you can squeeze the peel with your hands to remove excess water. Trim the pointed ends, roll each piece of peel the short way across, and slice into ½-inch strips. Measure 3 cupfuls.

Place the sugar, corn syrup or honey, and water in a deep 4-quart saucepan. Bring to a boil, stirring to dissolve the sugar. Cover tightly for a few moments to melt down any sugar crystals clinging to the side of the pan. Add the peel, and boil steadily, stirring occasionally, until most of the syrup has been absorbed and that remaining is very thick. To prevent sticking and scorching, stir more often toward the end of the cooking time, which is hard to predict.

Empty the peel into a colander set over a deep bowl, and let stand 10 minutes for excess syrup to drain. Then, use tongs or two forks to transfer the peel to a single layer on a rack set over aluminum foil-lined baking sheets, and air-dry at room temperature for 3 hours if you want peel to be used in baking. If you want it candied for snacks, use two forks or kitchen tongs to remove it while still hot from the colander; place strips in a single layer on a piece of waxed paper heavily sprinkled with pure cane sugar.* Sift or shake more sugar on top, and toss with forks to coat all sides. Then, transfer the strips in a single layer on racks to dry. The time needed depends largely on the kind of oven you use. If it is electric, preheat to 140 or 150 degrees Fahrenheit, and turn off the heat but leave the light on. If the oven is gas, there is no need to preheat—the pilot light will suffice. If you use a convection oven, set the temperature for 140 to 150 degrees Fahrenheit, and leave the door ajar about 1 inch. Check every few hours, and remove when peel is slightly chewy, and no longer sticky. It keeps for months in a tightly covered container.

> *Like pastries, jams remind me vividly of my childhood, of visiting relatives, of sitting on low sofas surrounded with bright silk cushions, of being enveloped by perfumes, faint and delicate or rich and overpowering.*
>
> *. . . Candied orange peel, quince paste, coconut, fig, date, rose, tangerine, and strawberry jams would be brought in as soon as we arrived, together with pyramids of little pastries, and accompanied by the tinkling of tiny silver spoons, trembling on their stands like drops on a chandelier.*
>
> Claudia Roden, A Book of Middle Eastern Food, 1972

Quince paste

MAKES ABOUT 70 (1-INCH) SQUARES

The welcoming scene evoked by Claudia Roden in her 1972 cookbook is centuries old in the countries of the Middle East, where the art of cooking with sugar is said to have begun. Sweets such as the ones she describes are traditionally served to newly arrived visitors, along with glasses of ice-cold water or strong

*Do not use blended sugar for this recipe. It attracts moisture from the air, and will melt or become sticky.

Quince paste (continued)

black coffee. Quince paste, for example, was made by the Arabs and Persians for centuries before the former introduced it to Spain. From there the popularity of fruit pastes and preserves spread throughout Europe, to England, and to the Americas in colonial times. The popularity of quince in the early days of our nation is unquestioned. Twenty-two recipes using the fruit appear in *Martha Washington's Booke of Cookery,* transcribed and annotated by Karen Hess (1981), and more than a dozen in *The Sensible Cook,* a seventeenth-century Dutch cookbook that had a major impact on the foodways of the Dutch in Holland and in New Netherland. Copies of *De Verstandige Kock* were brought here by the Dutch colonists who settled in New York and the lower Hudson Valley. My recipe is based on one from the 1989 edition, translated and edited by a modern Dutch immigrant, Peter G. Rose. I have updated it still more, using a 700-watt microwave oven with a turntable to reduce the cooking time significantly.

> 1 to 1¼ pounds semiripe to ripe
> quinces (2 large or 3 medium)
> ½ cup California Gewürztraminer or
> other German-style wine such as
> Rhine or Mosel
> Sugar equal in volume to the cooked
> purée, plus additional sugar for
> coating

Peel and core the quinces, and cut them into ¾-inch chunks. Set an open 8-ounce canning jar upside down in the center of a 3-quart microwave-safe glass casserole, surround the jar with the prepared quince and wine, and cover with vented lid. Microwave (see pages 33~35 for details) on high 15 minutes, or until the quince pieces are soft and easily pierced with a cake tester or wooden food pick. In a food processor with a metal blade, reduce quince and its syrup to a smooth purée, scraping down sides of the workbowl as necessary. Measure purée; you should have about 2¼ cups. Stir in an equal volume of sugar, return the casserole, uncovered, to the microwave oven, and microwave on high for a total of 15 to 20 minutes, stopping to stir the paste down at 5-minute intervals. The stirring encourages even cooking, and prevents boil-overs and overcooking at the outer edges. When done the paste will be a medium amber color and so thick that it holds its shape when dropped on the surface of the boiling hot paste.

When the paste is done, stir to stop the boiling, and quickly pour it onto a 7 x 10-inch nonstick cookie sheet that has been rinsed or lightly sprayed with cold tap water. Tilt the cookie sheet over the sink so that only droplets remain. Quickly scrape the paste onto the cookie sheet and smooth the top with a rubber or metal spatula to as even a layer as possible. Work as fast as you can, because the paste sets quickly. Let cool on a rack. Then, with a flexible metal spatula, loosen the sides from the pan and turn the paste out (you may have to lift a short end with the spatula, then grab it with your fingers and gently pull it loose) onto a marble or plastic surface. Cut into 1-inch squares.

Using a sugar shaker, sprinkle another cookie sheet evenly with pure cane sugar (do not use blended sugar; it attracts moisture from the air and becomes sticky), and set the squares on the sheet, top sides down and close together. Sprinkle the squares lightly with more sugar, and dry in an oven that has been preheated to 200 degrees Fahrenheit, then turned off; if the oven is electric, leave the light on to create a little warmth. The pilot light in a gas oven serves the same purpose.

A convection oven is even faster. Set the temperature to 140 to 150 degrees Fahrenheit, and leave the door ajar about 1 inch. Drying times for all three methods are approximate, depending on humidity and the amount of moisture in the paste. After several hours, the pieces should be inverted again, and lightly sugared. When they are dry to the touch, layer them with waxed paper in an airtight storage container. They keep for weeks, if you can hide them from two-footed predators.

Cranberry-quince paste variation   Add to the ingredient list half a 12-ounce package of cranberries—washed, sorted to remove soft or spoiled berries, and well drained. Place them in the microwave cooking vessel with the prepared quince chunks, and substitute 1/2 cup of fresh lemon juice for the wine. Follow cooking directions in quince paste recipe.

Apple-quince paste variation   Substitute diced tart apple, peeled and cored, for half of the quince chunks, and sweet cider or bottled apple juice for the wine. A little ground cinnamon and allspice are nice; stir 1/8 teaspoon cinnamon and a pinch of allspice into the sugar before stirring it into the cooked fruit. Taste, and add more spice, if desired. Follow cooking directions for quince paste.

Anne Mendelson's tomato concentrate

MAKES 1 1/2 TO 4 CUPS

This one is for all you home gardeners with a glut of ripe tomatoes. It is so good that even nongardeners may want to stock up, using tomatoes from farmers' markets or farmstands. The recipe, Anne says, "should not be attempted with

Anne Mendelson's tomato concentrate (continued)

anything but red-ripe, dead-ripe, *super-ripe* fresh tomatoes at the peak of the season. In Italy they used to make this in summer by putting out trays of the purée in the sun every day and taking them in every night, until they were like semidried clay. My version stops short of that super-concentration."

> **5 pounds very ripe fresh tomatoes (do**
> **not use canned)**
> **½ to 1 teaspoon sugar (optional)**
> **Pinch of salt (optional)**

Core the tomatoes, and cut into quarters or eighths, slicing them straight into a large, wide saucepan or stockpot. Cover, and bring to a boil over medium heat, stirring occasionally to prevent scorching. Simmer, covered, until the tomatoes are completely soft and swimming in their own juice. The time will vary, depending on how crowded your pot is. Put through a food mill to remove seeds and skins—in this case a food processor will not do. Return the purée to the pot and simmer, uncovered, over low to moderate heat for 2 hours; stir occasionally, and adjust heat to keep the purée from scorching. After 2 hours it will be more or less volcanic; protect your hands and arms by wearing kitchen mitts when you stir it. You should now have 2 to 2½ quarts of purée. At this stage, you may fill freezer containers with the purée, cool it, cover tightly, and refrigerate or freeze, or continue with the reduction.

To prepare the concentrate, taste the purée. If it is too acid, add up to 1 teaspoon of sugar, with or without a little salt. But go easy. Sugar and/or salt will be concentrated in further cooking.

Pour the purée into several shallow ovenproof glass baking dishes or pie plates, to a depth of about 1 inch. Bake in a preheated 200- or 250-degree oven 4 to 5 hours, until purée is a dense, deep red paste. *Do not be tempted to try a higher temperature; it scorches easily on top.* Taste again after 4 hours, and decide whether you want to reduce it any more. When it is as dense as you have patience for, cool it completely before refrigerating or freezing in small batches in tightly covered containers. (Leave 1 inch headroom if freezing.) If it seems a little crusty on top at the end of baking, stir to smooth it out.

Use sparingly, like canned commercial tomato paste. The yield cited at the beginning of the recipe is correct. It varies widely, depending on the juiciness of the tomatoes and the final cooking time.

Variation   For each 5 pounds of tomatoes stir in at the first stage of cooking 1 large onion, or 3 medium onions, or 3 or 4 large shallots, and 2 large or 4 medium garlic cloves, all peeled and coarsely chopped. A little oregano doesn't hurt either, but it should be added during the last hour or two of cooking.

SAUCES—SWEET
AND SAVORY

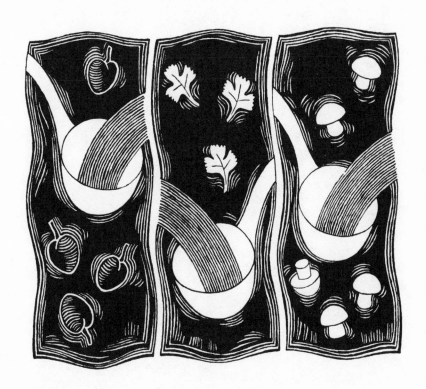

any American cookbooks published in the nineteenth century or earlier devote an entire chapter to sauces—principally ketchups. There were red and green tomato ketchups, of course, but also ketchups made from mushrooms, walnuts, and other unlikely (by today's standards) primary ingredients. Today, as we seek ways to eliminate rich and salty things from our diets, we are turning more and more to the light but intensely flavorful sauces introduced to the United States by families of Hispanic, Asian, and Mediterranean origin. In California, a major supermarket chain whose 325 stores include six that specialize in Hispanic foods recently began marketing a line of salsas and tortillas in some of its other stores. Both Mexican salsas and Italian pestos can now be found in supermarkets throughout the country. That is why this chapter starts with them, and goes on to Serbian *ajvar* and Mediterranean *aïoli*. When such sauces call for fat, it is not the solid animal and vegetable fats of the past, but lighter vegetable oils—olive, canola, and corn, for example.

Green chili is an old standby for Southwestern cooks. The table is not completely set if the green chili salsa is not handy to spoon over any and every dish.

Betty Shannon, *Green Chili*, 1981

Yellow tomato salsa

MAKES ABOUT 2 CUPS

The *salsas crudas* brought to the table in regions other than the Southwest are usually made with red tomatoes. Yellow tomatoes are slightly less acid than red ones, but the primary reason I chose them for this variation on traditional table salsa was the color. It is so appetizing.

1 small garlic clove, peeled
1 or 2 small hot chiles
2 tablespoons chopped onion, or
    to taste
1 pound yellow tomatoes
2 tablespoons fresh lime juice
About ¼ cup tightly packed corian-
    der leaves with tender stems (do not
    use central stalk)
Salt to taste

If using a food processor, mince garlic and chiles by dropping them through feed tube while motor is running. Add onion and process only to a coarse stage. Core tomatoes and chop coarsely by hand, then transfer to a small bowl, and stir in garlic, chile, and onion mixture and lime juice.

Wipe the food processor workbowl dry, and pulse/chop the coriander leaves, stopping to scrape down the sides as necessary. Stir the coriander into the tomato mixture, salt to taste, and let stand, covered, at least 30 minutes at room temperature before serving. Cover and refrigerate leftovers and use within a few days for best flavor.

Variation   Substitute red or green tomatoes for the yellow for a *salsa cruda* like those commonly used when New Mexico was still part of old Mexico. "They represent Mexican cookery that belongs to the United States," wrote Erna Fergusson in 1934 in the foreword to her *Mexican Cookbook*, published in Albuquerque.

CORIANDER

Salsa verde

MAKES ABOUT 1 TO 1¼ CUPS

You can make this popular Mexican sauce with ordinary green tomatoes, but the flavor is infinitely better with tomatillos, the small husk tomatoes used in Mexico and the American Southwest. They are often available in the fresh produce department of supermarkets and sometimes at farmers' markets and farmstands elsewhere in the country. I freeze this sauce to use in braising chicken and turkey parts in a skillet.

> 1 pound tomatillos, or green
>   (unripe) tomatoes
> 1 large garlic clove
> 1 small onion (about 4 ounces)
> About ¼ cup packed sprigs
>   fresh coriander
> 2 fresh jalapeños (1½ to 2 inches long)
> 1 tablespoon canola oil
> 1 (13¾-ounce) can chicken broth
>   (not condensed)
> Salt (optional)

Husk and wash the tomatillos. Pulse/chop tomatillos (or green tomatoes) in a food processor to a rough purée. Simmer chopped tomatillos or tomatoes in a 10-inch skillet (preferably nonstick), stirring occasionally, until their light, bright green color changes to pale olive green. Scrape into a large strainer, and let drain while you prepare the other vegetables and herbs. Discard juice.

Pulse/chop the garlic clove. Then, add to the processor the onion, coarsely chunked, the coriander sprigs, and the jalapeños, sliced crosswise into two or three pieces each, and process until finely chopped, stopping to scrape down the sides of the workbowl if necessary. Combine herb mixture with drained tomatoes.

Wipe out the skillet with a paper towel, add the oil, and heat until a spoonful of the sauce base sizzles when added to the skillet. Scrape remaining sauce into the skillet, and cook rapidly, stirring often, until dried out and mixture begins to stick. At this point, you may place the sauce base in freezer containers, cover tightly, cool, and freeze for up to 6 months.

To finish the sauce, skim fat from the canned broth, then add broth to the sauce base in a 10-inch skillet, and simmer over medium heat, stirring occasionally, until sauce thickens slightly. Taste, and add salt if desired.

Salsa fresca

MAKES ABOUT 1¼ CUPS

This nontraditional salsa was inspired by a recipe in a delightful 20-page cookbooklet, *El Plato Sabroso Recipes,* written and published by Doña Eloisa Delgado de Stewart of Santa Fe, New Mexico. It went through six editions between 1940 and 1953. The quantities in her ingredients list are vague by today's standards, so I have tried to be more specific, but this is really a sauce to be made to taste, and best, of course, with vine-ripened summer tomatoes. Despite its name—Spanish for Fresh Sauce—I think this salsa tastes best after 24 hours in the refrigerator, which allows the flavors to mellow. Do not add extra chile if you plan to serve it a day or so later; the spiciness increases markedly during storage.

> 1 small red chile, or canned drained
>   green chiles to taste
> 2 medium tomatoes (about
>   10 ounces total)
> 2 tablespoons chopped Spanish onion
>   or other mild onion
> ¼ cup orange juice, preferably fresh
> ⅛ teaspoon salt, or to taste

Hand chop the chiles, tomatoes, and onion—a food processor makes them too watery. Stir in remaining ingredients, taste, and adjust salt content. Serve at room temperature, but refrigerate leftovers in a tightly covered container. Doña Eloisa suggests serving the sauce with fried eggs or roast beef. I also like it with poultry and broiled fish, especially fattier fish such as salmon, mackerel, and shad.

Pesto is not just a pasta sauce made with basil

Most Americans think of pesto as the sauce for pasta that is made with fresh basil, garlic, pine nuts, and grated Parmesan or Romano cheese. In many Italian-American households, as in Italy, both the contents of the herb paste and its uses are far more varied. Parsley sometimes replaces part of the basil in the basic basil sauce. Other herbs may be used, or leafy greens — spinach, arugula, or watercress, alone or in combination with various herbs.

Pesto made with basil is added to cooked vegetables and stirred into soup — especially minestrone — at mealtime. In one of my favorite cookbooks, Italian Family Cooking, *Edward Giobbi, an Italian-American artist, uses traditional basil pesto as an ingredient for light sauces for steak, grouse, shrimp, sweetbreads, and green tortelloni. My friend Ruth Nesi makes a pesto-flavored vinaigrette salad dressing, and I make a lighter version with plain yogurt and pesto.*

Ruth Nesi's pesto and her salad dressing

MAKES ABOUT ¾ TO 1 CUP

Ruth began freezing pesto because the Manhattan apartment balcony garden her husband, Jim, plants each summer produces far more basil than their family can eat during the season.

> **2 to 4 peeled garlic cloves**
> **2 cups packed basil leaves**
> **½ cup olive oil**
> **½ cup pine nuts or shelled walnuts**
> **¼ cup (about 1 ounce) grated Romano
> cheese**

Drop the garlic cloves through the feed tube of a food processor with the motor running. Stop the processor, scrape down sides of workbowl, add the basil, and pulse/chop it coarsely. With the motor running, pour the olive oil through the feed tube. If you want to use the sauce immediately, add the nuts and cheese, and continue to process until you have a dark green paste with some texture remaining from the nuts.

To freeze for later use, omit the nuts and cheese, and pack the *pesto* into plastic ice cube trays. Once they are frozen, empty the cubes into a freezer-weight plastic bag, exhaust the air as much as possible, seal, label, and freeze for up to a year. Before serving the pesto stir in the nuts and cheese. One cube thinned with a tablespoon or two of water from cooking pasta dresses one serving of pasta.

Pesto salad dressing

MAKES ABOUT 1$\frac{1}{3}$ TO 1$\frac{1}{2}$ CUPS

1 teaspoon cold water
$\frac{1}{2}$ teaspoon Dijon-style mustard
$\frac{1}{2}$ cup wine vinegar or balsamic vinegar
$\frac{2}{3}$ to $\frac{3}{4}$ cup olive oil
Pesto to taste (page 203)

Mix the water, mustard, vinegar, and olive oil with a whisk in a small bowl or place in small, tightly covered jar, shake to blend, then add pesto, 1 tablespoonful at a time, tasting as you go. Refrigerate, but bring to room temperature before serving on salads or as a sauce with fish, chicken, or turkey fillets.

Variation   For a creamy version, stir dressing into nonfat or lowfat plain yogurt, using 1 part pesto dressing to 2 parts yogurt.

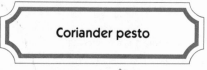

Coriander pesto

MAKES ABOUT $\frac{3}{4}$ CUP

Here is a strictly cross-cultural herb paste inspired by America's three most popular ethnic cuisines: the preparation technique is Italian and the flavors represent both oriental and Mexican cuisine. A few spoonfuls of coriander pesto are delicious in rice salad or steamed rice. It also makes a piquant salad dressing thinned down with plain nonfat or lowfat yogurt. If the musky herb is too strong for your taste, substitute fresh parsley leaves (preferably the flat-leaf Italian variety) for half the coriander in this recipe.

1 garlic clove, peeled
2 cups packed fresh coriander leaves
**   with their tender stems (discard**
**   central stems)**
$\frac{1}{4}$ cup dried hulled pumpkin seeds
$\frac{1}{3}$ cup mild salad oil
1 teaspoon oriental sesame oil

**½ teaspoon crushed dried red pepper,
or to taste
⅛ to ¼ teaspoon salt (optional)**

With the motor running, drop the garlic clove down the feed tube of a food processor and chop. Scrape down the sides of the workbowl, add the coriander leaves (and parsley leaves, if desired) and the pumpkin seeds and pulse/chop to a fine purée. Slowly pour the oils down the feed tube until a paste forms. Stir in the red pepper, taste, and add salt, if desired. Scrape the pesto into a freezer container or small jar, and cover tightly. Use within a few days or freeze for a few months.

Watercress: an all-purpose plant

Native wild watercress was growing in New England when the first settlers arrived. Most colonists followed the example of John Winthrop, the first governor of Massachusetts, who ordered seeds from London for his garden. The watercress we buy today in stores all across the country is believed to be a spontaneous hybrid of European cress and the wild American variety. Its uses range from a salad green and condiment to a soup ingredient. The colonists served it as a boiled vegetable with meat.

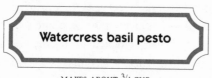

Watercress basil pesto

MAKES ABOUT ¾ CUP

Salt and pepper are optional for this pesto because the cheese is salty and watercress has its own peppery flavor. I use this paste on hot pasta and in cold pasta salads and potato salad.

**1 large garlic clove, peeled
¾ cup packed fresh basil leaves
2 cups packed fresh watercress leaves
   (a large bunch)
¼ cup toasted sunflower seeds,
   preferably unsalted
¼ cup olive oil
¼ cup grated Parmesan or Romano
   cheese
Salt and pepper (optional)**

Watercress basil pesto (continued)

With the motor running, drop the garlic clove through the feed tube of a food processor (fitted with the chopping blade) until the garlic is chopped fine. Stop the processor, add the basil and watercress leaves and the sunflower seeds, and pulse/chop the mixture to a fine texture, stopping to stir down the sides of the workbowl as necessary. With the motor running, pour the olive oil slowly through the feed tube until a paste forms. Stir in the cheese, and taste. Add salt and pepper, if desired. The pesto may be used at once, or refrigerated, tightly covered, for a week or so or frozen up to 6 months.

NOTE

Discard only the central stems of the watercress; the tender young stems on which the leaves grow contribute extra flavor and a somewhat crunchy texture.

Arugula variation   Substitute arugula leaves for the watercress and prepare as in recipe above.

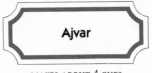

Ajvar

MAKES ABOUT 4 CUPS

This Serbian relish is traditionally served with meats in its nation of origin. But it is also wonderful as a dip for raw or blanched fresh vegetables; as a cooking or table sauce for fish, chicken or turkey, or a topping for baked potatoes. Mixed with plain yogurt, it also makes a good salad dressing. While it can be made any time of year, it freezes well—so I try to put up enough during the fall harvest season to last most of the year. Pronounced eye'-var, this recipe came to me from Jacqueline M. Newman, who got it from her friend Ivanka Karacic Jeftic, a well-known Yugoslav cookbook author. Ivanka's recipe makes a mild sauce, minus the garlic and red chiles that I use. Ivanka uses corn oil, while I prefer olive oil.

> 1½ pounds red, yellow, or orange
>   bell peppers
> 2 (2- to 3-inch) red jalapeño chiles, or
>   ½ to 1 teaspoon dried crushed red
>   pepper (optional)
> ¾ pound eggplant
> 1⅓ cups white vinegar, divided
> 4 cups water, divided

2 tablespoons coarse (kosher) salt,
   divided
2 to 6 garlic cloves, minced
About ⅔ cup olive, canola, or corn
   oil, divided
1½ teaspoons table salt
½ teaspoon paprika (if using red
   peppers)

Stem, devein, and seed the bell peppers and the chiles, and cut them into chunks. Peel the eggplant and cut it crosswise into 1-inch slices.

Put ⅔ cup of the vinegar, 2 cups of water, and 1 tablespoon of kosher salt in a saucepan of at least 2-quart capacity. Bring to boil, add  eggplant slices, return to boil, and boil 5 minutes, stirring a couple of times so the slices cook evenly. Drain in a colander while you boil the peppers and chiles 5 minutes in the same saucepan, using the remaining ⅔ cup of vinegar, 2 cups of water, and 1 tablespoon of kosher salt. Drain in a colander and reserve.

Meanwhile, sizzle the minced garlic in ¼ cup of the oil in a saucepan for 1 minute. Do not allow it to brown. Place the cooked, drained eggplant and pepper mixture in the workbowl of a food processor, in batches, if necessary, and purée. Stop to stir down the sides of the bowl as needed. Add the 1½ teaspoons of salt and the paprika, if using. With motor on, pour in as much of the remaining oil as the mixture will absorb. Return the sauce to the saucepan, and simmer over medium heat, stirring often, for about 15 minutes; mixture should thicken to dipping consistency. Fill hot, sterilized jars or several freezer containers, cover, cool, label, and refrigerate, or freeze.

How to roast bell peppers and chiles

To roast peppers, place them on their sides on a foil-lined broiler tray, and broil until skin blackens, turning with tongs as necessary. Let steam in a paper bag or covered bowl until skin pulls away easily. Hold under running water until they are cool enough to handle, then peel, and remove seeds and ribs.

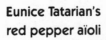

Eunice Tatarian's red pepper aïoli

MAKES ABOUT 2 CUPS

Aïoli is a garlic sauce sometimes called the butter of Provence because it is often used in that French Mediterranean province as the rest of the world uses butter. This beautiful pink sauce or salad dressing is a Californian version of the French original. The recipe is from a friend in Fresno. While it can be made with green bell peppers, the color is more appetizing when the sauce is made with red, yellow, or orange varieties. If you like spicy food, either use Mexi-Bell peppers or add a finely chopped jalapeño or other hot pepper to the sauce.

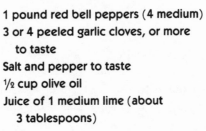

1 pound red bell peppers (4 medium)
3 or 4 peeled garlic cloves, or more
    to taste
Salt and pepper to taste
½ cup olive oil
Juice of 1 medium lime (about
    3 tablespoons)

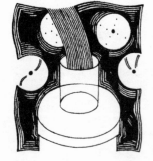

Roast and peel peppers (see box, page 207). Purée in a food processor with the other ingredients. If you plan to use the aïoli within a week, refrigerate it, tightly covered; or freeze at zero degrees Fahrenheit or lower to keep for up to a year. Serve on steamed new potatoes or with fish or seafood.

An ancestral sauce

Mushroom ketchup was widely used by our ancestors in America and England. Recipes for it appear in dozens of nineteenth-century American cookbooks and even earlier in English cookbooks. For many years the sauces were made with wild mushrooms, which would have provided more flavor than today's cultivated varieties. Although the name says ketchup, it is actually more like a Worcestershire sauce, a thin, spicy, dark-brown liquid to be sprinkled on steak and chops, or used as an ingredient in soups, stews, and sauces.

Mushroom ketchup

MAKES ABOUT 2 CUPS

This may seem like a lot of mushrooms for a little sauce, but you need not waste the chopped mushrooms that you strain out before bottling the ketchup. They may be used to make *duxelles,* a coarse purée of mushrooms and onions to use as a seasoning in sauces, soups, and stews. The dried oriental mushrooms called for really enhance the flavor. This recipe is adapted from Angus Cameron's recipe in *The L.L. Bean Game & Fish Cookbook,* by Mr. Cameron and Judith Jones (1983).

2 ounces dried oriental mushrooms
1 cup very hot water
1¼ pounds cultivated mushrooms
2 tablespoons salt
½ cup each of cider vinegar and
   tawny port
¼ teaspoon each of ground allspice,
   ground mace, ground nutmeg, and
   black pepper
Pinch of ground cloves
1 inch anchovy paste from a
   tube (optional)
2 dashes Angostura bitters

Place the dried mushrooms in a small bowl or a 1-quart canning jar, cover with the water, weight with a saucer or an empty jar to keep the mushrooms submerged, and let stand 30 minutes, until they are soft. Lift out the mushrooms with a slotted spoon, pour the soaking water through a paper coffee filter set in a strainer over a jar or deep bowl, and reserve. With scissors, cut the soaked mushrooms into pieces, discarding the stems, which are tough. Then, wash the cultivated mushrooms under cold running water and set them on a double layer of paper towels to drain. Transfer both kinds of mushrooms (halve or quarter the cultivated variety if they are large) to the workbowl of a food processor, in batches if necessary, and pulse/chop fine; do not liquefy. Transfer the mixture to a 1-quart refrigerator container,

Mushroom ketchup (continued)

stir in the salt, cover tightly, and refrigerate for 2 or 3 days, stirring occasionally. Then, drain the mushrooms in a fine-meshed strainer set over a deep bowl, pushing with a wooden spoon to extract as much liquid as possible. Place a handful of the chopped mushrooms at a time in a large white cotton handkerchief and twist it over the strainer to obtain still more liquid; set the solids aside to make *duxelles* (directions follow). When you have wrung out as much liquid as possible, pour it through a paper coffee filter (do not reuse the first one) set in a strainer over a 1½-quart saucepan; add the reserved filtered liquid from the oriental mushrooms, and all remaining ingredients, and boil, uncovered, about 30 minutes. Pour into hot, sterilized bottles, cover, and cool. Label and refrigerate for immediate use; freeze for long-term storage. Shake before using to mix in the sediment that settles during storage.

NOTE

Dried oriental mushrooms are sold in specialty shops, upscale supermarkets, and neighborhoods with many Asian customers; if you cannot easily obtain them, omit the dried mushrooms and water, and use 2 pounds of cultivated mushrooms instead.

How to make and use duxelles

Under cold running tap water rinse the finely chopped mushrooms left over from the preceding Mushroom Ketchup recipe to remove excess salt, then squeeze a handful at a time in a towel to remove as much liquid as possible. Discard the liquid. In a food processor, pulse/chop a peeled medium onion fine. Cook the mushrooms and onion together in a skillet with a little olive oil or mild cooking oil and butter over moderately high heat; stir often. When the mushroom pieces start to separate and brown lightly, add salt and pepper to taste. If desired, stir in a little Madeira or Marsala wine and continue cooking rapidly until liquid has evaporated entirely. Pack into small freezer containers, cover tightly, and cool. Refrigerate for a few days, or freeze for a few months. Use the *duxelles* by the tablespoonful or more to season soups, stews, poultry stuffing, and sauces.

"Duck" sauce, really plum sauce, is so named because it was served with duck during the early days of Chinese restaurants in America. It is made from plums, apricots, chilies, vinegar, and sugar—a sweet and pungent condiment that has since become a standard dip sauce, particularly popular with egg rolls or roast pork.

Irene Kuo, *The Key to Chinese Cooking*, 1977

Sweet-and-sour duck sauce

MAKES ABOUT 5½ CUPS

My version of the traditional Chinese sauce serves both as a dipping sauce and a glaze for pork and poultry. To make a glaze, thin the sauce with a little oil and vinegar, and baste the roast during the last 20 to 30 minutes of cooking. Because of its high sugar content, it burns easily.

3 pounds firm, ripe red plums
½ pound onions
1 cup rice wine vinegar or cider vinegar
1 teaspoon ground coriander
½ teaspoon each of dried crushed red
    pepper, ground allspice, and
    crushed garlic
2½ cups sugar

Pit plums and cut into ½-inch chunks. Peel onions, and pulse/chop finely in a food processor. Place all the ingredients except the sugar in a 4-quart saucepan, bring to boil over medium heat, stirring occasionally, and boil about 30 minutes.

Remove from heat, purée in a food mill, and return purée to the pan. Add sugar, and bring to a boil, stirring constantly. Boil about 30 to 45 minutes, or until a small amount holds its shape on a chilled saucer. Stir often to prevent sticking. Ladle into hot, sterilized jars, seal, cool, label, and store at least a week to mellow.

I'm mad about mustard—
Even on custard.

Ogden Nash,
Custard and Company, 1980

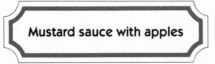

Mustard sauce with apples

MAKES ABOUT 2 CUPS

I'll pass on Ogden Nash's mustard custard, but I do like the mustard in this sauce, especially when it is served with pork, ham, duck, or goose. The recipe was inspired by one in a 1928 cookbook.

1 tablespoon Dijon-type mustard or
  grainy mustard
3 tablespoons olive oil
¼ teaspoon paprika
½ teaspoon salt
1 tablespoon sugar, or more to taste
Juice of 1 medium lemon (3 or
  4 ounce)
1½ teaspoons cider vinegar
3 or 4 apples (about 1 pound)

Place all the ingredients except the apples in the workbowl of a food processor with steel blade, and turn it on and off quickly to mix. Replace the chopping blade with a medium shredding disc, peel and core the apples, and shred them directly into the sauce. Transfer to a serving bowl or a refrigerator container with a tight lid; stir to make sure all the apple shreds are coated, then taste and adjust seasoning.

If you do not have a food processor, whisk the sauce ingredients together in a 1-quart or larger bowl, peel the apples and shred them on a grater, and stir them into the sauce. Apples are easier to shred by hand if you peel them whole, and use the stem and blossom ends as finger grips for holding the fruit against the grater.

Refrigerate the sauce in a tightly covered container if it is not to be served at once, but bring to room temperature before serving. It keeps at least 2 months in the refrigerator, but the flavor is best when used within 1 month.

Green tomato and horseradish sauce

MAKES ABOUT 6 CUPS

Sometimes old recipes can be misleading, as I learned the first time I made this sauce. It was overcooked and oversalted. And no wonder! The original recipe, in a book published almost a century ago in Canada, called for day-long cooking and a whole cup of salt! But I liked the combination of ingredients, so I worked out a version that cooks in an hour. It is particularly good with boiled fresh (or smoked) tongue and almost any kind of grilled fish.

1 pound green tomatoes
1/2 pound green bell peppers
1 pound onions
2 tablespoons plus 1 teaspoon coarse
  (kosher) salt, or 2 tablespoons
  uniodized salt or pickling salt
1 cup sugar
1/8 teaspoon ground cloves
1/2 teaspoon ground cinnamon
2 1/2 cups cider vinegar
2 (6-ounce) bottles prepared
  horseradish packed in vinegar, or
  about 1 cup grated fresh
  horseradish

Core the tomatoes, stem and seed the green peppers, and peel the onions. Cut the tomatoes and onions into chunks, and pulse/chop all three vegetables in a food processor to a coarse texture. Transfer the prepared vegetables to a 1 1/2-quart bowl (not aluminum), stir in the salt, and let stand 8 hours or longer. Drain, rinse, and drain again. Place the vegetable mixture in a wide 2 1/2- or 3-quart

saucepan, add the sugar, spices, and vinegar, and simmer about 1 hour, or until thick, stirring occasionally. Add the horseradish during the last 5 minutes of cooking. Ladle, boiling hot, into hot, sterilized jars, seal, cool, label, and store a week or two before serving. This recipe is easily halved.

There never was a more indefatigable preserver, pickler, curer, spicer, or canner than the Dutch housewife. Very little escapes her expert touch—and as a consequence she got in the habit centuries ago of loading every table with many "sweets and sours."

To such an extent that over the centuries it became a fixed tradition of Dutch hospitality for her to put on the table (especially for "company") precisely seven sweets and seven sours. The "company" would often count them! indeed would gaily demand them if missing.

J. George Frederick, *Pennsylvania Dutch Cookery*, 1935

Spicy chili sauce

MAKES ABOUT 3 PINTS

A good relish to make when you have a bumper crop of tomatoes or can get them on sale at a market or farmstand. If the original yield is too much for your family, the recipe is easily halved. Add the spices about an hour before the sauce is done—the flavor will be better. I often use a mixture of this sauce with mayonnaise for fish salads, or stir some into melted butter to serve with broiled fish or meat.

6½ pounds firm, ripe tomatoes
½ pound onions (3 medium)
¾ pound red or green bell peppers
2 cups cider vinegar
½ cup sugar
¼ teaspoon cayenne pepper
½ teaspoon each of ground mustard,
    ground mace, and ground cloves
1½ teaspoons ground cinnamon
2 teaspoons salt

Core tomatoes and cut into chunks. Peel onions and cut into chunks. Stem and seed the bell peppers and cut into chunks. Place prepared vegetables in the workbowl of a food processor, in batches if necessary, and pulse/chop to a rough purée. Transfer the mixture to a wide 4-quart saucepan, add vinegar and sugar, bring quickly to a boil, and simmer about 3½ hours, or until slightly thicker than ketchup. Stir in spices and salt after 2½ hours. Stir often, especially toward the end of the cooking time, to prevent sticking. Ladle into hot, sterilized jars, seal, cool, label, and store at least 2 weeks before using.

> So far as I know, every ketchup on the market has a sweetish, artificial, shallow flavor that revolts the descendants of Maine's seafaring families. [But] such was the passion [for grandmother's homemade ketchup] in my own family that we could never get enough of it. We were allowed to have it on beans, fish cakes and hash, since those dishes were acknowledged to be incomplete without them; but when we went so far as to demand it on bread, as we often did, we were peremptorily refused, and had to go down in the cellar and steal it — which we also often did. It had a savory, appetizing tang to it that seemed — and still seems — to me to be inimitable.
>
> Kenneth Roberts, *Trending Into Maine,* 1938

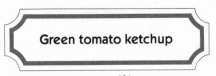

Green tomato ketchup

MAKES ABOUT 5½ CUPS

Maine's seafaring families undoubtedly developed a taste for ketchup when sea captains returning from voyages to Asia brought word of a spicy condiment the Chinese called koechiap or ketsiap, and the Malaysians called kechap or kechup. Imitations of these sauces (or condiments, if you prefer) began appearing in the seventeenth century — imitations made with cucumbers or walnuts or mushrooms, and later, tomatoes from the Americas. The oriental ketchups were based on fish brine with herbs and spices, and versions of this are still in use today throughout Southeast Asia. My version is based on an old American recipe devised by a Pennsylvanian to use up green tomatoes that had to be harvested before the first frost. It is both peppery and fruity. The tomato, apple, and onion combination makes it a good relish to serve with everything from hamburgers to pork and ham roasts. If the yield is too much for your household, the recipe is easily halved. It also freezes well.

Green tomato ketchup (continued)

> 1 pound onions
> 1 pound green tomatoes
> 1 pound tart green apples
> 1½ tablespoons coarse (kosher) salt,
>   or 1 tablespoon uniodized salt or
>   pickling salt
> 2 cups white vinegar
> ½ teaspoon each of hot red (cayenne)
>   pepper, ground cloves, and ground
>   cinnamon
> 1 teaspoon ground mace
> 2 teaspoons ground mustard
> ¼ cup sugar
> Green vegetable coloring (optional)

Peel the onions and tomatoes and slice thinly in a food processor. Peel and core the apples and slice thin in a food processor. Layer the onions, tomatoes, and apples in a 1½- or 2-quart bowl (not aluminum); sprinkle each layer with some of the salt. Let stand about 12 hours, or overnight.

The next day, drain well, and purée the mixture in a food processor. Place all the ingredients except the food coloring in a wide 4-quart saucepan. Bring quickly to a boil, stirring once or twice. Boil steadily about 30 minutes, or until mixture is almost as thick as bottled tomato ketchup. It will thicken more as it cools. Add the vegetable coloring, if desired. Ladle into hot, sterilized jars, seal, cool, label, and store at least 1 month before using.

Variation   Ripe tomatoes may be substituted for the green ones. If so, do not use the food coloring.

An appetite for gooseberries

Thomas Jefferson, our nation's third president, was so fond of gooseberries that 34 entries for the fruit appear in his garden book. Thomas Jefferson's Garden Book, *anno-tated by Edwin Morris Betts (1985), covers the years 1766 to 1824 and includes relevant extracts from his letters and other writings. In Jefferson's travels he often looked for new plants and seeds. While America's Minister to France, he wrote from Fontainebleau in 1785: "Their cherries and strawberries are fair, but I think lack flavor. Their plums I think are better; so also their gooseberries, and the pears infinitely beyond anything we possess."*

During his last year in the White House, Jefferson wrote to Bernard McMahon, a Philadelphia seedsman and florist, to thank him for a sample of gooseberries: "... they were certainly such as I had never seen before in any country, and will excite strenuous efforts in me to endeavor to raise such. for this purpose early in the next year I shall ask of you some cuttings of your bushes, and before that shall send a pretty copious list for a supply of the best kinds of garden seeds, and flowers. I shall be at home [Monticello, in Charlottesville, Virginia] early in March for my permanent residence, and shall very much devote my [time] to my garden."

In the Jefferson household gooseberries were made into French-style pies and pastries, and a favorite English dessert, gooseberry fool: stewed, strained berries mixed with rich egg custard and topped with whipped cream.

One hundred and sixty-one years later, Elizabeth David suggested a different use for the puckery fruit. "At one time, in France as well as in England, a green gooseberry purée seems to have been the accepted sauce for mackerel," she wrote in Spices, Salt and Aromatics in the English Kitchen *(1970).*

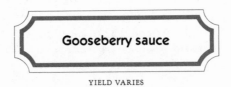

Gooseberry sauce

YIELD VARIES

Green gooseberry purée is just tart enough to offset the oily richness of salmon and shad as well as mackerel. You can make this sauce with frozen cooked berries or fresh ones puréed in a food processor. Simply strain out the seeds, thin to sauce consistency with water, add just enough sugar to take away that puckery feeling, and heat it to a boil in a small saucepan. Making it into a butter sauce is optional. To do so, add room temperature butter, a half tablespoon at a time, shaking the pan over low heat to incorporate the butter as it melts. For each ³/₄ cup of purée, allow 1¹/₂ teaspoons of sugar (or to taste) and 1¹/₂ to 2 tablespoons of butter. One pint basket of berries usually yields ³/₄ cup of purée.

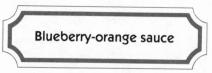

Blueberry-orange sauce

MAKES ABOUT 2 CUPS

This quick, easy, and lightly sweetened sauce is good over ice cream or frozen yogurt, and especially delicious with crêpes or over fresh, unsweetened fruit or berries.

> 1 dry pint fresh, ripe blueberries OR
>   1 (12-ounce) package frozen
>   unsweetened blueberries
> ½ cup sugar
> 2 teaspoons grated fresh orange peel,
>   orange part only
> 2 tablespoons orange-flavored liqueur
>   (Grand Marnier preferred), or 1
>   teaspoon orange extract

If using fresh berries, place a single layer in the bottom of a 2-quart microwavable glass measure, and crush them to release some juice. Add remaining berries, sugar, and orange peel, and microwave (see pages 33~35 for details), uncovered, on high 2 minutes; stir, and microwave 2 minutes longer. If using frozen berries, place a single layer in the bottom of the measure or casserole, and let defrost a few minutes, so they can be crushed to start the juices flowing, and add 30 to 60 seconds additional cooking time. Let cool to room temperature before stirring in the liqueur or orange extract. Pack into a refrigerator container or hot, sterilized glass jars, cover tightly, and refrigerate. The sauce can be served as soon as it is made, but it tastes even better after a week's rest in the refrigerator.

Spiced brandied fruit sauce

MAKES ABOUT 3 CUPS

A Christmas gift of imported French glacé cherries in brandy reminded me that holiday cakes made with brandied preserved fruit would be particularly delicious, and far less expensive to make if I brandied the fruit at home. My sauce is also good over ice cream, and a little of it is delicious in stuffing for roast duck or goose.

If you like raisins, add ½ cup to the glacé fruit and increase brandy so all the solids are covered.

> **1 jar or package (1 pound) glacé**
> **mixed, diced fruit and peels (about**
> **2 cups)**
> **¼ cup diced crystallized ginger**
> **½ teaspoon each of whole allspice and**
> **whole cloves**
> **About 5 inches stick cinnamon**
> **1½ cups brandy**

Mix the fruit with the ginger in a clean, scalded 1-quart canning jar or an apothecary jar with a tight lid or a glass-topped canning jar. Place the allspice and cloves in a metal tea ball, and bury it and the cinnamon in the fruit.

Cover fruit with brandy, and seal jar. After 3 weeks, taste a piece of fruit. If it is spicy enough to suit you, discard the spices and reseal the jar. If not, leave the spices a while longer. The sauce keeps indefinitely at room temperature.

Chestnut trees were growing in China at the dawn of history . . . and in this country at the time of its discovery. The chestnut was a great favorite with the Indians; they used it whole in stews and ground in bread. It grew in profusion from New England to the Gulf of Mexico, and it continued to grow and bear until the turn of this century when, in 1904 to be exact, the tree was attacked by a blight brought in from Asia by way of Chinese chestnuts.

Morton Gill Clark, A *World of Nut Recipes,* 1967

Chestnut dessert sauce

MAKES ABOUT 1 PINT

I used to make this sauce only when I could get raw chestnuts. Higher than usual prices in the winter of 1990 led me to try this recipe instead with canned French chestnuts. The syrup masks the smoky flavor of the canned nuts, many of which break into small pieces during the canning process.

Chestnut dessert sauce (continued)

> **2 cups raw chestnuts or 1 (15.5-ounce)**
> ** can of whole chestnuts**
> **Water**
> **1 cup packed light brown sugar**
> **¾ cup brandy**
> **About 2 inches vanilla bean**

Buy at least 1¼ pounds of raw chestnuts, or more if it is late in the season, when they are more apt to have developed mold during storage. Peel and skin as described on page 42. Place them in a single layer in a large, deep skillet, cover well with boiling water, and simmer them until soft and starting to break apart. If the water level drops below the nuts, replace it with boiling water. Cooking time varies, depending on the size of the nuts and how well you can control the water temperature—allow 20 minutes or longer.

When the nuts are ready, use a slotted spoon to transfer them to a hot, sterilized wide-mouth 1-pint jar or a half-liter European-style canning jar with glass lid and wire closure; reserve 6 tablespoons of the cooking water for the syrup. Set the filled jar in a water bath to keep hot while you make the syrup. Place the sugar, brandy, vanilla bean, and reserved cooking water in a 1½- or 2-quart saucepan, bring to a boil over moderate heat, stirring, and continue to boil about 15 minutes, until the syrup thickens slightly. Remove the jar from the water bath with a jar lifter, fill it almost to overflowing with the syrup, clean the rim (and threads, if using a standard canning jar), seal, cool, and refrigerate.

If you are using water-packed canned chestnuts, save the canning liquid to use in the syrup; add cold tap water if necessary to reach the 6-tablespoon level. If the nuts were dry-packed, use tap water alone. Set aside the nuts, drained if necessary, while you sterilize the jar and make the syrup. Pack the nuts into the jar, cover with boiling hot syrup, and seal as described in the previous paragraph.

NOTE

If you can get only an 8-ounce jar of roasted chestnuts, you should reduce the amount of syrup, using ¼ cup water, ½ cup packed light brown sugar, ¼ cup plus 2 tablespoons brandy, and about 2 inches of vanilla bean, prepared as above.

BAKING AND DESSERT–MAKING WITH HOME–PRESERVED FOODS

In [eighteenth century] working class rural households, rich confections like raspberry jam might be spread across the top of a freshly baked pie (made with raised crust), or mixed with vinegar and served hot over pork. Where formality was in order, jams and jellies were generally eaten as spreads on cake, not bread.

William Woys Weaver, *Sauerkraut Yankees*, 1983

ams, jellies, preserves, and marmalades as spreads for breakfast toast and muffins are relatively new. As recently as the early 1930s menu cookbooks were still suggesting sweet preserves to be served like pickles and relishes as condiments at breakfast, midday dinner, and evening supper. Cooking was plainer then, and preserved foods made meals more appetizing, especially in winter when fresh produce was scarce. Historically, preserves and other sweet spreads have also been used as ingredients in other recipes. The following recipes suggest possibilities beyond the obvious ways of adding relishes to fish, meat, or poultry sandwiches, or salads.

Some recipes in this section require high-altitude adjustments if you prepare them at 2,500 feet or more above sea level. Less leavening (baking powder and/or baking soda) and more liquid will be needed because biscuits and quick breads rise faster at higher altitudes. Frostings also cook faster at higher altitudes.

Pastel jelly frosting

MAKES ABOUT 2 CUPS

In the 1930s this frosting and the topping recipe that follows were recommended as cake toppings. I came across them in a loose-leaf booklet based on a popular radio cooking show, *General Foods Cooking School of the Air*. They really suit today's lifestyles remarkably well—being quick and easy to make, and fat-free.

You need not worry about the risk of salmonella poisoning from raw or undercooked egg whites in the next two recipes as long as you follow the

Pastel jelly frosting (continued)

directions for cooking them until their temperature registers 160 degrees Fahrenheit. If that seems like too much trouble, you may substitute the equivalent of one egg white in powdered egg white solids, reconstituted as the package label directs. They can sometimes be bought at bakeries, and are also sold by mail order. See Source List, page 250.

> ¹/₂ cup jelly, plus more for garnish
> 1 egg white, unbeaten, or its
>   equivalent in powdered egg white,
>   reconstituted as package label
>   directs
> Dash of salt

Place jelly in a small bowl and set over hot water. Beat at low speed with a cordless hand mixer, an eggbeater, or a whisk until jelly is no longer lumpy. Add egg white and salt, and increase speed to high, beating continuously until frosting is stiff enough to stand in peaks when the beaters are withdrawn. If you have used a raw egg white, continue beating until the temperature throughout registers 160 degrees Fahrenheit on a cooking thermometer, preferably an instant-read model. Move the thermometer around in the frosting, and do not allow it to touch the bottom or sides of the bowl. If you plan to serve the cake within 2 hours, spread the frosting on the cooled cake, and dot with additional jelly. For later use, spoon the frosting into a dish, cover tightly, and refrigerate. It will remain spreadable, and can be used at your convenience within a day or two.

Raspberry jam topping

MAKES ABOUT 2¹/₄ CUPS

> ³/₄ cup Raspberry Jam (page 56)
> 1 egg white, unbeaten, or its
>   equivalent in powdered egg white,
>   reconstituted as package directs
> 1 teaspoon fresh lemon juice
> Dash of salt

Melt jam in a small bowl set over hot water. Add the egg white, lemon juice, and salt, and follow directions as in preceding recipe.

Variation   Mix the chilled topping into vanilla yogurt, and freeze to make a quick sorbet. Or swirl it through softened vanilla ice cream or frozen vanilla yogurt, and refreeze.

Jelly roll

8 SERVINGS

American women have been baking jelly roll–type cakes as far back as Eliza Leslie, whose first cookbook, *Seventy-five receipts for pastry, cakes, and sweet-meats* appeared in 1828.

When I was growing up in Arkansas in the 1920s and 1930s, jelly rolls were a frequent dessert at our house—most often made with Concord grape jelly, a family favorite. Nowadays I tend to substitute angel cake batter adapted from a Swans Down cake flour baking booklet for the traditional whole-egg sponge cake batter, and raspberry jam for the jelly.

> **4 egg whites**
> **1/8 teaspoon cream of tartar, or**
>   **1 teaspoon fresh lemon juice**
> **Pinch of salt**
> **1/2 cup sugar, superfine or regular**
>   **granulated**
> **1/2 cup cake flour, sifted before**
>   **measuring**
> **1 teaspoon vanilla extract**
> **Powdered sugar**
> **3/4 to 1 cup jelly or soft jam**

Preheat oven to 300 degrees Fahrenheit. Coat a 9 x 13-inch jelly roll pan with nonstick vegetable spray, line with parchment or waxed paper, and lightly coat again with the spray. In a large bowl beat egg whites with the cream of tartar or lemon juice and salt until foamy. Beat in the sugar, 2 tablespoons at a time, until the whites maintain soft peaks that curl over when the beaters are lifted (they should not be stiff and glossy).

Return measured flour to the sifter (or a sieve, if you have no sifter), and sift about 1/4 of the flour at a time onto the egg white mixture, folding each batch in before you add another. Fold in vanilla extract, and spread batter in prepared pan. Bake about 20 minutes, or until cake springs back when lightly touched in the middle.

Lightly sift powdered sugar evenly on a doubled strip of paper toweling several inches longer than the cake. Remove cake from oven and invert it at once

Jelly roll (continued)

onto the sugar-coated paper toweling. Peel off and discard the parchment or waxed paper. Roll the warm cake, starting from a narrow end, and cool. When it is cool, unroll carefully, and spread with jelly or jam to within 1 inch of the edges. Reroll, and use a wide, long spatula or a small cookie sheet without sides to transfer the jelly roll to a serving dish or tray. Shake powdered sugar from the towel onto the roll, adding more if needed to coat it lightly.

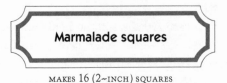

Marmalade squares

MAKES 16 (2~INCH) SQUARES

The original marmalade cakes probably date from plantation days, when nobody gave a second thought to using half a dozen eggs, plus eight egg whites, in a single recipe. My marmalade squares are a 1990s compromise, with a topping that is far less rich than that of the old Virginia recipe on which it is based. The Virginia recipe appeared in the *New York World's Fair Cookbook* by Crosby Gaige (1939). "There are many 'Lee' recipes in Virginia, and many families which claim authentic 'receipts' from the old kitchens which once cooked for the Lees," Gaige wrote, adding that his recipe came from a cookbook of the period that had been standardized for baking in modern ovens. The results were more like meringue-topped *petit fours* than traditional cakes. Peach, quince, or raspberry marmalade were suggested as the filling, topped with a baked meringue. If you substitute a citrus marmalade, as I have done, bake the bars at least one day ahead of serving. Either refrigerate them or freeze them overnight to allow the characteristic bitterness of the marmalade to meld with the other ingredients.

> 6 tablespoons butter or margarine
> 1/4 cup sugar
> 1 cup flour plus 2 tablespoons,
>   measured by the scoop and level
>   method, and divided
> 2 eggs
> 1/2 cup citrus marmalade — Lemon
>   (page 85), Key Lime (page 88),
>   Pummelo (page 92), or other spread
>   of your choice
> 1/2 teaspoon baking soda
> Pinch of salt

In a food processor mix the butter, sugar, and 1 cup of the flour until mixture resembles cornmeal. Empty into a greased and floured 8-inch square baking pan or dish. Do not use nonstick spray — both the cookie layer and the topping tend to stick. Pat the dough mixture evenly into the pan, and bake 25 to 30 minutes in a preheated 325-degree Fahrenheit oven.

Prepare the topping: While crust is baking, beat remaining ingredients together in a small bowl. Pour it over the baked dough, return pan to oven for 25 to 30 minutes longer, or until topping has set and is lightly browned. Cool completely in pan before cutting into squares.

These not only freeze well, they taste best, I think, when taken right from the freezer. The fat and sugar content keep them from becoming rock-hard.

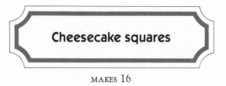

Cheesecake squares

MAKES 16

Variations on a theme by Maida Heatter, inspired by Florida Cream Cheese Squares in her *Book of Great Cookies* (1977).

5 tablespoons plus 1 teaspoon butter
¹/₃ cup light brown sugar
1 cup all-purpose flour, measured by
**   scoop and level method**
¹/₂ cup (about 2 ounces) chopped
**   pecans**
8 ounces light cream cheese
**   (Neufchâtel)**
1 cup Strawberry-Rhubarb Jam
**   (page 51), or any raspberry jam**
**   (pages 56 or 57), or a citrus**
**   marmalade (see Index)**
¹/₂ teaspoon vanilla extract
1 egg

Place a rack on the second lowest level of the oven, and preheat to 350 degrees Fahrenheit. Grease and flour an 8-inch square cake pan; invert the pan over the sink and tap to remove excess flour. Do not use nonstick spray. Like the preceding marmalade bars, these tend to stick.

In a large bowl use an electric mixer on low speed to cream the butter with the sugar. Mix flour and chopped nuts and gradually beat into sugar mixture, stopping as needed to scrape down sides of bowl with a rubber spatula. The

Cheesecake squares (continued)

mixture will be crumbly. Reserve 1 cup of it for topping; with your fingers press the remainder into the baking pan, and bake 15 minutes.

Prepare the filling: Using the same bowl, beat the cheese on low speed until creamy; add the jam or marmalade, and continue beating, increasing to medium speed, until mixture is well blended. Beat in vanilla and the egg.

After 15 minutes, remove crust from the oven, scrape the filling into the center, and use the rubber spatula to spread it evenly on top. Sprinkle reserved crumb mixture evenly on the filling, return pan to oven, and bake 25 minutes longer.

Remove pan to a rack to cool completely, then cover with plastic wrap and refrigerate at least 1 hour before serving.

With a metal spatula, release the sides of the cake from the pan, then quarter it. If necessary, cut one quarter into 4 squares and lift out with a flexible spatula. Use plastic food wrap to cover tightly, and refrigerate or freeze. Like the marmalade bars, these taste great while still frozen.

Nineteenth-century recipes using preserves as baking ingredients were mostly rich with butter and eggs and ultrasweet — like Mrs. Thomas L. Rosser's jam pudding in Housekeeper's and Mother's Manual (1895). The pudding batter was made with three eggs, plus a teacup each of butter, sugar, and jam, and was baked in puff pastry.

Macaroon thumbprint cookies

MAKES ABOUT 32

These were inspired by a recipe for Viennese bar cookies that are baked in strips on a cookie sheet. Drop cookies are just as easy to make, and far easier to remove from the cookie sheets, especially if you line them with baking parchment paper. I generally make these macaroons with either pecans or almonds, but other varieties of nuts may be used. Just be sure they are unsalted and raw—roasted nuts are apt to burn during the baking. Peanut macaroons with grape jam or preserves make a big hit with children. The almond base is an especially good choice with apricot, peach, or cherry jam.

⅔ cup pure cane sugar, divided*
1½ cups raw nutmeats
Whites of 1 or 2 large eggs
1 (4-ounce) jar of thick homemade jam,
     preserves, or marmalade

*Blended sugars are not recommended for meringue-type cookies because they attract moisture from the air.

Set a rack on the second lowest level of the oven and preheat oven to 325 degrees Fahrenheit. Cut baking parchment paper to fit cookie sheets, and "glue" them in place, using dabs of vegetable shortening, butter, or stick margarine.

Combine ¼ cup of the sugar with the nuts in a food processor, and pulse/chop until mixture resembles fine cornmeal. The sugar speeds this process by acting as an abrasive. It also helps keep the nuts from becoming oily. Scrape the nut mixture into a bowl of at least 1-quart capacity, stir in the remaining sugar, and add the first egg white beaten until frothy. Blend with a fork until the mixture sticks together enough to be kneaded. If necessary, add some of the second egg white. With a spoon or a food scoop with 1⅛-inch diameter bowl, form into balls about 1 inch across. (If you use the scoop, scrape it against the side of the bowl each time to remove excess dough.) Set the balls about ½ to ¾ inch apart on the parchment-lined baking sheets. Dampen your fingertips in water, and with a thumb, press the center of each cookie to form a well for the filling, and smooth out any cracks in the sides. Bake about 15 minutes, until surfaces are dry (and lightly browned, if using almonds) and the centers are still soft to the touch.

While the cookies bake, zap the uncovered jar of jam in the microwave just long enough to melt it to a spoonable stage, about 30 seconds in a 700-watt oven.

Remove the macaroons from the oven, fill the cavity of each one with ½ teaspoon or slightly more of jam, then transfer them from the parchment to a rack to cool. Store in single layers in tightly covered containers. For crisper cookies, store in lightly covered containers. I think they taste best if stored at least a day before serving.

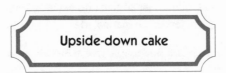

Upside-down cake

MAKES ONE 8~INCH ROUND OR SQUARE CAKE, 6 TO 8 SERVINGS

A recipe contest conducted by the Hawaiian Pineapple Company (now Dole Packaged Foods Co.) in 1925 attracted 60,000 entries, 2,500 of which were recipes for pineapple upside-down cake. Whose was the first is anybody's guess.

My recipe has a 1930s cake batter atop a thinned-down fruit preserve. Sliced fresh or canned fruit is optional.

> 1 (8-ounce) jar Apple Ginger (page 62)
> Defrosted undiluted apple juice
>   concentrate
> 2 apples (optional)
> 1/4 cup butter or margarine
> 1/2 cup sugar
> 1 egg
> 1 teaspoon vanilla extract
> 1 cup plus 6 tablespoons all-purpose
>   flour
> 2 teaspoons baking powder
> 1/8 teaspoon salt
> 1/2 cup milk (low-fat or skim works fine)

Preheat the oven to 300 degrees Fahrenheit for an ovenproof glass dish or 325 degrees for metal. Generously butter the bottom and sides of the baking dish or pan. Heat jam or preserves in a small saucepan with a few tablespoonfuls of undiluted apple juice concentrate until it resembles a medium-thick syrup, then pour it into the baking dish or pan. Arrange peeled apple slices, if desired, in an attractive pattern over the syrup.

Mix the batter: In a bowl of at least 2-quart capacity cream butter with sugar. Beat in the egg and vanilla. Combine flour, baking powder, and salt, and add the dry ingredients alternately with the milk to the butter mixture, to make a thick batter. Spoon batter evenly over the apple-jam mixture, and bake 45 minutes, until cake has browned lightly and begins to pull away from the sides of the pan.

With a table knife, loosen the sides of the cake from the pan, and invert it onto a serving dish. With a rubber spatula remove any topping that has stuck to the pan and place it on the cake. Serve warm or at room temperature.

Variations Other possible fruit and sauce combinations: papaya slices and Papaya-Pineapple Marmalade (page 98); peeled apricot halves and Pineapple-Apricot Marmalade (page 89); peeled pear wedges and Ginger Marmalade (page 93); canned, drained pineapple rings and Apricot Jam (page 44); carambola slices with Carambola-Orange Marmalade (page 91).

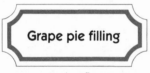

Grape pie filling

MAKES 4 TO 5 CUPS

My mother used to make Concord grape pie with fruit from a vine that grew along our back fence in Harrisburg, Arkansas. Her recipe had come from a sister-in-law in Missouri. Aunt Yettie's grape pies had a baked-on topping of beaten whole egg instead of a lattice crust or a solid top crust. Today I skip the egg and the top crust altogether, and substitute a scoop of premium frozen vanilla yogurt. What's a pie filling doing in a preserving book? Simple. I precook and freeze the grapes during the fall harvest season, so I can have my favorite pie any time of year.

2 quarts (3 pounds) fully ripe Concord grapes

Wash and drain grapes. Slip pulp from skins into a 3-quart saucepan, and reserve skins in a small bowl.

Bring pulp to boil over medium heat, stirring. Boil about 10 minutes, or until seeds begin to separate from pulp. Transfer to a strainer set over a bowl, and push pulp through with a wooden spoon to extract as much of it as possible. Return pulp to the saucepan, add the grape skins, and bring just to a boil. Ladle into freezer containers, cool, seal, label, and refrigerate or freeze.

Concord grape pie

MAKES ONE 8– OR 9–INCH PIE

Pastry for single or double crust
For 8-inch pie
2 cups grape pie filling
   (preceding recipe)
1 cup packed light brown sugar
2 tablespoons flour, or
   1 tablespoon cornstarch
For 9-inch pie
3 cups grape pie filling
   (preceding recipe)
1½ cups packed light brown sugar
¼ cup flour, or
   2 tablespoons cornstarch

Preheat oven to 425 degrees Fahrenheit.

Line a pie pan with pastry, and flute the edges if using a single crust. Stir sugar into the filling until dissolved. In a custard cup, stir a few spoonfuls of the filling into the flour or cornstarch until no lumps remain. Stir this mixture back into the filling until thoroughly combined, pour it  into the crust, and top with a lattice crust, if desired, or bake as is, about 30 to 35 minutes, or until the edges and top crust, if any, are lightly browned. Serve at room temperature with pouring cream, vanilla ice cream, or vanilla yogurt. An 8-inch pie makes 4 to 5 servings; the 9-inch pie, 5 to 6. The filling should be a little runny.

An 1850s recipe for ice cream

Take a gill of fresh currant juice, make it very sweet, and stir in half a pint of cream, and freeze it. In the winter, or when fresh currants are not to be had, beat a tablespoonful and a half of currant jelly with the juice of one lemon, sweetened, and put to it half a pint of cream.

Currant Ice Cream recipe in *The Country Kitchen*, 1850,
published by *Americana Review*, 1965

Apricot sherbet

MAKES ABOUT 4 SERVINGS

This sherbet, and the other flavor combinations I have suggested, are all variations on a theme by chef/author Jacques Pepin. In a recipe that appeared in *The New York Times* Sunday magazine section in the summer of 1990, Jacques used strawberry jam to replace part of the sugar in a strawberry sherbet. I have carried his idea one step beyond, by using only jam or marmalade and vanilla yogurt for sweetening. As some of my jams and marmalades are fairly tart, you may want to add a little sugar by the tablespoonful or its equivalent in sugar substitute for a sweeter dessert. My recipe is a rule, in the old-fashioned sense of the word: a rule of thumb, in which each cook adjusts the recipe to personal taste. I have chosen apricots to illustrate the point, but you can make equally fine sherbets with any fully ripe fresh fruit, or even with frozen, unsweetened fruit or fruit canned in juice or in heavy syrup. If you choose to omit the alcohol, the flavor will differ slightly, and the sherbet may be more crystalline, because alcohol, like sugar and other natural sweeteners, inhibits freezing.

> **1 pound fully ripe apricots, peeled and**
> **pitted**
> **½ cup vanilla yogurt**
> **¼ cup or more to taste of Apricot Jam**
> **(page 44)**
> **¼ cup Jasmine Markarian's Apricot Cor-**
> **dial (page 241; optional)**
> **Sugar to taste**

Place the pitted apricots, yogurt, apricot jam, and apricot cordial, if desired, in the bowl of a food processor or electric blender, and blend or process until puréed. Taste, and add sugar by the tablespoonful if desired. Keep in mind that freezing makes sweetness less apparent. If you add sugar, continue blending the mixture briefly to dissolve the sugar crystals. Either freeze in an ice cream freezer, following manufacturer's directions, or pour into a shallow metal baking tin, and freeze until solid throughout. Cut into chunks with a table knife, empty into a food processor with steel blade, and process, starting with pulse action, then run continuously until smooth; stop to scrape down sides as necessary.

Pack into a freezer container, eliminating air bubbles; place plastic wrap directly on top of the sherbet, then seal with the container's own cover. Return

Apricot sherbet (continued)

to freezer to firm up. Best if eaten the same day it is made. If mixture freezes too hard to scoop, let covered container stand on a refrigerator shelf for about 30 minutes before scooping.

Reduced-calorie variation   Substitute low-fat or nonfat yogurt and ½ teaspoon vanilla extract for vanilla yogurt, use one of my reduced-calorie spreads, and add sugar substitute to taste. The texture will be more like that of an ice.

Flavor variations to try   Strawberries, with Strawberry Jam (page 50) or Strawberry-Rhubarb Jam (page 51), and kirsch

Strawberries, with any Orange Marmalade or orange spread (see Index), and orange-flavored liqueur or Orange-flavored Sherry (page 242)

Raspberries, with Raspberry Jam (page 56) or Peach Melba Jam (page 54), and *framboise* (raspberry brandy)

Blueberries, with Blueberry-Orange Spread (page 115) or Spicy Blueberry Jam (page 69) and orange-flavored liqueur

Plums, with Damson Plum Jam (page 53) and slivovitz (plum brandy)

Dark sweet cherries, with Half-and-Half Cherry Preserves (page 65) or Cherry Currant Jam (page 47) and kirsch

Bananas, with Lime Marmalade (page 87) or Key Lime Marmalade (page 88)

Pears, with Gingery Pear Butter (page 113) or Ginger Marmalade (page 93), and Poire William or *eau de vie du poire*

Paradise Conserve (page 181) with Paradise Jelly (page 82), and cranberry cordial

Mango, with Mango Spread (page 123)

The thin-skinned, juicy, extremely sour Key lime (also known as the Mexican, West Indian, or golden lime) originated in Southeast Asia many centuries ago, and it is thought that Columbus brought seeds to Haiti in 1493 and established the thorny little trees there. The limes were thriving on the southern tip of Florida well before the Civil War, and the name by which they are best known comes from their association with the Florida Keys. Key limes were a thriving commercial crop there until 1926, when a

hurricane wiped out the groves. Now there are only a
scattered few Key lime trees left, and it is exceedingly rare
to get a piece of restaurant pie anywhere that has been
made with real Key lime juice.

. . . When condensed milk was readily available after
the Civil War, many Southern cooks used it in place of
perishable dairy products. In the Keys as far back as the
1890s, a simple pie combining egg yolks, condensed milk,
and lime juice in a graham-cracker crumb crust was a
well-established local favorite. It is essentially the same pie
that persists in cookbooks and restaurants today, though it
is generally made with Persian lime juice and sometimes is
baked in a regular crust with meringue on top or egg
whites folded into the custard.

John Egerton, *Southern Food,* 1987

Key lime marmalade sherbet

MAKES ABOUT 4 CUPS, OR 8 ($^1\!/_2$-CUP) SERVINGS

This recipe represents my attempt to have the flavor of Key lime pie without the fat content of crust and egg yolks. This sherbet remains soft and scoopable because of its high sugar content. Now that Key limes are being imported regularly from Haiti, we no longer have to substitute juice and peel from the larger, greener, seedless, and less sour Persian variety. Either raw egg whites or egg white powder (see Source List, page 250) may be used. I prefer the powder because it has been heat treated to meet USDA standards for salmonella negativity.

> 1 (15-ounce) can sweetened
>   condensed milk
> 3/4 cup **Key Lime Marmalade** stock
>   (page 88), or 1/2 to 3/4 cup fresh Key
>   lime juice
> 2 tablespoons rum (optional)
> 3 large egg whites, or the equivalent
>   in egg white powder, reconstituted
>   as the package label directs

Empty the condensed milk into a large bowl. Stir in the Key Lime Marmalade stock or the fresh strained Key lime juice, and the rum, if desired. In another

Key lime marmalade sherbet (continued)

bowl beat the egg whites or reconstituted egg white powder with an egg beater, a whisk, or an electric mixer until soft peaks form when the beaters are withdrawn. Fold the egg whites into the milk mixture, pour into a 1-quart freezer container, cover tightly, and leave undisturbed until uniformly frozen throughout, and flavors have melded, preferably for 24 hours.

BEVERAGES

aking alcoholic and nonalcoholic beverages was an important duty of an American housewife from colonial times through the early part of this century. Even during Prohibition some continued (illegally, of course) to make fruit wines and beer for family consumption. My childhood memories include being awakened in the middle of the night by the sound of bottles of home brew blowing their temporary corks, and of squabbling with my brothers over whose turn it was to use the bottle capper after fermentation had ceased.

The popularity of these homemade drinks was reflected in cookbooks of the period, which contained lots of recipes for fruit and berry wines, shrubs (brandy- and wine-based sweet beverages), punches, mulled wine, mead (honey wine), syllabubs (creamy wine drinks), and both alcoholic and nonalcoholic beers. Raspberry vinegar in those times was a sweet syrup to be mixed with cool water for a refreshing summer drink.

Cider and beer were the breakfast beverages of choice long before coffee and tea came into widespread use.

"Apprentices and journeymen received grog from their masters as 'coffee breaks' during the day," wrote Virginia T. Elverson and Mary Ann McLanahan in A Cooking Legacy (1975). "At meals during the seventeenth century, a bowl of cider, beer or 'noggin' was passed after the host had first toasted his guests with a swallow."

Even the Quakers and Shakers, religious groups that forbade spirits except for medicinal purposes, made their own folk wines, cider, and beers. Cider, fruit wines, and ginger beer were drunk by the Shakers when the purity of available drinking water was questionable.

Cherry bounce was a popular social drink in colonial times. By the nineteenth century it had become an acceptable tonic for monthly "female complaints," writes William Woys Weaver, editor of the 1982 edition of *A Quaker Woman's Cookbook* by Elizabeth Ellicott Lea published originally in 1845. Cherry bounce was a potent tipple made with wild cherries and rum, rye whiskey, or brandy. In *America Eats* (1989), Weaver describes cherry bounce as a folk version of ratafias, which were drinks and ices that originally used an expensive Dalmatian cherry liqueur called *Maraschino di Zara*. Wealthy American colonists obtained maraschino from Venetian traders who shipped it to both England and America.

Few of us would go to all the trouble today of making such a variety of beverages when we can buy good quality cordials and liqueurs almost everywhere. That is why I have limited my Beverages chapter to three recipes for drinks that are not obtainable in stores.

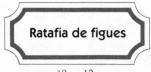

Ratafia de figues

MAKES 10 TO 12 OUNCES

Ratafias are homemade liqueurs that were popular a century and more ago. They were made with all manner of things—freshly roasted coffee or cocoa beans, fruit, fruit peel and leaves, flowers, and herbs. Most of the old ratafias were based on brandy or pure grain alcohol. I find brandy works best with most fruit except for dried apricots, which have enough flavor of their own to transform tasteless vodka into nectar. This ratafia, like the one for Jasmine Markarian's Apricot Cordial that follows, can be used as a sauce for ice cream as well as an after-dinner drink. As a beverage, it tastes best mixed with additional brandy.

1 package (12 ounces) dried figs
½ pound rock candy, or 1 cup plus
2 tablespoons sugar
1¼ cups brandy

Place all ingredients in a clean, scalded, glass-topped quart mason jar or apothecary jar, and seal. Let stand 3 months. Stir or shake occasionally to dissolve the rock candy or sugar; the latter tends to settle. Taste after 1 month and add more sweetening, if you wish, but remember that dried figs are extremely sweet.

Decant ratafia into a clean, scalded bottle of 10- to 12-ounce capacity, and seal tightly. Refrigerate the figs in a tightly covered container. To serve as sauce, offer the fruit, cut up, in a few spoonfuls of the syrupy cordial.

Rock candy is useful in beverages

Rock candy makes a convenient substitute for granulated sugar in homemade beverages because it dissolves rapidly and evenly, while beverages made with granulated sugar must be shaken or stirred every day or so until all the sugar crystals have dissolved.

Jasmine Markarian's apricot cordial

MAKES ABOUT 1 PINT

The apricot's botanical name is *Prunus armeniaca,* which may explain why some people have attributed its origin to Armenia in western Asia. But most experts agree that the luscious peach-colored fruit first grew in China and spread westward from there, eventually reaching California. It is probably no accident that the San Joaquin Valley there has both an Armenian-American colony and apricot orchards. Jasmine is a member of that colony, and this is how she describes making the delectable beverage at her home in Fresno:

"Choose a glass jar with cover. Place alternating layers—1 inch—of dried apricots and rock candy to within 1½ inches from top. Choose very flavorful apricots (important). Fill jar with an inexpensive brand of vodka. Close jar tightly, and place in a cupboard or on kitchen drainboard.

"After one month, open jar, taste for sweetness, and if necessary add more rock candy. Stir well but carefully with a wooden spoon. Close again, and after one month repeat procedure. After one more month (three months in all) drain into decanter.

"If the apricots are flavorful and meaty they may be used over again (I might add some fresh dried ones)."

Jasmine uses the drained apricots in sweet breads and fruit cake or chopped and served with a little of the cordial as a topping for rich vanilla ice cream. To keep the drained fruit for several months, refrigerate it in a tightly closed container.

Jasmine Markarian's apricot cordial (continued)

Here is my version; as a beverage it is delicious alone or mixed with brandy.

About ¾ pound dried apricots
About ¾ pound rock candy
About 2 cups 80-proof vodka

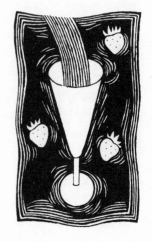

Fill a clean, scalded, glass-topped quart mason jar or apothecary jar with alternating layers of apricots and rock candy, starting with an inch-thick layer of apricots, lightly packed. Cover mixture with the vodka, seal tightly, and set aside for 3 months. Taste for sweetness (and adjust it, if you wish) at the end of the first month. Stir the mixture, recap it, and repeat the procedure at the end of the second month. After the third, strain the cordial into a decanter of at least 2-cup capacity, cover, and store at room temperature. I follow Jasmine's suggestions for storing and using the drained fruit. Because most of the apricot flavor has gone into the cordial, the fruit does not make good preserves or apricot butter.

Orange-flavored sherry

MAKES 1 BOTTLE

Orange-flavored sherry originated in Spain, or so I was told during a tour of California vineyards and wineries in the 1960s. A California product was said to be available then, but I never located a bottle during that trip. So I made my own, and usually serve it in the Spanish fashion, as an aperitif with toasted almonds.

2 medium oranges
1 bottle (fifth) of good quality dry
sherry

Use a swivel-blade vegetable peeler to remove strips of peel as thin as possible from the oranges. Decant the sherry into a clean, scalded, glass-topped quart mason jar or an apothecary jar. Twist each strip of peel over the surface of the wine to release the oil that carries the flavor. Drop the peel into the wine, seal the jar, and store for at least a month in a cool, dark, dry place. Decant into a pretty jar with a tight stopper, and serve, chilled or over ice, with a thin half-slice of fresh orange or a twist of orange peel. Or pour a few spoonfuls over fresh fruit an hour or so before serving.

Guavas, pineapple, soursop, cocoplum and other fruits grew wild in the island and were used by the Indians when Ponce de León began the colonization of Puerto Rico. Since then, the Spanish conquerors brought more fruits and food plants from Spain and other regions: papaya from Central America . . . tamarind and mangoes from India . . . and citrus fruits and pomegranate from Spain.

Berta Cabanillas and Carmen Ginorio,
Puerto Rican Dishes, 1956

GLOSSARY

Airtight seal: See *Seal, vacuum.*

Alum: A fine white powder, ammonium alum, sold at drugstores and in food store spice sections. In pickling, it is used in minute amounts to help keep vegetables and fruits crisp.

Ascorbic acid: Vitamin C, which is widely available in drugstores and health food stores in tablet form. In preserving and pickling it helps prevent browning of fruits such as peaches and pears.

Ascorbic acid mixture: A blend of sugar, ascorbic acid powder, and an anti-caking agent that serves the same purpose as plain ascorbic acid. It is sold in food stores in areas where much canning and preserving is done and sometimes can be found in drugstores as well.

Blanch: To cover with, and sometimes cook briefly in, boiling water. Some fruits are blanched so they can be peeled easily. Walnuts need blanching to prevent browning of other ingredients in conserves and compotes.

Blended sugar: A combination of cane sugar (sucrose) with other forms of sugar, such as dextrose and fructose. Unless otherwise indicated, it may be used interchangeably with cane sugar in preserving and pickling recipes in this book.

Boil, full rolling: Large bubbles rise and break on surface of a liquid so rapidly that vigorous stirring does not interfere.

Boil, steady: Medium to large bubbles rise regularly to surface of a liquid and break there, but reduced bubbling occurs when liquid is stirred.

Butter, fruit: Fruit purée cooked (with or without sugar or other sweeteners) to a consistency that spreads like butter.

Calcium hydroxide: See *Pickling lime.*

Canning, open-kettle: Preserving foods by cooking them in uncovered saucepans and packing them, usually while hot, in hot, sterilized jars, which are then sealed, cooled, and stored.

Canning, pressure: Processing sealed jars of food under pressure at 240 degrees Fahrenheit (at sea level to 2,000 feet above; adjustments must be made at higher altitudes). This method is necessary for low-acid foods to destroy bacteria which can cause spoilage and food poisoning, including botulism. See pages 10–11 for additional information.

Canning, water bath: Processing certain acid and/or sweet foods to destroy bacteria, enzymes, molds, and yeasts that can cause spoilage. Filled, sealed jars are boiled (or simmered) for specific lengths of time in water deep enough to cover them by an inch or so at top and bottom. For additional information, see page 11.

Chutney: A pungent relish of East Indian origin made from fruit, herbs, and spices.

Compote: Fruit cooked or stewed in syrup.

Conserve: Crushed or ground fruit made from a mixture that usually contains some citrus and often raisins and nuts as well.

Funnel, canning: A wide-stemmed funnel designed to fit the necks of standard home canning (mason) jars.

Gel test: See page 7.

Headspace: Air space between the top of the food and the jar lid. It allows for expansion during cooling and/or freezing.

Jam: A mixture of crushed and/or ground fruit that tends to hold its shape but usually is not as firm as jelly.

Jars, mason: Glass containers with threaded necks made especially for home canning, pickling, and preserving. They range in size from 4 ounces (½ cup) to half-gallon. Most brands use two-part self-sealing lids. Tapered mason jars, larger at the mouth than at the base, can be used for freezing as well as canning.

Jell test: See *Gel test.*

Jelly: A clear spread made from fruit juice (or wine and pectin) that is firm enough to hold its shape when turned out of its container.

Lid, self-sealing: A two-part metal closure consisting of an enamel-lined metal lid with sealing compound and a threaded metal band, or ring, to hold the lid in place. When used as a manufacturer directs, it produces a vacuum seal that can be verified by the position of the lid after a jar's contents have cooled. Directions for use come with packages of lids, bands and lids, and cases of jars. All are packed in units of twelve.

Mandoline: This is the French name for a utensil often labeled a slicer/shredder or slicer/grater in the United States. Mandolines are modern replacements for the old-fashioned vertical hand grater/slicer. I have often thought the old name should be taken literally because as often as not I sliced or grated my fingers as well as the food. Virtually all the plastic and steel mandolines today come with a food holder that is a buffer between your hand and the sharp grating and slicing blades. These moderately priced utensils usually have interchangeable steel inserts for making different size slices and strips of vegetables. Look for them in housewares catalogs and housewares shops and departments.

Marmalade: Usually defined as tender jelly with fruit suspended in it. The word marmalade is derived from *marmelo,* the Portuguese word for quince, and the first marmalades were made from that fruit. Many nineteenth-century American marmalade recipes use other fruits as well.

Nonreactive: A term used to describe cooking and serving utensils made of materials that do not react with acids and brine (a salt and water solution) to discolor foods or form toxic substances. Nonreactive saucepans and pots include all of those with undamaged nonstick interiors, plus pots and pans made from flameproof glass, glass-ceramic, stainless steel, enameled steel, and enameled iron. Uncoated iron and copper form toxic substances when used for cooking high-acid foods; uncoated aluminum darkens some fruits and may become pitted if salty mixtures are left standing in them.

Paste, fruit: A confection made by cooking fruit purée with sugar until it can be poured and cut like fudge.

Pickling lime: This fine white powder, chemical name calcium hydroxide, reacts with acid ingredients such as cucumbers, tomatoes, and melons to make them wonderfully crisp. At least two manufacturers make the product in 1-pound boxes or bags, and you will find it in many supermarkets and other stores that carry canning supplies. For mail order availability, see Source List, page 250.

Preserves: Whole fruits or large pieces in a thick syrup that may be slightly jellied.

Salt, pickling or canning: Medium crystal salt packed without additives that interfere with the pickling process. Sold in 5-pound bags and 26-ounce round cardboard containers.

Salt, coarse (kosher): Large crystal salt processed with only a tiny amount of anti-caking agent and no additives that interfere with pickling. If pickling or canning salt is unavailable, coarse (kosher) salt is preferable to table salt for most recipes using cucumbers.

Scald: Rinse with boiling water.

Seal, vacuum: Airtight seal that helps preserve food. In general, it can be recognized with home canning jars and lids when the center of a self-sealing lid is depressed and remains that way after a jar has cooled. Occasionally, it is necessary to tap the center lightly with a finger to complete a seal. If the lid pops up again, the jar should be either repacked, following the original directions, or used promptly. If the food does not require prolonged storage for mellowing (as most pickles and relishes do), check the recipe to see if the unsealed jar should be refrigerated or stored at room temperature.

Simmer: Tiny bubbles rise slowly and break below surface of a cooking liquid, so that it barely shivers.

Stock: The home preserving equivalent of *fonds de cuisine,* the French term for a seasoned cooking liquid to be used for making broth, sauces, and glazes. For preserve-making, stocks consist of cooked fruit, berries, and/or other solid ingredients and their cooking liquid that can be refrigerated or frozen until you are ready to make preserves and other sweet spreads.

SOURCE LIST

All of the ingredients and utensils called for in this book are sold at retail stores, but specific items may not always be available in every community. However, manufacturers usually will provide the name of the nearest retail dealer on request; and some manufacturers sell certain items by mail direct to consumers. The following list is intended as a guide.

Ascorbic acid mixture: Sold in food stores and drugstores. Fruit Fresh brand is made by Benckiser Consumer Products, Danbury, CT 06810. Toll-free, call: (800) 284-2023. Mrs. Wages Fresh Fruit Preserver, by Dacus, Inc., Tupelo, MS 38803-2067.

Lids: Plastic lids for canning jars to be stored in refrigerator or freezer are available in regular and wide-mouth sizes through the mail order catalog of Miles Kimball, 41 West Eighth Ave., Oshkosh, WI 54906.

Low-methoxyl pectins: Four brands are sold in food stores and shops that carry canning supplies. Ball 100% Natural Reduced Calorie Fruit Pectin and Kerr Pure Fruit Pectin for Lite Jam & Jelly are national brands; if they are not available where you buy the same companies' canning jars and lids, ask the store to order some; Slim Set Jelling Mix, a product of MCP Foods, Inc., Anaheim, CA 92803, and Mrs. Wages Light Home-Jell are more likely to be found in, respectively, Western states and the Pacific coast area, and in the South and Midwest. For information about Pure Fruit Pectin for Lite Jams & Jellies, write Kerr Glass Manufacturing Corporation Consumer Products Division, P.O. Box 76961, Los Angeles, CA 90076; Mrs. Wages Light Home-Jell is available both in stores and by direct mail order from the manufacturer, Dacus, Inc., Tupelo, MS 38803-2067.

Pickling lime: One-pound boxes and bags are sold in food stores and shops that carry canning supplies. The manufacturers are Ball Corporation Consumer Products Division, Muncie, IN 47305-2326 and Dacus, Inc. Dacus's Mrs.

Wages brand is also available by direct mail from the manufacturer at the address on page 249.

Powdered egg whites: Available in half-pound and two-pound packages from Maid of Scandinavia, 3244 Raleigh Ave., Minneapolis, MN 55416. Toll-free order line: (800) 328-6722; in Minnesota, (800) 851-1121. A half-pound package contains the equivalent of 50 to 55 large egg whites.

Spice, or flavoring, oils: Sometimes sold in the prescription department of drugstores. Other retail sources include specialty herb and spice shops such as Aphrodisia, 282 Bleecker St., New York, NY 10014, and Maid of Scandinavia (see powdered egg white listing for address and telephone numbers). Both shops have mail order departments.

SELECTED BIBLIOGRAPHY

Andrews, Julia C. *Breakfast, Dinner and Tea.* New York: Appleton & Co., 1865.

Angier, Bradford. *Free for the Eating.* Harrisburg, Penn.: Stackpole, 1966.

———. *More Free for the Eating.* Harrisburg, Penn.: Stackpole, 1969.

Appert, Nicolas. *The Art of Preserving All Kinds of Animal and Vegetable Substances for Several Years.* London: Printed for Black, Parry, and Kingsbury, 1812.

Brantley, William F. *A Collector's Guide to Ball Jars.* Muncie, Ind.: Rosemary Humbert Martin, 1975.

Brown, Helen Evans. *Helen Brown's West Coast Cook Book.* Boston: Little, Brown, 1952; New York: Alfred A. Knopf, reissue, 1991.

Centennial Cookbook, Manhattan, Kansas: American Association of University Women, 1961.

Child, Mrs. Lydia Maria. *The American Frugal Housewife,* 22nd edition. New York: S.S. and W. Wooch, 1838.

Colbrath, M. Tarbox. *What to Get for Breakfast.* Boston: James H. Earle, 1882.

Cranberries. Washington, D.C.: American Folklife Center, 1984.

Dickinson, Maude. *When Meals Were Meals.* New York: Crowell, 1967.

Duncumb, Elizabeth. Manuscript receipt book. Warwickshire, England: Sutton Coldfield, circa 1791.

Early, Eleanor. *New England Cookbook.* New York: Random House, 1954.

Fernald, Merritt Lyndon, and Alfred Charles Kinsey, revised by Reed C. Rollins. *Edible Wild Plants of Eastern North America.* New York: Harper & Bros., 1958.

Flowers, Barbara, and Elisabeth Rosenbaum. *The Roman Cookery Book.* New York: British Book Centre, 1958.

Grigson, Jane, and Charlotte Knox. *Cooking with Exotic Fruits & Vegetables.* New York: Henry Holt, 1986.

Hall, Thomas. *The Queen's Royal Cookery,* 5th edition. London, circa 1734.

Haughton, Claire Shaver. *Green Immigrants, The Plants That Transformed America.* New York: Harcourt Brace Jovanovich, 1978.

Hess, Karen. *Martha Washington's Booke of Cookery.* New York: Columbia University Press, 1981.

Hill, Janet M. *Canning, Preserving and Jelly Making.* Boston: Little, Brown, 1917; revised, 1927.

Homespun, Priscilla. *The Universal Receipt Book,* 2nd edition. Pennsylvania: Isaac Riley and J. Maxwell printer, 1818.

Hooker, Richard J. *A History of Food and Drink in America.* Indianapolis: Bobbs-Merrill, 1981.

Hughes, Mary B. *Everywoman's Canning Book.* Boston: Whitcomb & Barrows, 1918.

Hyun, Judy. *The Korean Cookbook.* Chicago: Follett, 1970.

Kavasch, Barrie. *Native Harvests.* New York: Vintage Books, 1979.

Lin, Florence. *Florence Lin's Chinese Regional Cookbook.* New York: Hawthorn, 1976.

McGee, Harold. *On Food and Cooking.* New York: Charles Scribner's Sons, 1984.

McNeill, F. Marian. *The Scots Kitchen.* London: Blackie & Son Ltd., 1929.

Microwave Cooking Handbook. Clifton, Va.: International Microwave Power Institute, 1987.

Nathan, Joan. *The Jewish Holiday Kitchen.* New York: Schocken, 1979.

——. *An American Folklife Cookbook.* New York: Schocken, 1984.

Neil, Marion H. *Canning, Preserving and Pickling.* New York: David McKay, 1914.

Niethammer, Carolyn. *American Indian Food and Lore.* New York: Collier, 1974.

Randolph, Mrs. Mary. *The Virginia Housewife.* Philadelphia: E.H. Butler & Co., 1860.

Rorer, Mrs. S. T. *Mrs. Rorer's Philadelphia Cookbook.* Philadelphia: Arnold and Co., circa 1886.

Schneider, Elizabeth. *Uncommon Fruits & Vegetables.* New York: Harper & Row, 1986.

Simmons, Amelia. *American Cookery,* Harriman, Tenn.: Pioneer Press, 1966.

Solomon, Jack and Olivia. *Cracklin' Bread and Asfidity.* University, Alabama: University of Alabama Press, 1979.

Stone, Ruth. *Pioneer Cook Book.* Topeka, Kansas, 1970.

USDA Complete Guide to Home Canning, Agricultural Information Bulletin No. 539. Washington, D.C., 1988

Weaver, William Woys. *A Quaker Woman's Cookbook.* Philadelphia: University of Pennsylvania Press, 1982.

——. *America Eats.* New York: Museum of American Folk Art and Harper & Row, 1989.

——. *Sauerkraut Yankees.* Philadelphia: University of Pennsylvania Press, 1983.

Wilson, C. Anne. *The Book of Marmalade.* New York: St. Martin's/Marek, 1985.

Wolcott, Imogene. *The Yankee Cook Book.* New York: Ives Washburn, 1963.

INDEX

Recipes appear in boldface.

A Note About the Author

Born in Kansas and raised in small towns in Arkansas during the Depression, Jeanne Lesem learned early to appreciate the role of homemade preserves and pickles as condiments to make plain food taste special. She learned to cook while helping her mother prepare meals in the family's large, old-fashioned kitchen in North Little Rock, Arkansas. After earning a B.A. in journalism at the University of Missouri, she began a career with news agencies that led eventually to New York, where she became the first full-time food reporter, then food editor, of United Press International. Since her retirement in 1984, Ms. Lesem has continued to write occasional articles about food for newspapers and magazines. She is a member of the Culinary Historians of New York, and she lives in New York City.